# YOU DON'T
# UNDERSTAND ME

## ABOUT THE AUTHOR

Dr Tara Porter has worked in clinical settings with young people since 1992. Since qualifying as a clinical psychologist in 1997, this has primarily been with girls and adolescents as part of the Child and Adolescent Mental Health Services (CAMHS) in the NHS in north London, a region of extreme social-economic, ethnic and religious diversity. She has also been involved in teaching teachers about mental health through the Anna Freud National Centre for Children and Families and regularly writes about mental health in schools in the *Times Educational Supplement (TES)*. She is an associate clinical tutor at UCL and also works privately.

# YOU DON'T UNDERSTAND ME

## THE YOUNG WOMAN'S GUIDE TO LIFE

### DR TARA PORTER

Lagom

First published in the UK by Lagom
an imprint of Bonnier Books UK
4th Floor, Victoria House
Bloomsbury Square
London, WC1B 4DA
England

Owned by Bonnier Books
Sveavägen 56, Stockholm, Sweden

facebook.com/bonnierbooksuk/
twitter.com/bonnierbooksuk

Trade paperback – 9781788705127
Ebook – 9781788705134
Audio – 9781788705141

A CIP catalogue of this book is available from the British Library.

Typeset by Envy Design Ltd
Illustrations by Graeme Andrew
Printed and bound in Great Britain by Clays Ltd, Elcograf S.p.A.

1 3 5 7 9 10 8 6 4 2

The names and identifying characteristics of some persons described in this book have
been changed.

Every reasonable effort has been made to trace copyright holders of material
reproduced in this book, but if any have been inadvertently overlooked the publishers
would be glad to hear from them.

Lagom is an imprint of Bonnier Books UK
www.bonnierbooks.co.uk

For Ella; for Charlie; for Joe.
For always.

# CONTENTS

*About the author*                                                    ii

*Introduction*                                                        1

## CHAPTER 1: ATTACHMENT AND BELONGING                                7

Toxic parenting                                                       19

What helps is one good attachment                                     23

Attachment in teenage years                                          26

## CHAPTER 2: YOUR FAMILY                                            29

The pendulum of adolescence                                          33

Families are complex systems                                          34

Parenting as a verb                                                   37

Overparenting                                                         39

Discipline, boundaries and rules                                      43

Your acceptance of your parents' parenting style                      48

Siblings                                                              56

Families: the best of times and the worst of times                    62

## CHAPTER 3: FRIENDS     65

Patterns in female friendship     69

Fitting in – finding your tribe     77

Problems in friendships: socially awkward

    socially anxious and Autistic Spectrum Disorder     81

Boundaries     89

So now I've told you friendship is gonna be this way     92

## CHAPTER 4: EMOTIONS, THOUGHTS AND FEELINGS     91

What are feelings? Emotions? Thoughts?     95

Your emotional mind and your rational mind     99

Where are you in relation to your feelings?     104

Strong negative emotions: negative coping strategies     107

The foundations of good mental health     113

Actively managing your feelings     120

## CHAPTER 5: ANXIETY AND WORRY     133

What is anxiety?     136

Internal and external triggers for anxiety     139

The spiral of anxiety     141

The spiral of anxiety in a social context     144

Why is *now* so stressful?     145

Anxiety management     148

Behavioural management of anxiety     161

Don't do your best, don't be the best –

    live your best life     171

## CHAPTER 6: EDUCATION AND QUALIFICATIONS    173

Education and mental health    177

There is another way: setting realistic expectations    187

The truth about university    194

Study smart not long    199

The right to be a little bit naughty    207


## CHAPTER 7: FOOD, EATING, WEIGHT AND SHAPE    209

Beware the healthy eating messages    212

Your body shape    216

Your inaccurate body image    220

Dieting    226

How dieting leads to overeating: the 'what the hell?' effect    233

A perfect storm: willpower and dieting    237

All-or-nothing eating and yo-yo dieting    240

Body satisfaction    242

How to eat    244

Food, eating, weight and shape: how to get sanity in an insane world    247


## CHAPTER 8: SCREENS AND THE INTERNET    251

24/7 culture    255

The impact of stimulation on mental wellbeing    259

Addicted to your screen?    262

The internet typhoon    263

Values and The Happiness Trap    264

Deciding and keeping to your values    270

Comparison and perfectionism    273

Loneliness and vulnerability                                    279
It's not enough; I've had enough; I'm not enough                282
Screen freedom or screen slave?                                 283

## CHAPTER 9: ATTRACTION, RELATIONSHIPS, SEX AND LOVE                                                287

LGBTQ+                                                          290
Love and the wise mind                                         293
Why are you attracted to someone?                              294
The thrill of the chase                                        300
Playing hard to get?                                           304
Love and self-respect: congrats, hun                           308
Nurturing your sexuality                                       310
Final thoughts on love                                         318

*Last Words*                                                   319
*Acknowledgements*                                             321
*Want to know more?*                                           323
*Endnotes*                                                     325

# INTRODUCTION

*Psychology: the scientific study of the human mind and its functions, especially those affecting behaviour in a given context.*

In my career as a therapist and psychologist, I have talked with hundreds of girls. This book is based on these conversations: on the girls' stories, hopes, fears, thoughts, feelings, behaviour, failures and triumphs. It is what I learnt from listening to them and what I had to learn in order to help them; it has grown out of these girls' struggles and successes.

*You Don't Understand Me* is about how to navigate young womanhood, providing a toolkit for growing up emotionally competent and confident. The world for girls and women has changed beyond all recognition in one generation. Over the 25 years of my clinical practice, I have observed the opportunities and power of teenage girls increase exponentially. You, girls, are outstripping boys academically; the gender balance for entry into medicine and law is now equal; we see teenage girls and young women flexing their power – in feminism with #metoo and in climate change with the school strikes. The technological revolution means that girls today are the first generation of women who are screen natives: there has never been a time when the internet wasn't a part of your life and you work a screen instinctively. These changes mean that many of you leave your teenage years with a freedom and a platform that were unimaginable to women a generation ago.

Some things are clearly going right for girls and young women, but other things are going badly wrong. It's clear that with that greater freedom, choice and empowerment there also comes immense challenges. We are all aware that mental health problems are on the rise among young people, but the statistics are somewhat misleading. In fact, rates of mental illness among boys and younger girls are relatively stable. However, mental health problems among teenage girls and young women are sky-rocketing. Self-harm among girls of 16–24 years old has shot up from around 6 per cent in 2000 to around 20 per cent now.

It is distressed girls like these that I have met in a therapy room. There, I have tried to listen to their experience, through the lenses of both my clinical knowledge and the collective wisdom I have gained from listening to other young people – their peers and the generations before them. I try to help each young woman understand her internal world so as to navigate her external one. And sometimes, something powerful happens in my therapy room: by helping these girls forge order out of the chaos in their minds, it gives them the agency to think differently, which in turn helps them to act differently, to make different choices and consequently to feel better.

In this book, I draw together the commonalities of those experiences to share them with you. What you will read here is the sum of their collective wisdom alongside my observations and musings from listening to them. I want to give you the tools to understand yourself and treat yourself with compassion, to use the freedom girls now have wisely and not at the expense of your mental health. I don't want any more girls to self-scar or starve, to be paralysed with panic, to think the world would be better without them. Enough, already. I want you girls to be armed with the self-knowledge not just to survive but to thrive. To soar and fly with confidence and a clear mind. I want to do myself out of a job.

To all my current and ex-patients: firstly, thank you, oh thank you, for sharing your stories with me. Secondly, none of the case examples are you. Why? Because I had to make them up to protect your privacy. Quite frankly, it took me a long time to get my head around how I could do that because I was worried that it might make the book seem less true or honest. So, what I did was this: I made myself a rule that I would only use a case example if I could think of two or three young people I'd worked with who'd had that problem, and I combined their stories. Then I took out all the extraneous detail and added some new detail for colour. I did this to protect your stories, which you have trusted me with, and I did this because the reason for including the case studies is to illustrate a wider point, and the key thing is *that point* and not how old you were or what you look like. So, to be relevant to more people, I placed the things I learnt from you all into a fictional person.

A note about language. This book is written about the commonalities I've observed while working with teenage girls and young women. Not all of it will be relevant to all girls and women, as you are, of course, a diverse group, and a lot of it will be relevant to some boys and young men. I have not worked with enough young people who identify differently to this, or young people in transition, to claim any specialised knowledge of their psychology. I hope what you read here captures something of your identity. I see gender as socially constructed and self-determined, which, in some ways, makes a book targeted just at girls and young women a contradiction. However, I justify it as the data we have shows that young women are currently suffering more with mental health difficulties (and they are more interested in studying psychology) which suggests some need or demand for a gendered book. I use language in the style of the young people I see, which is generally quite gender-neutral ('guys' and someone who's a dick or a prick can be any gender). I also use the words mum, dad and parent quite fluidly to account for all people in those roles for you including step-parents, guardians, foster parents and the like.

This book is obviously not exhaustive in its content. It grew out of my clinical experience rather than research studies, and there are some topics and issues which I don't feel I have the clinical or personal experience to cover. Indeed, as I wrote this book, I became painfully aware of lots of areas I had little experience or knowledge of. For example, I know a lot about anorexia, dieting and intuitive eating, but found I knew little about body positivity. Why am I telling you this? I am telling you this because as you read this book, I hope you will sometimes have the experience of being known and recognised. But, of course, I don't know you, and I may capture your thoughts brilliantly in one area and not at all in another. One of my favourite psychology articles ever is called 'On Knowing What You Don't Know' and there is a lot I don't know. I apologise for those oversights and will continue to educate myself.

I've also included a section at the end called 'Want to Know More?' where I give references and some ideas for further exploration, particularly (I hope) on some of the stuff I don't know much about.

Finally, this book is not primarily about mental illness; it is about mental health – the everyday psychology of girls and young women. I hope it will help those of you who are suffering from a mental illness but also that all of you will find something of themselves to recognise in here. I hope that it will help you put into words something that is in the shadows of your mind that you are struggling to express. Most of all, I hope you will feel understood.

# CHAPTER 1

# ATTACHMENT AND BELONGING

'Although we may love our children with all our hearts, not all children will feel our love . . . The first two or three years of life is when the brain is being wired for relationships'

**RICHARD BOWLBY, BRITISH PSYCHOLOGICAL SOCIETY**

'They fuck you up, your mum and dad. They may not mean to, but they do'

**PHILIP LARKIN, 'THIS BE THE VERSE'**

I wonder why you have picked up this book. Perhaps someone gave it to you because they are worried about you, or they just thought you'd be interested. Maybe you are thinking about studying psychology for A level and want to know what it is all about. Or you are feeling a bit lost and want to understand yourself some more. Perhaps you are feeling worried or sad, or not yourself and want some help. Maybe you are hurting yourself, or other people.

I'm imagining you as I write. I'm imagining you like someone I might see walk into my therapy room – usually curious about therapy but often sceptical about whether I'm going to understand *her*; and often sad or worried, or lost or lonely, and usually a bit stuck – but sometimes heading in the wrong direction, with her eyes cast down. And always, always unique. She is certainly more gorgeous, smarter and funnier than she thinks she is. I wonder if you're thinking, 'Well, she's wrong about that; I'm not.' Yes, honestly, you are.

All the young women I meet are unique, yes, but there are commonalities. Themes. Things I've learnt and continue to learn, from listening to you. I'm going to share some of those here, to illustrate some psychological ideas to help you think about what is going on for you. Not all of the stories are going to be relevant to you and, looking through the table of contents, you might have a sense of which chapters are going to most connect to you and want to skip forward. This particular chapter may not be instantly interesting to you, as a lot of it relates to a time you may not consciously remember. Maybe you are tempted to dive into a chapter that relates more directly to your worries, such as Chapter 7: Food, Eating, Weight and Shape or Chapter 5: Anxiety and Worry. Feel free to do so, although I think that would be a mistake. The journey into your own psychology starts with what happened to you as a baby. You may not consciously remember it but, believe me, your first days and months run right through you, like the writing runs through a stick of rock candy. What happened to you then, in your first relationships, is imprinted into your brain. As you grew, it fundamentally shaped you. It's powerful stuff and worth understanding.

In psychology we call this attachment. Animal parent and offspring, especially mammals, try to stay close to each other after birth. Ethological psychologists working in the early- and mid-part of the last century first established this. Perhaps you know some of these experiments? A baby gosling will look for a moving stimulus in the day after its birth and will start to follow it around, even if it is a toy train or a pair of welly boots. A baby monkey separated from its mother will cling to a cloth mother-substitute for comfort, even when this doesn't provide food. Young children separated from their parents while in hospital or orphanages and not given adequate connection show a range of psychosocial and emotional difficulties. Have you ever have seen footage of Romanian orphanages from 1989? Hundreds of children were kept in shocking conditions. Leaving aside actual abuse, the emotional deprivation and the lack of a parent figure caused a range of severe psychological and intellectual impairments.

The attachment bond created between the parents and a baby,

and young child, was investigated and the theories around it popularised by a psychologist called John Bowlby. There is a strong instinctual drive in both parent and infant to stay close, propelled by evolutionary purposes for survival of the species. As the baby naturally looks to a parent, so most parents are drawn to the child and the reciprocal pleasure both receive

Harlow's monkeys went to a wire 'mother' for food but generally clung to the soft mother for comfort.

from that sets up a positive cycle. Occasionally a parent isn't able to do this, and this is usually because they haven't experienced attachment themselves as a baby: they haven't had this imprinted into their brain. A good attachment ensures that the child's basic needs of food, shelter, consistency and comfort are fulfilled.

For a child, attachment is having the feeling that someone will care for you, that they are interested in you, that they are on your side. As you get older, you may not agree with the ways in which your parents are on your side and you may think their rules are stupid – why do you have to learn the piano? Sit up straight? Put your phone away? – but (mostly) you can see that your parents are doing this in what they believe to be your best interests. Their hearts are in the right place. You may love them or hate them or oscillate between the two, but you recognise that your parents are there for you.

Or maybe you don't. For some, the attachment bond is damaged or broken. Maybe you feel lost, like you are floating free without an anchor.

*Mia was referred to me when she was 17. She was suffering with low mood and a teacher at school had noticed signs of self-harm. On the surface, she was still functioning: she was going to school, hanging out with her friends, doing her work. But when you scratched that surface, she didn't think she was any good at anything or would amount to much, and she thought that she had no future.*

*Mia was the youngest of three children. She had been very close to her mum, who had passed away years before when she was in primary school. She could only remember her mum ill and, while it had been awful when her mum died, her life had continued much as before. Although she wasn't close to her father, who had always worked long hours as the main breadwinner, she and her older siblings had had a nanny who had been with them long before her mother died, and Mia had been very close to her. Her nanny had cooked for them, been there when she got home from school, driven her around and been interested in her on a daily basis. They were close and Mia felt loved by her. When she had turned 15 and could get around by herself, and she and her siblings could make themselves something to eat, her dad had decided they didn't need a nanny any more. But Mia missed her dreadfully; she would regularly go to see her old nanny and the new children she now looked after. A year after that, Mia's nearest sibling went to university and she was the last child at home. She had previously been involved in competitive swimming but she got injured and decided to give up, as she wasn't getting any further with it, other people were better and it was all such a hassle getting herself to training.*

The first attachment bond is generally between a baby and their parent,[1] and most young people, even the most troubled and mentally distressed young people who I see in CAMHS – Child and Adolescent Mental Health Services, the NHS provider for mental health treatments for under-18s in the UK – come into therapy attached to a good-enough parent. 'Good enough' is another psychological concept, popularised by a psychoanalyst called Donald Winnicott. Psychoanalysis is one type of therapy that emerged in the early part of the twentieth century. Those early psychoanalysts looked a lot to the relationship their patient had had with their mothers when they were looking for reasons for mental distress.

Winnicott's message was hopeful. He didn't believe in a perfect parent but thought that psychological health resulted from the messy-but-loving chaos of family life. He paved the way for what has been proven by later research: parenting doesn't have to be 'perfect' and, in fact, that it is in the imperfections that the psychological work is done; it is in the rupture and repair where we learn to tolerate each other's idiosyncrasies. This is the best preparation for adult life. He knew that attachment sometimes does go seriously off course but even then it is repairable. Young people generally only need one person who they think cares about them to form attachments and for them to be OK in the long term.

---

1   The baby–mother bond has been studied in most depth probably due to the more obvious physical bond between a mother and baby (e.g. pregnancy, giving birth and breastfeeding) but socio-political factors such as expectations and opportunities also meant that women were traditionally more often in this role of primary carer. There is no evidence that a baby more easily attaches to a female than a male, however, and mostly I use the word parenting to describe the range of people who are the main carer for children, which of course may be foster carers or grandparents who are acting as parents.

There's a famous experiment with a mother and a baby that shows the intricate dance which is attachment. There's a link to it in the 'Want to Know More?' section at the back. It's called the 'Still Face' experiment. It begins with the baby and the mother smiling at each other and interacting – when the baby points at something, the mother reacts; when the baby reaches out her hands, the mum takes them in her own. Mother and child are engaging with each other and their emotions are in sync. For the 'still face' part of the experiment, the mum does just that – for a period of two minutes, she presents a still face and doesn't engage with her baby at all. The baby tries to get her mum to notice her but nothing she's done previously – pointing, for instance – gets her mother's attention and she becomes increasingly distressed.

I show a video of this experiment when I teach and, as my audience watch the clip, I watch them. Generally, the audience is surprised at how hard the baby works to re-engage with her mother and is sad at her distress when she can't: their faces mirror the reaction of the baby. As the baby gets distressed, the audience makes a noise of pain 'oooowww', and eyebrows start to furrow and mouths turn down. They share the baby's pain and confusion in a show of empathy.

Please rest assured that the momentary rupture in the bond between mother and baby does no long-term harm: we are often all ignored in our baby years, as our parents need to cook meals, sleep or look after other children. What the clip doesn't capture is that the attachment bond occurs not in a moment but over years. If we think in terms of what the baby is learning, what connections are being made in the baby's brain, we guess they might be strengthening a connection for 'Mum is sometimes interested in me' while her mum is interacting and cooing with her; then, as her mum ignores her, the baby might make a connection that 'Mum sometimes is not interested in me'. Those are OK brain connections to have: they reflect real life. As long as we have the connection that someone is generally there for us as a baby and small child, we can tolerate the times that they aren't. It seems that the brain connection that says 'Mum sometimes isn't fun and kind and nice' does not destroy the connection that she sometimes is. They exist in parallel. As long as the rupture in the attachment isn't too frequent, lengthy or severe, it is repairable.

Your attachment pattern is based on the understanding, communication and responsiveness of your parent or other attachment figure not in a single instance but over your childhood – your lifetime, even. Some parents choose routines; some choose co-sleeping. Some parents work; some stay at home. Some stay calm; some get angry. Children have tantrums and bicker. They scream and shout, disobey and act out, but as long as there is some degree of connection, care and consistency across time, the attachment survives. Family life, even happy family life, isn't always pretty.

*When we talked about Mia's sadness, it seemed that she thought it was normal. She felt empty. She thought everyone felt like she did. She knew that doing the competitive swimming had, in a way, kept her so busy that she hadn't allowed herself to think about it. In therapy, tears rolled down her cheeks as she remembered her primary-school years. Her mum had picked her up from school frequently. She remembered holding her hand and being swung along – warmth, happiness, fun. She had thought the world was a good place. She missed feeling like that: safe, secure and protected. Her nanny, too, had been very maternal, in the traditional sense of the word. Her life was well managed. When she sat in the kitchen of the home where her nanny worked now, she felt some of that again. She felt jealous of those kids who still had that warmth, that busy-ness, that bustle. Her home felt empty, lonely and cold in comparison.*

Attachment is the cradle that rocks your development from a baby to a fully formed adult, and understanding what it is and was like for you may be key in understanding who you are. It certainly doesn't decide everything about you but the interaction between your personality and your attachment relationship will have helped create who you are today. You've probably heard about nature and nurture, right? Nature is what you are born with and nurture is the environment you grew up in. The nature of your birth characteristics interacts with the nurture of your attachment relationship. For someone born with an intrinsically independent personality, their parents not paying them attention as they get older might feel like fun or freedom. For a more anxious child, it might feel worrying. Your personality will interact with your parents' nurturing style to create a completely unique creation: YOU!

Your attachment blueprint will guide your friendships and intimate relationships now and throughout your life. Psychology is not a neat science: We cannot isolate variables as you can in chemistry or medicine and neatly predict that X child receiving Y parenting will create Z attachment, because X, Y and Z are infinite in number. As with your fingerprint, your birth personality is unique and the interaction between this and your first attachment relationships creates you. Even in a roughly similar nurture environment, such as within a family, there are infinite number of environmental factors which can impact on a child. Identical twins will not both wake up at exactly the same time, nor cry at the same pitch, nor be picked up for comfort or food simultaneously. And so begin the infinite variables that imprint upon you to create your individuality and how you relate to others.

How you have felt in your relationships within your family, and what you have gleaned from the stories told and the photos viewed, will tell you something about your attachment to your family. As I am imagining you, the reader, as a teenager or young person, you may feel pretty fed up with your parents right now but try to think back. Have you felt solitary and lonely? Smothered and cocooned? Or somewhere between these extremes? Did you like your parents' style? Did you want to be closer or pull away? Did you feel scared and anxious to please at home, and try to avoid conflict at all costs? Or did you feel secure enough in your relationships to challenge your parents often, and were there lots of arguments? Did you feel intruded upon, with no sense where your parents ended and you started? Were you accepted or rejected? Did you feel palmed off or a nuisance? Were you characterised in a particular way as the difficult one, the favourite one, the clever one or the pretty one? Were we told 'you are just like me' or 'we don't do that in this family'? These are just a small selection of the infinite combinations that you may have experienced. And then, of course, there is the question of how all this interacted with your nature and in what ways it affected you. How does this impact on your friendships and relationships now?

This is the crux of it. Your past attachment relationships cast a forward shadow into your current and future relationships. Does your attachment relationship with your parents play out in your friendships and romances right now?

Every patient I see has a story of being parented. The shy, gothy girl who feels defeated by her mother's glamour and can only rebel by being as grungy as possible. The only child infantilised by an overbearing mother-hen, living vicariously through their precious daughter. The party girl who feels her parents just don't get her and wants to leave them behind to hang out her friends.

*Mia's dad wasn't mean or unkind. They rubbed along well enough. He did practical things for Mia – it's just he was sort of emotionally absent. If Mia tried to talk to him about emotional things he just said, 'Oh well, I'm sure you'll figure it out,' or, 'Life's not fair,' and then would change the subject or busy himself with something else. When I met Dad a few times for reviews, he seemed emotionally blank, though in a way he always took my advice. For example, I could feel Mia's loneliness, so advised that they spend more time together. And he did but it felt perfunctory, as though it was a thing to be ticked off a list. I wondered why. Had he always been like that or had his wife's death broken him? There was a sense of him being done with parenting. He needed Mia to grow up, move on and, of course, in time she did.*

*The therapy was important for Mia. It emotionally 'held' her. It allowed her to grieve, not only for the loss of her mother, but also the loss of the relationship that she would have liked to have with her father. But it also allowed her to move on and work out what she wanted in life. Therapy reminded her of what she had had in the past and what she wanted from life in the future. She made wise choices about who to be friends with and who to love. She came to our last session with one eye on the clock. She wanted to meet her friends who were waiting for her close by: she was done with therapy. As she should; she'd moved on from my temporary attachment and my work with her was done.*

Often, I see the attachment break down in the teenage years through misunderstanding or due to children and parents simply forgetting to keep connecting with each other and passing like ships in the night. And, of course, it is very common for teenagers to feel their parents just don't understand them (hence the title of the book!). Sometimes it's clear that both parents and child are lovely but are very different people, and that it is hard for them to understand each other. Sometimes teenagers find it difficult to show any of themselves to anyone at all, even their parents. I have seen shy, socially anxious or socially awkward young people who can't let their parents into their lives. They know their parents love them but they don't 'get' each other. It's worth remembering that the attachment bond is a two-way street. It is the parents' responsibility to make it work as they are the adults, whatever their own history. However, the child brings their own pre-existing personality to it: a child may feel insecure despite having the most caring parents.

However, there is another group of kids who show up in services with effectively no parenting at all or with minus parenting: parenting that has done actual harm.

## Toxic parenting

*Sara presented in therapy initially with suspected anorexia, as she was barely eating, but within the first few sessions, this had changed and she was binge eating. Then her eating seemed to return to normal but she was smoking and drinking a lot. Therapy felt like a whirlwind; each session presented a new problem and it felt as if I was starting afresh. Some weeks she was happy and had nothing to talk about; some weeks she had been thinking about suicide. Nothing*

*I said seemed to go in and I didn't feel our relationship was growing. However, she kept coming.*

*She'd told me her relationship with her parents was 'fine' but I got the sense from her parents that they saw taking their daughter to therapy as a little like dropping off a computer to be mended; they seemed slightly frustrated with me that it was broken in the first place and annoyed that I was taking so long to mend it. Her difficulties, they appeared to assume, were a problem entirely separate to them, entirely located in her. Did I know what I was doing? In fact, I wasn't sure I did at that stage. I couldn't get a grip on her at all.*

Working in therapy with young people is like trying to complete a jigsaw puzzle that is constantly changing and growing, and with half the pieces missing. Young people who have been abused or neglected don't all behave or think in the same way: sometimes they are low, broken and lack confidence; sometimes they blame themselves. Sometimes they are acting out at school; sometimes they are thrill seekers engaging in risky or illegal behaviours. Young people who have been abused can be very changeable in therapy and struggle week-to-week to keep to a theme or a sense of progress. They sometimes 'act out' in therapy – not coming regularly or coming late, or breaking the boundaries of therapy by sending emails in the middle of the night. But these are all pieces of a patient's jigsaw puzzle that help to make sense of the whole picture.

Why do young people who have suffered abuse behave like this? They behave like this because that is what they have learnt relationships are like. Babies are not responsible for the success or otherwise of their first attachment, they are biologically primed to attach to whoever is around, and if that someone is unresponsive, cold, inconsistent or hurts them, that gets wired into their brain as the way they should relate to others. They are primed to seek warmth and affection. If they don't, if they felt a sense of abandonment and rejection instead, the brain is wired to believe 'The world is not a safe place. No one will care for me if I am sad or worried; I must be on my toes and be one step ahead to keep myself safe. I am not going to let myself care for anyone.'

*Sara told me a story about her breaking a cupboard door when she was younger. Her mum had locked her outside of the house as a punishment. She remembered crying and banging on the door, and her mum shouting at her that she could come in when she was going to behave herself. Generally, as a therapist, I try to keep my face fairly neutral to anything anyone might say to me. But Sara saw the shock and horror in my face as she told this story and I saw her surprise at my reaction: she didn't know this wasn't normal. Then she opened up about numerous similar times, when her parents had hit her or ignored her, or similarly punished her.*

*Sara believed that her parents wanted the best for her and she thought they were disciplining her through the use of physical punishment. However, it was clear to me that the physical 'discipline' was at times driven by their anger and frustration, and there was a lack of warmth in their relationship with her. Social services became involved and, as a result, there was a change in her parents' behaviour: the physical abuse stopped. But the physical abuse – shocking and damaging though it was – was secondary to the mental and emotional harm Sara received from the lack of warmth in the relationship. It had left her lacking confidence or security, and feeling unloved, lonely and uncertain in all her personal relationships. She acted out in numerous ways with alcohol, drugs and relationships.*

As children grow up, if they only know relationships as inconsistent or harsh then that is how they will act to other people, too. Their attachment relationship is the blueprint for how to act in the future. A catch-22 is set up, as, desperate for love and affection, they draw people into intense friendships but then behave in extreme, on–off, mean ways. They can end up rejecting a friend before the friend rejects them, protecting themselves as they don't trust that anyone else will protect them. Or they provoke a rejection from the other person, who is understandably fed up with their nonsense, and that acts to reinforce their belief that they are unworthy of love and kindness.

The early animal experiments again give us some clues about this. Some poor little monkeys, left only by a wire mother rather than a soft terry-towel mother, grew up to have poor social skills, unable to relate to other monkeys, and became poor mothers themselves.

Similarly, a baby and child whose cries are consistently not answered, or only answered inconsistently or harshly, will learn a sense of helplessness, and their brain becomes wired into hopelessness – that they have no future. They are likely to develop a belief that they are no good and don't matter.

Abused children in their teenage years are often similar to a tornado in their social relationships, razing to the ground everyone in their way. In mental health services, this extreme on-and-off, risky behaviour is often referred to as 'borderline', which is a shortening of the diagnosis of 'borderline personality disorder'. I dislike this diagnosis because it is implicitly judgemental and also because the word 'personality' suggests these symptoms are permanent. This is not the case: the damage done by lack of attachment early on can be healed by a different attachment relationship later. People diagnosed with borderline personality disorder can recover.

In my experience, authorities such as Social Services generally do not take cases where children are being emotionally abused as seriously as they do physical or sexual abuse. I understand why this is. Physical abuse and sexual abuse are categorical behaviours: that means they either happened or they didn't, and they encompass emotional abuse, too. Emotional abuse by itself is a what we call a 'continuum behaviour': shouting, being mean, being cold and distant are behaviours that we nearly all do sometimes. Emotional abuse is defined not by whether these behaviours happened or not but on the context, frequency and severity of that behaviour. It is only emotionally abusive if it happens a lot and is not backed up by an otherwise warm and kind relationship. The complexity of this means it is hard to identify and even harder to prove.

It is also a disaster because it is emotional abuse which is most damaging to kids' mental health. The bruises and cuts of physical abuse heal but being hit has very serious consequences for that child's sense of being loved and cared for and of knowing how to relate to people in the future. Those baby monkeys weren't hit; they weren't starved of food or water; they were 'simply' denied basic comfort and that had a long-reaching impact upon their lives.

## What helps is one good attachment

Most children don't suffer abuse at the hands of both parents and it seems that one good relationship is enough to offer the benefits and protection of an attachment relationship. This is also important to know if one of your parents has left or died. Young people who have been let down by one parent, or experienced their loss, often act out their distress at the remaining parent. It is almost like you are testing out that attachment relationship by showing your worst side. There is often no way to show the anger and despair to the person who has let you down; instead, you may find you project those feelings onto other people who you do trust. You instinctively test out the boundaries of their attachment.

Also, it seems that there is an optimal window for attachment and it is most important if that relationship comes in the first two years of life. For example, of the babies adopted into loving families from Romanian orphanages after horrific early neglect, those who were adopted younger found life easier in the long term.

However, most young people thankfully have not had the horrific experience of a Romanian orphanage and generally the damage by a broken attachment is not irreversible. Another relationship can provide that attachment later. That might not be perfect but can still be reparative. It can become imprinted on their brain that someone, somewhere, cared, and that sense of being cared for gets wired into their brain and becomes a better map for other future relationships.

In therapy, young people can repair that relationship if they experience something differently. Indeed, any good adult relationship where you experience someone caring, where you feel that you matter, can make a difference to how a young person recovers from this situation. Therapists call this being held in mind. That might be with a teacher, social worker or youth worker.

*In truth, in therapy with Sara I did very little. I believed her; I bore witness to her pain. I tried to understand how she felt; I tried to help her understand what impact the abuse had had on her and I stayed calm and carried on. I didn't over-react or under-react – I just listened, believed, understood. For a long time, she continued to be up and down: sometimes she didn't come; other times she came regularly and shared good news and bad with me; she showed me photos of things she'd done and even brought a friend to meet me. I realised that I was her attachment figure. In the absence of 'good-enough parenting' she'd adopted me in that role.*

*What I did in therapy was offer her a secure attachment relationship. I was calm and caring; she allowed me to care. She shared and let me in, and then tested the relationship, and saw that it was safe and good. It created a new brain pathway where people didn't always let you down. She moved on with her life.*

Young people like Sara have said to me at the start of therapy 'you are paid to care' but that is not true. We are paid to see people and offer treatment, but you really can't pay anyone to genuinely care. Of course, you can pay someone to pretend to care but I think most teenagers would smell that a mile off. By its very nature, caring isn't fake or put on. Caring is a side effect of getting to know someone and understanding them. And it can only be genuine: I remember my patients in my heart.

A good and healthy attachment relationship imprinted on your brain and alive in your everyday world provides a framework for life. Bad things may well still happen to you but you will be more able to move on from them. However, even with good-enough parenting, the patterns of your parental attachment may continue to reverberate through your life. He had a point, that Larkin.

## Attachment in teenage years

The developmental task of adolescence, according to us psychologists, is to separate and individuate from your parents. It is normal around the age of puberty to start loosening the attachment bond with your parents and start to attach more to your peers as part of the process to move you towards adult life. When you are involved in a wider social circle, you start the process of comparing your parents to others and questioning how they do things. You will find your parents lacking – because they are human and so not perfect. Perfection is an unhelpful concept in human beings (more, much more, about perfection later).

Typically, parent–child attachment in adolescence involves 'rupture and repair'. If the attachment is strong and good, it is OK to argue, disagree and have some shouting and slammed doors. And yet, as every young person will stumble and fail at times on their path to adulthood, it is helpful for you, despite the conflict, to know that your parents or other attachment figures are there to return to. Rupture and repair in adolescence means that one minute you feel uber-critical and irritated with your parents and stomp off to your bedroom, but then later feel worried and lonely and run downstairs for a cuddle. This pattern links back to your earliest relationship with your parents as a baby and toddler: toddlers toddle off to find a toy, fall over and run back for comfort. With adulthood looming, worries about the future can surface: 'What am I going to do? Why don't I know yet? Everyone else knows. Am I going to be good enough?' Parents and home are important as a secure base when your first adolescent-adult steps falter and you need the emotional, practical and financial help.

If you don't have that attachment relationship, it is going

to be difficult for you, but it can also cause problems when the attachment is too strong or stifling. It is a warning sign to me if a family says (sometimes smugly) 'we never argue' or 'we are best friends' because it is often through arguing that the developmental task of separation is achieved. Without some disagreements between parent and child it is hard to establish the right level of distance in that relationship for that child to move forwards in their adult life. When this goes wrong, adult-children look too much to their parents for help or parents interfere too much in their child's life. Some young people find it difficult to separate from their parents as they are scared of failing. I've worked with many a bright patient, often heading off to university, who is terrified of how to cope with everyday living tasks such as getting a bank account or shopping.

In your late teens and early twenties, when you are setting off in life, it is of course OK to retreat back to your parents for help in times of difficulty, but be careful: you don't want your parents to solve all your problems as that will mean they are super-involved in your life. I've seen some young people rely excessively on their parents well into their twenties – for money, for help, for support – and then moan that their parents are nosey, interfering or controlling. I've had to say to them, well, yes: if you still expect you parents to pick your washing up off the floor and organise your meals, you are going to be treated as a child. Other times, I've had to encourage parents to be cruel to be kind, to give their young person a little push to fly the nest or take responsibility.

I guess the message is that if you're in your early adulthood and you feel your parents are over-involved in your life, you need to ask yourself 'Does this come from me? Am I over-relying on them and expecting them to do a lot of stuff for me? Or does it come from them?' Sometimes, the reluctance to separate is fuelled more by the parents who are unwilling to relinquish their parenting role. If you have 'helicopter parents' who swoop in to solve all your problems, you may be grateful in the short term but in the longer term you will be infantilised. I will talk in the next chapter about overparenting and how it can make the family system get stuck.

I read this in a parenting book for parents of teenagers: 'We [parents] need to give them [adolescents] space and hold them tight all at the same time. No one said this was easy.' The corresponding advice I would give to young people is, 'You need to move physically and/or emotionally away from your parents, but not too far. If they are basically OK, treat them kindly, so they are there when you fall. And you will fall, hopefully not too deeply or for too long, but no one gets through life without falling.'

To those young people with toxic parents or no parents: I am sorry. It is much, much tougher for you. Try to find some alternative attachment figures to support you – a relative, therapist, social worker, teacher, friend's mum or some good friends – and be honest with them about what has happened to you and what you need. You will have to survive this. Having no attachment relationship with a parent is a tough hand to be dealt in life. Let's try to understand how that has affected you and help you to thrive, not simply survive.

Attachment is an intricate dance between parent/carer and a child. It's a dance that can last for life, or we can learn new steps or new dances completely. It's good to learn to dance young but if you don't, it doesn't have to be the end of the story. You can learn the attachment dance at any age.

# CHAPTER 2

# YOUR FAMILY

'How few people break away from the expectations
of their parents to live their own, authentic lives.
Guilt and fear keep so many of us ensnared. Who
can stand the emotional blowback that comes from
choosing a different path?'

**REBECCA WALKER,** *BABY LOVE*

'But you will learn someday
That wherever you are and whatever you face
These are the people who'll make you feel safe in this world'

**TIM MINCHIN, 'WHITE WINE IN THE SUN'**

So, if attachment is an intricate dance between parent and child, being in a family is that dance happening in a nightclub. Your parents run it and they choose the music, the drinks, the clientele and the décor. When you are a baby, they hold you in their arms as they dance, passing you back and forth. And as you grow, you hold their hands as you take a few toddler steps and sway to and fro. Or you do that thing where you hold their hands and stand on their feet as they gently move them. Then you progress to dancing holding your siblings' hands, adjusting to their style so you don't bump into them too much or step on their toes; or sometimes you deliberately do exactly that to wind them up. As a family, sometimes you all dance together and sometimes it's like you are dancing to a different tune. Sometimes other people join and dance with you; sometimes they stay and sometimes they go. And right at the end of the evening, someone in the family might get tired or hurt, and they might need to be carried again, for a slow dance, clasping their arms round their parent's neck.

And then you turn into a teenager and suddenly you notice their décor is a bit shabby, and your parents are a bit embarrassing in the way they dance, and the music they play, well, it's invariably stuck 20 years ago, and you don't want to dance there at all. You start to wonder if it's all a bit pathetic. And you worry about your friends seeing it at all, and some days, OMG, you just HATE how awful it all is. Your friends are going to the new place that has opened that has really cool music and great cocktails. And you want to go too.

If you are securely attached, your parents are probably a bit sad to see you go and you feel a bit sad leaving them (you used to think they were so cool). So to make yourself feel better you pick a fight so you can blame them for you leaving and storm out. And they miss you at first but, actually, in time, they find some new dances without you. Then, later on, they come and dance with you at your club and you find you do play some of their old tunes there. And when you go back, you notice that they have updated the décor and they have a new cocktail menu, which looks a bit like yours.

That is what happens if you are lucky. But there are lots of ways for it to go wrong. Maybe your parents didn't dance cradling you in their arms when you were a baby – they dropped you or left you alone on the dancefloor where you got hurt. And as you got to be a teenager, they didn't care so much whether you were there or not, and when you left, they didn't check out where you were going.

Or maybe you were unlucky in the opposite way: maybe they cared too much. Maybe they never ever put you down, never encouraged you to take those first steps yourself. They never let you dance on your own, or find your own rhythm or style, because they were too worried about there being glass on the floor or the other children being rough, or other imagined dangers. Or just when you started to dance alone or with someone else, they swept you up into their arms again and told you it wasn't safe for you. And when you finally got your own nightclub, they really wanted it to be exactly the same as theirs and felt upset or criticised that it wasn't.

*Edie was a much-loved only child of older parents, conceived through IVF. She came to see me for treatment of an eating disorder. She was 16 years old but it was hard to remember that because she seemed much older. I heard that she had always been a sensible child and there was a particularly flat hierarchy in the home, the three of them as a team together. She had done lots of activities as a younger child and her parents were friends with the parents of the other children who did her activities: the weekend was often busy with her routine. In primary school, Dad was a governor at her school and Mum usually went on the school trips as a parent helper. Any small thing happening in Edie's life, such as a vocabulary test or sports game, was planned out in family life. If there was any disagreement, it was fully and respectfully discussed.*

*When Edie had become interested in animal welfare a couple of years previously, they all became interested in animal welfare. Investigating ethical eating, she moved to a vegetarian diet, a move supported by her parents who also then became vegetarian. Then she started asking questions about where their food came from and slowly moved to a vegan diet. By the time she reached me, she was eating fruit and veg and some pulses, but no fats and no carbs. She was dangerously underweight.*

## The pendulum of adolescence

As I mentioned, the psychological task of adolescence is individuation and separation. To grow up and leave your family – not just physically but metaphorically, too. At the end of adolescence, when you are an adult, you get to be your own person and make your own choices. Some of these will be very different to the choices your family would make; some of them will be the same.

Like a pendulum swinging away from its resting point, during the period of adolescence young people tend to swing further away from their family's way of doing things, as if to accentuate the differences between themselves and their family, but in adulthood they tend to swing back to a point that's closer to the way their parents have lived their lives.

Important change happens in that swinging away from your family – and not just for you, for society. Each generation of adolescents pushes on the boundaries. I look on with admiration at your generation's commitment to climate change and Black Lives Matter. My generation insisted that we would not to be defined by our marital status – we wanted to use 'Ms' not 'Mrs' or to keep our name when we married; your generation pushes the progress further with gender-neutral or personal choice in pronouns.

However, sometimes in adolescence, the pendulum swings you too far from your parents and it's easy to forget that they know stuff, that they pay for stuff and that their own equilibrium needs to be respected. It can make it a stormy time.

## Families are complex systems

In this book, I am trying to draw out the commonalities, similarities and the frequently occurring patterns that I have seen in the psychology of young people. It is difficult to do so because obviously you are also all unique. When we add families into the picture, it becomes infinitely more difficult to find those commonalities because when there are more people there are more possible patterns. Similarities become trickier to spot. The more people in your family, the more relationships you have, and we quickly get into an exponential level of complexity. A web of complexity.

In psychology, we often make an analogy between a family and a system like a plane engine. There are so many moving and connected parts. How do we understand it? How do we capture the essence of it?

Your parents could be married, single; divorced or re-married; they could be gay or straight, dead, ill or health freaks. They might be indulgent or neglectful; over-anxious or under-engaged; strict or lenient. They might be kind or mean; generous or selfish; affectionate or cold.

You might have no siblings or loads of siblings; you might be part of a complex web of half-siblings and step-siblings; you might be the oldest, youngest or bang in the middle. You and your sibling(s) of the same sex or different sexes could have lots in common or nothing in common, get on or hate each other, or oscillate between the two. There might be a big, small or no age gap. Each of those factors, and a million others, will impact with your own psychology in a myriad of interactions to create an absolutely unique, constantly moving system of a family.

Added to that, your family doesn't exist in a vacuum. There is not only a myriad of interactions between you and your family, and within a family, but also between your family and the rest of the society within which you live, work and play. You and your family will be influenced by decisions made and the culture of the society within which you live, and possibly by that of your family's previous country. There may be religious or traditional expectations embedded in these. You may be influenced by your immediate community: is it safe? Friendly? Prejudicial? Welcoming? Similarly, schools have particular styles and expectations, as do the way your peer group acts and the friendship group you fall into.

There is often a cultural clash between young people and their parents as each generation evolves. Screens and the internet are a big one at the moment, with the older generation often not understanding the online community of TikTok or Instagram. I have also met a lot of girls who struggle with the generational aspects of migration: of the difference between the culture within which they live and the culture, religion or social norms within which their parents were born.

Thus, a family is a complex machine, wired and plumbed into a larger, even more complex system. It makes the commonalities of experience between you all harder to find. You all exist within utterly unique systems.

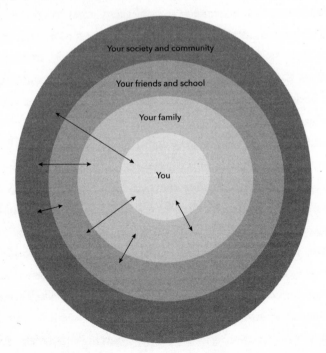

## Parenting as a verb

When I started to talk to publishers about this book, they nearly all said the same thing: 'It's really good but can you write a book for parents instead of teenagers?'

Do you know how many books there are on parenting teenagers? When I put 'parenting teenagers' into Amazon, it gives me more than 20,000 results. Why on earth did the publishers all feel that we needed another book on parenting you, when there are 20,000+ out there already? Do parents have an insatiable appetite for books on how to be a parent?

I think that is because towards the end of the last century, sometime before you were born, parenting turned into a verb, a 'doing' word, rather than a noun, a 'being' word. That means many of you are the first generation to be 'actively parented' rather than to 'have parents'. Previously, most parents used to practise a sort of benign neglect, where they looked on at their children from the sidelines fondly but got on with their own lives without feeling the need to get too involved in their children's lives. This relied heavily on 'nature' in the 'nature–nurture' debate: children were important because of the genetic bond between you and, it was assumed, they would probably turn out fine for the same reason. Somewhere pre-2000, though, the 'nurture' angle started to take far more prominence. Parents were encouraged to take an active role in developing their child: a Baby Mozart-type mentality was encouraged and educational black-and-white toys started appearing, marketed on their ability to strengthen brain waves and stimulate. Children became a project to be worked upon, to be given every opportunity to reach their potential.

Surely that's 'a Good Thing' to have parents who are actively interested and engaged, and thinking how to do the best job they possibly can? For them to invest time, money and energy into you? Who are mindful of your needs, involved in your lives? I'm sure that for those of you without a thoughtful, kind parent, it may feel a dream scenario. But, of course, that sort of parenting has its disadvantages too.

What I do see in my therapy room are kids who have suffered when parenting has become something to be done to them, rather than their parents being people in a relationship with them. These teenagers feel the pressure of being the subject of all their parents' efforts: the Kumon maths and violin lessons; the Harriers clubs and uni applications; the exam results and the tutoring. Listening to your generation and your parents, the image that sometimes comes into my head is of childhood as an assembly line where bits are being added to the raw material of a baby – the grades, the accomplishments, the best possible university – to create a good product at the end. An assembly line of a childhood where the outcome is a 'successful' young woman. I don't think your childhood should be like that: I think it should be a relatively unstructured time for you to have freedom and explore, to wonder and wander, while still having some chores to do and some rules and structure within which to do them.

Back to my nightclub analogy again: in this type of parenting, your parents are not dancing with you, having fun and laughing, they instead have become a bit obsessed with making it the best nightclub, with top reviews on TripAdvisor. I call this an outcome-parenting style. It's all about your output.

If your parents are like this, it is probably unconscious: your parents themselves are a product of their time, after all. This style of parenting is part of the current zeitgeist: it's reflected in the toys in the shops; the messages back from your schools; the articles in the newspapers; the shows on TV. Culturally, it has become synonymous with being a good parent, and most parents aspire to be that.

However, I'm just not sure making a child feel like a product to be worked on and improved has been good for the mental health of a whole generation of you. Some of you seem to have internalised that mindset of 'doing' stuff instead of 'being' who you are. It can make you feel that your worth is just the sum of your achievements and that doesn't seem to be very good for you. More on this theme later in the book.

## Overparenting

Generally, the younger the child, the more they like having an attachment figure around; it helps them feel secure and I would say it is a good thing for younger kids. But as you hit your teenage years, and especially if you are the youngest or an only child, it can become a bit intense having someone there all the time. This is especially true if that parent continues to make you their full-time job. Some parents don't have enough in their own life to satisfy them or can start to think of your success as an indication of how good a mum or dad they are. They become over-invested in your life and that makes it hard for you to individuate and separate.

Sometimes, this is because a parent has their own issues with anxiety and, as we will see, anxious people want to control their environment to help themselves feel safer. If you have an anxious parent they may want to micro-manage every aspect of your life both to eliminate risk but also to feel in control. The anxiety appears in the cloak of love – 'it's only because I care'. They may well have spreadsheets, school run rotas and rigid routines. Of course, there are advantages to that type of parenting (you are never short of a lift home) but as you hit adolescence, the lack of freedom can be stifling and the anxiety contagious. Extreme parenting can also be exacerbated in families with only one child, where the singleton becomes the apple of their parents' eye.

Wealth can be an exacerbating factor in this sort of extreme parenting too, as a wealthy parent can often outsource chores and have more time to micro-manage their children's schedules. There is a certain type of expectation that can come from having wealth, as parents may have become used to getting what they want in life. That can heighten the idea of their child being an output of their time, money and energy: this type of parent might unconsciously be expecting a successful child for their investment. Sometimes, when a child isn't achieving, parents look for medical diagnoses, searching for an explanation for their child not fitting their expectations. For some of you, to have your dyslexia or ADHD diagnosed will feel like a relief and you'll finally get the help you need. The right diagnosis at the right time can be transformative. However, for others of you, being dragged round to various different specialists may make you just feel like a problem child; it can make you feel like you are not good enough or don't fit in to the standards of the family.

Some parents of young adults, unsure of their own role as their children leave home, can unwittingly convince their child they are hopeless and won't manage without them. For these parents, facing their child's competence would only make them more aware that their child is growing up – and growing away from them – and that they're no longer as needed as they once were.

If they never push their child out into the (big, bad) world, that child internalises the message they can't cope and never learns to stand on their own two feet.

So maybe you recognise something of your own parents in one of the descriptions. And maybe you are thinking, 'So what? What difference does it make if my parents want to over-protect me and pay for everything and drive me places?' Well, in the later teenage years, say 16 and older, you should be getting a degree of freedom and making some of your own decisions. Having your parents swoop in and solve every problem is not a good thing: it can infantilise you or turn you into a bit of a dictator, used to getting your own way. Or, with parents like this, you can begin to become a bit 'pretty and precious'[2] and the normal hurly-burly of life can seem unfair or difficult compared to the special treatment you receive at home. It becomes too easy to retreat back there to be adored, as it's a much more comfortable space than the real world.

Ultimately, it can make it hard for you to separate from them, which might be fine for you if you want a life just like theirs. But if you want a different life, and you recognise your parents' anxiety/love/time/investment in you, that can make you feel horribly guilty. You know your parents are so nice and that they might feel implicitly criticised or upset by your choices, and that makes you feel like you are being mean. Some young people I see feel constrained by their parents' expectations, by the unlived lives of their parents and the lives their parents had imagined for them. That can contribute to you not separating from them at all, as the fallout is too hard, or it can push you to rebel too much

---

2 We will be talking more about 'pretty and precious' in Chapter 7 – Food, Eating, Weight and Shape.

against their boundaries so you hurt them, or you, in the bid to get a sense of yourself.

I want to give you back an inalienable right, and this is one of the key messages in this book: as an adult, you have the right to be your own person. You don't need to feel guilty if that conflicts with what your parents want you to become. However lovely your parents have been while you were a child, your late teens are a transition time between the child you were and the adult you are yet to become. Your relationship with your parents needs to grow and change to allow this to happen.

*I saw Edie's family together and, as therapy proceeded, I had to encourage her parents to say no to her eating disorder. In setting this boundary, that she had to eat, a side of Edie came out that none of them had ever seen before. There was screaming, crying and slamming doors, but only around food and eating. Edie then felt horribly guilty for being so mean to such kind parents who loved her so much. It felt as though all her separation and individuation needs were being played out through the eating disorder: it was the only way she got to separate from and be different to her parents.*

*I discussed the need for separation and individuation with Edie and her parents and encouraged them to think how the parents could have boundaries as a couple and Edie could have space. As she began to gain weight and recover, I had to help her parents see that their over-involvement was actually stifling her independence and setting her up to have unrealistic expectations of other relationships. She didn't have space to make a mistake without them solving it, or to explore a new interest and drop it again, as her parents would have swamped the interest with time and attention. I encouraged her to use other sources of self-expression, that her parents weren't involved in, other than not eating. They needed to withdraw and let her fly on her own for a bit and she had to find healthier ways to express her independence.*

Of course, your freedom to be who you want to be as an adult should be balanced by the responsibility of listening to your caregivers' views in this transition time, especially if you are living in their house and spending their money. When they pay, they say, so having your own weekend or evening job is one way of getting more autonomy. Your parents have rights too: you don't have the right to disturb their sleep, for example, or vomit on their carpet. The more responsibility you take, such as doing your own laundry or keeping your life organised and tidy, the more freedom you will get. But ultimately, it is your life and once you are an adult you have the inalienable right to live it in your own style, even if your parents don't like it, and you shouldn't feel guilty about that. They need to let you go. Most parents can do that but some struggle and some can't do it at all.

## Discipline, boundaries and rules

I would hazard a guess that half of the 20,000 books written about parenting are about how your parents get you to do what they want. They want to make their lives easier, for you to comply quicker, for life to run smoother. But why is there such an insatiable desire for these sorts of books about discipline now?

Well, I think there are a few things going on here. Parenting-as-a-verb requires getting a lot of stuff done. Society is fast-paced, which means that children's compliance with adult authority is more necessary to be able to fit it all in, and non-compliance is also more annoying to your parents when there is a time pressure.

In addition, having put so many hours into parenting, they think they deserve your compliance – all that Baby Mozart and taking you to ballet class. They don't just ignore you like their parents did them! Aren't you grateful?!

This has coincided with a time where hierarchy in society has flattened: a generation ago, I called my parents' friends Mr and Mrs X; the teachers in school could hit you with a cane and no one had heard of children's rights. The authority of adults was unquestioned and previous generations complied more with direct instructions because they didn't think they had a choice. (Or, at least, they hid their non-compliance better because otherwise they could get smacked.) Your generation have more of a voice, more of a say, more power. You can communicate with each other and with the world more easily, which means that you see that there are different ways of doing things, rather than only knowing your parents' little fiefdom, as was previously the case. This may lead you to challenge the way your parents do things or who they are as people or who they want you to be.

Thus, it seems to me that parents buy parenting books because there is a perfect storm going on: parents on the whole give more and expect more from you, but there is less compliance in society and you have more knowledge and power. Teenage years are about experimenting with identity and pushing the boundaries of the orthodoxy. As we have seen, this is generally a good thing because it is how society progresses. When you push against your parents' boundaries, or when they don't have boundaries, it can lead to you making mistakes; when parents have reasonable boundaries – firm but with some space for you – your mistake-making is generally within safe limits.

Most of these parenting books offer advice about two dimensions of parenting: how strict to be and how warm to be. That sets up four different dimensions of parenting depending on these different parameters.

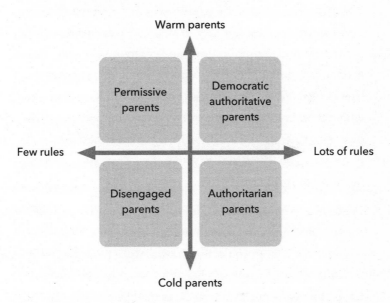

So, one scale is about how strict your parents are, running from strict, firm parents with lots of rules at one end to very lax, go-with-the-flow parents at the other end. The other scale of parenting is how warm they are, running from loving and affectionate to distant and critical.

Whilst I've represented these as separate groups of parents this is an oversimplification: they largely do not split neatly into 'warm' or 'cold' or 'strict' or 'lax'. Parenting styles are more of a tendency than a type and parents might respond differently about different topics or at different times. For example, your parents might be relaxed about you drinking and strict about schoolwork, or vice versa. They might be warm and affectionate most of the time but grumpy and snappy when they come in from work. Nevertheless, these dimensions can be used to think about four different tendencies in parenting style:

- Authoritative, democratic parents who have plenty of rules and boundaries but will talk to you about them and have plenty of time, attention, love and affection for you. You generally feel that although they are pretty strict as parents, they are mostly not too unreasonable. If you have a parent who parents like this (most of the time) you have won the parenting lottery. You are more likely to keep their rules and not lie to them. You think they have legitimacy as a parent: more about this later.

- Permissive parents are also full of time, attention and love for you but don't call you out on your behaviour. They tend to give in to you, so you get your own way. Or are the 'we're so cool', 'more-of-a-friend', 'here-try-a-joint-at-the-kitchen-table' type of parents. If your parents are more like this, it is harder for you to do well at school, unless you are self-motivated. It can also be harder for you to separate because it's more difficult to rebel as there are no rules. It can be risky if you push to find your parents' limits – that might mean you are not safe.

- Authoritarian parents are firm and strict, which means there is little fun, warmth or affection. They are very interested in the rules, schoolwork, music practice. They believe in children doing as they are told. They definitely love you but do so by wanting obedience.

- Disengaged parents don't care enough to make rules and are cold and uncaring with it. They pretty much ignore you except to punish you – and not when you break the rules, because the rules aren't clear or imposed, but when you annoy them. Kids will often play up to get attention. Generally, this is the poorest type of parenting and at its extreme, this is abusive. If your parents parent you like this, please try to talk to another adult outside of the family home.

I wonder if you recognise your parent anywhere here? How does your parents' style of parenting interact with your own personality style and your social network?

If you do recognise your parents in these descriptions, a little warning: it's not going to be helpful to throw this information in their face in the middle of an argument. If you think, on reflection, that they are too strict or not huggy enough for you, try talking to them. Be upfront that you read this in this book and maybe show it to them. Ask them which one they think they are. Tell them you find them a bit authoritarian about going out in the evening or that you wish you had a more affectionate relationship with them and see what they say. I can't promise that they will hear you, but that is the right thing to do.

*Simone was the middle of three girls. She was suffering and so was her family. Her parents were at their wits' end over how to manage her. She was constantly arguing and pushing boundaries at home. She often came home drunk; sometimes she came home high. Her parents thought she was always causing difficulties with her sisters: winding her older sister up by stealing her stuff or bossing her little sister around with rules she herself didn't keep. However, when they tried to tell her off or discipline her, it would escalate into rows and then later Simone would become really upset and guilty, and feel unloved. On occasion, she had self-harmed and that horrified her parents.*

*Simone's parents recognised that she had always had a different personality from the rest of the family. They had clear expectations, many of which were linked to their religious beliefs and their community. They were conformist and mild-mannered. They thought they that they were pretty liberal compared to the rest of their community but felt that every time they gave her an inch, Simone took a mile. For instance, she had promised she'd get home from a party at 11pm but it was 1am before she got in and she was drunk. Of course, her parents loved her, they admired her spirit, but they had to admit that it was easier when she was out of the house. Everyone else was so calm. There were no rows or drama when she wasn't there. Simone had always been a child who asked 'Why?', followed by 'No' and she was very strong willed.*

## Your acceptance of your parents' parenting style

While all of you will become more independent as you get older, the rate at which you become independent differs considerably. This will not only depend on you and your parents' personalities and relationship but will be influenced by the multiple layers of the systems your family is embedded in: your friendship group, your school, your community, your religion and society standards as a whole. For example, there is research showing considerable difference in children's responses to parental discipline in different countries of the world and within cultural groups within a country. Some cultures are more individual and parents are not expected to set rules, and some cultures are more collective and parents are expected to do so.

However, within that, you yourself also bring your unique personality and expectations to this process: whether you rush towards or avoid independence, or perhaps you are super independent in some areas and super dependent in others. And all the shades in between. Some of you are very private and independent, others more anxious and dependent. Many grown women continue to feel very criticised by the slightest comment or look from their mum and never really break free from seeking their approval.

Whether you accept your parents' authority or rail against it depends firstly on whether you believe your parents should be allowed to set rules about things in your life (i.e. do you give them legitimacy to parent) and secondly, whether you feel obliged to obey.

## Legitimacy to parent

When you were younger you (probably) accepted your parents would set all the rules in your life. You might not have always obeyed the rules but you probably didn't question your parents' right to make them. Then, at around about 11 years old, you probably went to a larger school and moved away from constant, direct, adult supervision. You may have started to travel to school on your own. It's likely that your parents didn't know the parents of the other children you met there. You probably didn't consciously twig this at the time but your parents' ability to discipline you became more dependent on what you told them and not on their direct supervision of you or that of adults they know well. You likely developed your own friends and interests, and your own preferences in music and dress. While this is not always true, and there are some communities that keep their young adolescents closely within their grasp, in Western society, it is usual for parents to allow their children more freedom in early adolescence.

From that point to when you leave home, there will be a gradual unwinding of your parents' authority over aspects of your life. The concept 'legitimacy to parent' is about whether you and your parents agree about whether they, as parents, have the right to decide things for you. When you argue with your parent, sometimes it is simply about what you want but sometimes it is about whether they have the general right to decide that for you. Often, that is what you are fighting for. For example, do you or your parents get to decide:

- Issues about safety (e.g. do you wear a cycle helmet? Are you allowed to walk home late at night on your own?)

- Moral, religious and cultural issues and social convention (are you allowed to swear? Use 'God' as an exclamation of frustration? Have a boyfriend or girlfriend sleep over?)

- Family habits and chores (do you have to be at dinner? Go to Granny's on Sunday?)

- Academic, job and career issues (who decides what topics you choose to study?)

- Money (do your parents give you an allowance? Pay for your phone? Or are you expected to get a job and pay for them yourself?)

By the time you are an adult, you get to decide all of these things, but there are no hard and fast rules about when you should take over from your parents in this decision-making. Are all of these your choices yet? Or are all of them your parents'? And do you agree with your parents about which are yours and which are theirs? Generally, parents and children mostly agree that children get to decide their own personal issues (dress, friends, preferences) and parents get to decide family rules and safety. Choices about academic study tend towards a child's decision but I have met lots of children trying to live their parents' dreams in choosing a particular path, or who are put under a lot of pressure to study a particular subject.

But it can be complicated when it's not a clear-cut issue. Who your friends are is often a point of contention as you see this as simply your personal business, whereas parents often see it as an issue of safety or academics if they worry that certain friends are going to lead you into trouble or to neglect your studies. Arguments can move quickly from the specifics of whether you are going to that friend's house on that night till what time to the generic of whether it is your decision or theirs.

When teenagers agree that an issue is their parents' decision, they are giving their parent legitimacy to parent. There is an often unspoken paradox at the centre of adult authority over adolescents, which is that adults kind of rely on your *consent to be parented*. Often, authority is implicit or based on goodwill but the more outspoken among you may say to your parents 'You can't make me' or simply ignore their rules.

Things seem to go wrong for the children I see when they have pushed and got that independence too early (or, to put it another way, their parents have let them have it too soon) or because they are too afraid of upsetting their parents and haven't pushed to get that independence at all (or their parents haven't encouraged them or let them have it). At the extreme, I've seen 13-year-olds beyond their parents' control and 19-year-olds who are completely under their parents' authority.

Permissive parents tend to let you have too much independence too young, and while this can be fun, it is also dangerous. You are an adult for a long time and while you might be in a rush to get it started, there will be situations you don't understand yet and plenty of people who want to exploit you.

## Inclination to obey and lying

So, as you get older, even if you accept your parents' legitimacy to set a rule and don't openly argue with them about their right to make it, you may feel that you don't have to keep to it. Many young people accept that their parents are allowed to set rules about drinking alcohol or coming home on time, for example, but also don't necessarily keep these rules as they think that they are grown up enough to accept their concerns but also to assess the situation and make a judgement.

This might put you in a position where you decide to lie. In fact, this is *highly likely* to put you in a situation where you lie. Research repeated across different countries consistently shows that 95 per cent of adolescents lie to their parents. Is there any other sin that we all do so often that is so universally reviled? You typically lie by telling partial truths and leaving out key information that your parents would want to know, or by avoiding the topic by changing the subject – picking a fight and storming out is a popular technique here. And sometimes you tell the odd bare-faced lie. The topics of your lying? Most commonly, drinking and your schoolwork.

Please don't quote that statistic to your parents as a justification for lying when they catch you. Parents don't like that 'everyone else does it' defence. It's likely to rile them further. They want your relationship with them to be different: they want you to be the 5 per cent who don't lie (or, possibly, to be the 5 per cent who lie to researchers about lying to their parents . . .).

Research indicates that you tend to lie *less* when there are *more* rules and lie *more* when there are *fewer* rules. That seems a bit weird, doesn't it? Why would you need to lie if there aren't many rules?

Well, it seems that you lie less when you have the sort of democratic, authoritative parents who, while having lots of rules, are warm and kind and who you are able to talk to and, if necessary, negotiate the rules. When the rules aren't explicit but you suspect your parents would disapprove, you do that half-lie shuffle – for example, avoiding the topic; giving partial information; distracting parents with one issue to avoid another; saying, 'Sophie's parents are letting her go,' without mentioning that Zahra's, Moya's and Karlie's parents have all said no way.

Why do you lie? Well, again the research shows that you lie because you don't want to upset or argue with your parents. See! You may lie but you are nice: you don't want to upset them. Teenagers lie because you are programmed to push at the boundaries of whatever freedom you are given and lying, it seems, is part of the pull away from your parents and your drive for independence. How this might sound in your head is: 'I want to go to a rave. Mum and Dad don't want me to take drugs or stay out late. I don't want to lie to my parents.' There is no squaring this circle. These wants are contradictory and you can't do them all. Psychologically, you don't like this: it is called 'cognitive dissonance', which is the discomfort you feel when you know contradictory things to be true. Your mind goes into overdrive trying to reduce this dissonance. Criticising your parents to justify to yourself lying to them or ignoring them is commonplace. 'I'll tell them I'm staying at Iona's (true: I'll stay there after the rave); I'll say we are going dancing but I don't exactly know where (true: it's only getting announced at the last minute); it's only because my parents are so crazily over-protective – any normal parent would let me go.'

I am in the psychology business not the morality business, and so I am not here to give you a lecture about the evils of lying. It seems that lying, not telling the whole truth or just not talking about the things your parents won't approve of are almost an intrinsic part of adolescence. They do not make you a bad person, they simply make you a normal person of your age. My observation is that, pragmatically, it generally isn't a good strategy to lie as parents often find out and it damages your relationship with them. Also, parents tend not to freak out as much as you think they will if you tell them the truth. Parents, like most people in life, tend to care most (after safety) about how you treat them. They are more likely to sweat what you might think is the small stuff – that you do what you are told and what you say you'll do – than the big stuff. That boils down to trust and if you want your parents to trust you, the best thing to do is to show them that you are grown up enough to cope with the situations you are putting yourself in and not lie about it. So, it's best, if you possibly can, to negotiate. E.g., 'We are going to a rave, and I am staying at Iona's afterwards.' You will most likely find there is some compromise to be had. 'You can go the rave. You come home here afterwards so we can check you didn't

take drugs. We will pay for a cab.' At the rave, you can blame
your mum with a 'she's so strict' eye-roll. Most parents want you
to tell the truth so they can trust you more and give you that
independence and freedom that you want. Most parents want
you to be independent as much as you want it.

I acknowledge that this advice won't work with some parents,
particularly if your parents are extremely anxious or over-
protective, or if they are guided by orthodox religious beliefs or
conservative cultural standards.

*Simone hated being at home. She loved being with her friends at
school. She didn't hang out so much with the girls from her cultural
group and all her friends had so much more freedom than her. She
had to be back by 10pm. Her parents phoned her friends' parents
FFS; how embarrassing was that? In therapy, her mum sometimes
cried when she was trying to talk to her about it and she found that
excruciating. If it all upset her so much, why didn't Mum just back
off? From Simone's perspective, Mum was always in her business –
fussing about something. She loved her mum but wished she would
just leave her alone. In fact, she loved both her parents but why
did they make so much fuss?*

*'Does Simone remind you of anyone else in your family?' I asked.
Nervous laughter and exchanged glances between Mum and Dad.
She was so like Dad's sister: she'd gone her own way. She'd fallen out
with her parents as a teenager too and they hardly saw her now. They
didn't want to lose Simmie like that.*

*This was news to Simone; she didn't think she was like her auntie.
Is that what they were worried about? She wasn't going to mess
things up like that.*

There's lots of evidence that teenagers take more risks than adults and this seems primarily linked to wanting to fit in with friends, which means that you downplay potential dangers. Your parents are likely to have been around the block – hard as it may be to believe, they were young once and therefore probably understand risk better than you. You might find it is worth having their eyes over the situation you are putting yourself into. I don't want to terrify you into not taking any risks, as risk-taking is part of adolescence, but I do see the casualties caused: the ones who have been arrested holding drugs; had a bad reaction to drugs; been raped or got pregnant. These aren't urban myths – these things happen, infrequently, it is true, but every day, to teenagers like you.

## Siblings

It's hard to think of any other area, except perhaps falling in love, which evokes such strong emotions as the relationships with your brothers or sisters: full, step or half siblings are all capable of evoking the same strong emotions. Unlike falling in love, many of these emotions are negative: hatred and physical violence are quite common among siblings. Now, I'm sure some of that is about *them*. I'm sure they are annoying, messy, noisy and that they started it. I'm sure they did go into your room/borrow your stuff/lie to Mum/get away with it.

But not all of it is about them. Some of it is about *you*, too.

Let me tell you that all other people are annoying. Everyone has bad habits. I know it seems like your friends aren't nearly as annoying as your siblings, and of course they aren't because they are the same age and share the same interests, so they are more similar to you. But, by definition, habits are repetitive behaviour and they only start to grate over time. I expect if your friends had lived in your house your whole life, their little quirks and foibles would be as excruciatingly painful as your little brother being on the PS4 all day or your elder sister's need to always be right. What wears us down is being stuck with habits for a long time in close proximity, never being able to escape them. The likelihood is also that you will have some inbuilt social restraint that stops you from showing your worst side to your friends, that you don't have when you're around your family. Things can quickly escalate in a family setting where you're less worried about being polite or people liking you.

In psychological terms, there is a lot going on too. Your siblings are likely to raise difficult psychological issues for your developing self. As a teenager, you are changing all the time: everything about you changes over these years. You are uncertain of the future, unsure about what you want or, if you do know, whether you will be able to achieve it. Even between the years 16 and 20, it is likely that you will change how you look; where you live; who your friends are, and you will take over ownership of who decides things about your life. Rapid change is always disconcerting but it is particularly challenging in teenage years, as you become increasingly self-aware and judgemental about yourself. That makes for a perfect storm: you're rapidly changing and you're very self-conscious. When you are trying to get to know yourself at a time of change, of course you are going to make mistakes, do things that you regret, get pulled into stuff with your friends that is wrong and tell lies.

And you are doing all this under the constant scrutiny and backdrop of your siblings. You try out a new haircut and it doesn't suit you – they are there to comment. You get in trouble for coming in late – they are there looking smug. You get your first boy- or girlfriend – they are there to sing out that you are sitting in a tree. K.I.S.S.I.N.G.

All of this makes you doubt yourself and feel even more self-conscious.

In addition, there's the psychological process of projection. This means that you (unconsciously) project the parts of yourself you don't like into someone else – in this case, your brother or sister – and hate it in them instead. For example, the way you look or your tendency to not listen to your parents, or leave clothes on the bathroom floor. Psychologically, projection protects you from uncomfortable thoughts and feelings around not being good enough. Instead, you see those traits in those around you and react accordingly by telling them how awful they are. In other words, you demonise someone close to you on account of the very characteristic you don't like in yourself – and the people in closest proximity to you growing up tend to be your siblings.

*Simone hated her older sister; she was so bloody perfect. She said that her older sister never argued with her parents, did well at school and was admired in their community. She bossed Simone around, acted superior and moaned that Simone didn't show her respect. Simone experienced her as excruciatingly annoying – she thought she was such a goodie-goodie – why couldn't anyone else see that? Simone could barely be in the same room as her sister. She loved her little sister in lots of ways and they had fun together, but she didn't get to boss her around. Mum came down on her like a ton of bricks when she did it. It wasn't fair. And Simone hated it that everyone babied her little sister – that was completely unfair, too. Simone felt she got none of the advantages of being the eldest or the youngest.*

Psychology considers there to be an imagined thing inside of you called your 'ego' – essentially, your sense of yourself or your self-esteem. When you see your siblings making exactly the same mistakes as you yourself have made, your ego gets the chance for a little boost, to feel morally superior for a few moments. Is that a good thing? Probably not. It's an ego boost that comes from denial (that you make the same mistake) and comparison (I'm better than them). Psychologically, you are likely protecting yourself from facing your own faults, because facing our faults is painful. But, of course, both you and your sibling have faults, and neither of you are perfect. In fact, perfection doesn't exist as there is no one universally agreed standard for anything. Not for appearance, not for achievement, not for personality. We are all human and destined to get things wrong. Perfection is a very dangerous concept, from a mental health point of view (and because it is so truly awful for mental health we will come back to it in two other chapters, about anxiety and on the internet).

Intrinsic in this is comparison and indeed it is very difficult to not compare siblings: that someone is sportier, grumpier, lazier, smarter than the other. As humans, we instinctively compare and within a family, this can create caricatures that are hard to break out of. Indeed, many adults find they fall back into teenage roles when they return to their family home.

And finally, if that all wasn't enough in making sibling relationships stormy, you and your siblings are nearly always competing. The resource is often the attention or good opinion of your parents and the financial and practical resources they provide. By putting your sibling down, you place yourself in a good light.

I have a dog, Suki – isn't she adorable? Although we care for her as a family, she instinctively knows and responds to me as the 'head of the pack'. If I'm not there, she will gravitate to the next oldest person in the family, and so on. Humans are pack animals, too, and your core brain will unconsciously make you compete with your siblings.

Even as you are challenging your parents' legitimacy to parent and disobeying them, you will be jostling for your position in the pack. Though a part of you can't wait to leave home and get your own independent life, at the same time, you still want your family's good opinion. You are still capable of getting jealous of your siblings, even if you don't want what they are getting – e.g. if your mum or dad is hugging them or babying them and you don't want this, you may well still feel 'annoyed' (jealous) by this. This can be even more exacerbated in blended families. I expect within your family you sometimes find yourself fighting for something you really don't care that much about and afterwards you justify that to yourself as being because your family were being so annoying. But that's the pack coming through – the instinctive jostling for position.

All that habit, teasing, projection and competition can lead to jealousy. Rather than see all your siblings' best features as you do when you think about your friends, you focus on their worst. You do this because they are annoying habits that you have had to live with for years and because they make you feel superior, particularly if you share that bad characteristic. If your siblings are older than you, you may feel jealous of the freedoms they are offered, while competing to be as successful as them. If they are younger, you may feel more jealousy as you see the special relationship they have with your parents: you don't even *want* to be that close to your parents, as you want to separate, but it's still annoying. Younger siblings also represent your younger self, which is sometimes excruciating to see and, again, very annoying.[3]

How can you protect your ego, your sense of self, with all this comparing and jostling going on? Well, as an older sister you may try to boss your siblings around to stay superior in your own mind. Or as a younger sister you may needle them with whining or run to your parents every time they do something wrong. Your mind may filter your memory, so you remember everything you did right and everything they did wrong – every chore you did and every chore they didn't; every time your parents spoiled them and ignored you.

Do these strategies help? Well, that depends on what you mean by 'help'. Psychologically, they may help you survive it in the short term but, as you grow older, if you want to leave these patterns behind, it's likely you need to get some insight into them and some appreciation of your siblings' points of view. There is more than one reality in the sibling relationship.

*Simone recognised that sometimes she got sad and then she turned the anger inwards. She was angry at herself for upsetting everyone so much. She felt trapped and awful about herself, and that is when*

---

3   From my patients' experience, I would say that 13-year-old brothers are peak annoying. There seems to be a bravado and an arrogance 13-year-old brothers put on which is excruciating to their sisters. Of course, it stems from a deep insecurity on their behalf. They won't appreciate you telling them this, BTW.

*she had self-harmed. Why was she so different? She wished they'd just let her disappear. She could tell her parents loved her other sisters more than her as they didn't give them the trouble that she did. She was both annoyed at them for being so nice and disgusted at herself for being so mean to them. She oscillated between blaming herself and blaming them.*

## Families: the best of times and the worst of times

Families are all about invisible bonds. Ideally, those bonds are loose and flexible enough that, as a teenager, you can both metaphorically and physically wander far and truly be yourself. But, at the same time, those bonds are hopefully made from something so madly strong that – however far you wander and however different you are – they never, ever break. That is a good family.

But the thing about bonds is *you all are bonded*. That's a multi-way relationship. A messy tangle of bonds. If they fall, you are attached, too. As a child, you get used to the bond being there for your benefit but if you want a more grown-up relationship with your parents then you must accept that you have some of the responsibility for keeping all of you standing up.

*In therapy, I had to think about lots of different dilemmas: how could Simone's demands for more freedom be managed in the family without making her feel awful about herself? Did Simone's behaviour mean more to her parents than a simple teenage rebellion because of their family's context? How could Simone understand her parents' perspective? What things could Simone be given freedom on? And what were non-negotiables? There is no neat solution to these issues*

*– they were ongoing negotiations, an ongoing dance between Simone and her parents, but therapy gave them a respectful space to try to sort them out.*

So, your family will not be perfect. Indeed, they are likely to be your first introduction to the concept that nothing is perfect: your parents will make mistakes and your siblings drive you to distraction. But hopefully your family will provide a safe space – a mix-up of love, acceptance, competition, bickering and annoying habits – where you instinctively return for the licking of wounds when things go wrong. As one teenager said to me, 'Of course I'd give my sister a kidney if she needed one, but no, she's not bloody borrowing my phone charger.' Even if your family can be pretty rubbish, you may still find you are almost magnetically drawn back, perhaps unconsciously hoping it will be different this time, that you will get the family warmth you have sadly missed out on before. And your family generally do take you in, as in all likelihood and despite their and your mistakes, they want to make things right, too. Those family bonds run deep.

## CHAPTER 3

# FRIENDS

'From the days of Homer, the friendships of
men have enjoyed glory and acclamation, but the
friendships of women . . . have usually been not
merely unsung but mocked, belittled and
falsely interpreted.'

**VERA BRITTAIN, *TESTAMENT OF FRIENDSHIP***

'And I tried to remember any case in the
course of my reading where two women are
represented as friends.'

**VIRGINIA WOOLF, *A ROOM OF ONE'S OWN***

I don't think there is any other subject I have discussed as much with the girls and young women I see in therapy as friendship. Yet when I racked my brain for representations of female friendship, I could only think of the film *Mean Girls*. And whilst it captures something quite significant about school-based friendship between girls – the propensity for backstabbing, conniving cruelty – female friendship can be so much more, so much better than this. It seems that through the trials and tribulations of friendship when women are young girls and teenagers, something gets resolved, so that most grown-up women I know have a heap of close female friends to whom they would willingly donate a kidney. Female friendship is deep, complex and intense. As such, it is often painful and heart-wrenching in childhood but through adolescence often grows into one of the most important and beautiful parts of life.

Female friendship is such a crucial and joyous part of being a woman and yet it seems underrepresented in our public discourse and cultural life, in books, music, plays and films. Indeed, when it is represented, it is often bitchy and unkind, with women competing against each other for a man. When I googled 'quotes about friendship', I largely got quotes by male writers. I thought Jane Austen might have something to say about friendship but really, not much. Typically, in films, books and TV, the main focus of the female character is their romantic interest or their families. This tendency was highlighted by a famed American cartoonist Alison Bechdel, who popularised an eponymous test: in order to pass the Bechdel test, a film, book or television show must represent two women having a conversation together about something that isn't a man. Whilst there are signs that the tide is slowly turning, with films like *Bridesmaids* and *Booksmart*, where female friendship takes centre stage, sadly, many films still fail the test – even 35 years after it was first developed.[4]

Perhaps you don't agree with me that female friendship is one of life's hidden treasures. At the moment, it may be that your friendships are torturous and stormy. You may feel that no one likes you and you are totally alone. You may have friendships but feel insecure in them, or you may feel lonely or victimised. From my observations in my clinical work and in life, childhood and adolescent female friendships are like a blustery, turbulent ocean that you have to travel across to get to the security and pleasure of the beautiful calm bay of adult female friendship. Yes, the bay has the occasional wave that knocks you off your feet but friendship between women is generally like bobbing in warm, tranquil water. For the most part, it's a good, safe, reliable place to be, after a long and bumpy journey. Friendships between young girls or teenagers can sometimes be brutal and soul destroying but it seems that something deep and fundamental gets figured out through this process, so that most women emerge with a deep connection and warmth with their female friends. You may observe this with your mum and her friends.

---

4   The quotes I've used at the beginning of the chapter from Vera Britton and Virginia Woolf are from over a century ago, indicating that the lack of female friendship represented in culture is a long-standing problem. As you are the next generation of writers, artists and storytellers, can you sort that out for womankind, please?

## Patterns in female friendship

What do we know about female friendship? We know that the female sex looks more to friendship than the male sex from an early age and that, generally speaking, in childhood, when compared to boys, girls' friendships are typically less about shared interests and more about shared mental space. That means that when girls play and talk they are thinking about the same thing. I sometimes imagine that they create a shared thought bubble between their two heads.

At primary school, that's often a co-created imaginary game, but as girls get older it's often shared news, or gossip, or talking about their feelings. The shared thought bubble encompasses thinking about things from the other person's perspective and this is reflected when girls say things like 'she was really there for me'. It means 'being there' with them in their emotional experience, which we call empathy. Empathy is when someone has taken the time to listen, to understand and share your experience with you, and it's the second key message in the book. There will be much more about empathy to follow.

*Cassie was a popular young woman who came to me in the last year of school for therapy for her anxiety. She had always thought of herself as 'highly strung', although on the surface she seemed to have it all. It had all started to unravel about six months earlier, when Cassie had been slut-shamed online for getting with someone else's boyfriend when she was drunk and unflattering photos of the incident had been shared around. It had split her social group and people had taken sides. For the first time in her life, Cassie wasn't popular. It had left Cassie reeling and started her anxiety cycle.*

*We talked through her friendship history. In primary school, she had always had friends and, from the sound of it, other girls competed for her attention. She'd always been at the centre of things, always got invited to things. Why was that? What was she like then? She wasn't sure. She didn't think she was the most exciting girl in her class or the most fun – in some ways, she felt she had been more of a watcher than someone who joined in. She was seen as cool. The other girls told her their secrets and she was often whispering and gossiping. She recognised that she had held a lot of power – people had wanted to be her friend – and her friendships shifted multiple times over those years. That made me wonder about her relationship with her parents.*

Sometimes, primary-age girl friendships follow the relatively straightforward pattern of two girls pairing off together, taking the best-friend route, where they fit together like a jigsaw puzzle, getting all their emotional needs and sense of belonging from each other. While the pair of them will join other girls for a larger game, everyone in the wider group knows those two are best friends. If you had this friendship pattern, it was probably quite a stable and mutually dependent relationship for both of you because each little girl holds a similar amount of power in the dyad. It is a pattern of friendship often beloved by girls who aren't particularly confident and want a low-drama life.

If you were in a trio, you may have had a bumpier ride down the friendship pathway. They typically involve three roles, each with a varying amount of power: a leader, a best friend and someone who is being left out. The leader often will flip the role of who is her best friend and, consequently, who is being left out, by the power of her attention. This is an insecure triad for everyone involved but, counter-intuitively, it is often the leader of this trio who is the most insecure. In my experience, she often has attachment issues in her family, in that she may have felt uncertain of her parents' love or that they were there for her. The leader takes that role because she feels that she needs to keep her friends close due to something missing in the parental attachment relationship, and the best way to keep them close is to wield power. If you don't feel you have a good and trusting relationship at home, keeping two people clamouring for your attention is a sensible strategy. But as we're talking about primary age here, the leader's manipulation is, of course, unconscious. There is no blame for this little girl leader. She doesn't know what she is doing and often has her own issues.

### On/off friendships

This brings us to one of the most fundamental patterns in girl friendship – the on/off friend. All through your life, you are likely to meet 'on and off' people. They may be your friend, boss or teacher, or, if you are really unlucky, your parent or your partner. But for most of us females, the first introduction to the on/off friend is in the school playground.

What is an on/off friend? It is when you go into school on

Monday and someone runs towards you, singling you out and whispering all her secrets to you, giving you a sense of belonging. This attention makes you feel special. You are no longer alone: you are part of this special twosome. As humans, we are programmed to connect – connection is a need as deep as air, water, food. But with an on/off friend, the next day you discover she is doing exactly the same with someone else and you are left out. It can be utterly devastating. You're embarrassed – is everyone looking at you? Do they think you haven't got any friends? You feel alone. But of course, you still want that closeness back; we want what we can't have more than anything. You start competing for attention, in a game where the rules keep changing, and you want your leader's approval. The more you chase after the closeness you used to have with them, the more they pull away from you. 'What have I done wrong?' you wonder. And then, as suddenly as it was gone, the friendship is back again. But this inconsistency is anxiety provoking. You begin to feel second best, worried about what each day will bring.

The on/off friendship is addictive for young girls because it creates what we psychologists call a 'partial reinforcement schedule' to the high of belonging: the lovely feeling of being close to someone, of feeling accepted. A partial reinforcement schedule is when you get a reward sometimes, but not every time, for doing the same thing. We get addicted to things as humans because we keep chasing that pay-off, the good time we had last time. For example, people keep gambling because they want the feeling of winning again. You might get 'addicted' to the on/off friendship as you try to resolve the confusion of being left out or ignored by chasing the friendship of the leader, trying to make it right again. And frequently it plays out in trio friendships as the leader is being an on/off friend to her two friends-in-waiting, although it can be in a larger group too. The leader-friend generally doesn't have conscious intent but it is unpleasant and potentially damaging to those around her.

Why does the leader act like that? Do you remember 'projection' from the previous chapter about family, when you create in others the emotion you are struggling with yourself? In the on/off friendship it is often the case that the leader is working through her own insecurity by creating insecurity in the others. In this way, she gets to re-write a script in her head where she is no longer the victim of feeling insecure but instead holds the power. This is a pattern that most girls grow out of as they progress through school.

*Cassie told me about her relationship with her parents. They were divorced and she went between their homes. They both had busy lives of their own and, she told me laughingly, often she would arrive at one of their houses to find they had forgotten she was coming and were on their way out. But they'd always been pretty cool and permissive, letting her have friends back, turning a blind eye to drinking and smoking. She'd always thought she could tell them anything but when she told her parents about the incident where she had been slut-shamed, looking for support, they were furious with her. They were worried about how the pictures online might impact her future university and job prospects.*

*That had made her re-evaluate her relationship with her parents. She'd liked being independent when she was younger and had learnt quickly to get on with things by herself. She had, for example, faked her parents' signatures on permission slips and organised her own packed lunch for school trips because she knew that her parents would miss things like that. Often, there was no food in their houses and she'd be on her own, ordering in. All her friends thought her parents were great as she'd never been told to come home at a particular time but that was now making her feel unattached and unstable. She realised that she had always acted to amuse her parents and not trouble them too much.*

Social media has intensified the process of on/off friends, particularly WhatsApp: it makes it even easier to form little groups where power games are played through inclusion and exclusion. A, B and C make a WhatsApp group but A also has another group with just B (where they talk about C) and one with just C (where they talk about B). While B and C might have one in principle, it is rarely used as they both compete for A, and A divides and rules.

## Being liked vs popularity

The on/off trio friendship is influenced less by being a good friend and more by hidden power. And the issue of power is fundamental to secondary-school friendships.

For some of you, you will have progressed seamlessly with a group of friends from your feeder primary school to your secondary school. Others of you may have transferred into a school where you knew almost no one, though perhaps everyone else knew each other. That might have been a welcome chance to start afresh or an overwhelming stress.

Whatever the pattern, it is likely that this disrupted your friendships. The transition to secondary school is often a time that's writ large in my patients' minds, as it is a period of instability where most people are looking for their new group.

The instability can mean that you retreat to your usual patterns from primary school with a quick commitment to a new best friend or a revisiting of the unstable trio.

Classic studies of friendships in early and mid-adolescence indicate that, in the secondary-school years, that there is a confusion between 'being liked' and 'being popular'. In social psychology experiments, researchers have gone into secondary schools and asked teenagers in a single class, 'Who do you like?' and also, 'Who is popular?' Numerous studies show that there is only a small overlap between these two groups: the best-liked kids are usually only averagely popular; the most popular kids are not particularly well liked; a small proportion are both liked and popular.

Researchers found that 'being liked' is linked to 'the lack of unpleasant behaviours and the possession of prosocial and entertaining qualities' – such as being kind and co-operative; not starting fights; being able to tolerate being teased; being honest, fun and not stuck-up and not being disruptive to the group. 'Popularity', on the other hand, seems to be linked more strongly to notions of social power, status or dominance: being a leader, being fashionable or good looking, being cool, having money. For girls, popularity among other girls can also be linked to having boys like you.

Nearly every young person I've worked with in therapy has found it helpful to understand that distinction and to think where they want to be in those categories.

*In therapy, Cassie had to confront the limitations of her parents and the impact they had had on the way that she related to others. Yes, they loved her, but they weren't there for her in the boring everyday sense and they gave her few boundaries and little guidance. She realised how alone she felt at home and craved being able to talk about her feelings and her problems. This made her really sad. She didn't want cool parents any more, she wanted supportive parents. She slowly realised that in her friendships and romantic relationships, she had kept people at arm's length, making them compete for her attention and good opinion as she had vied for her parents'. She'd always had to hold the power – to be funny, clever, smart . . . but not vulnerable. She wanted something different for her future. She wanted to be more real.*

Acceptance and commitment therapy, a type of psychological therapy, can be very helpful in thinking about your own friendships. In this type of therapy, we ask people to identify their values. Values are like a life compass – they embody the type of person you want to be or the way you want to live your life. Values are not like goals, as goals are something to be achieved, to be ticked off a list. Russ Harris, a guru in this approach, lists around 60 possible values, including respect, assertiveness, power, independence, caring, friendliness, fun, equality, excitement, adventure, conformity, fairness, and humility.[5]

You can, to a certain extent, choose what you want out of friendship but you can't have it all. For example, it is hard in a friendship to have the values of power, assertiveness and independence and yet to also have conformity, fairness and humility. It is not wrong, per se, to want popularity more than you want to be liked – both have costs and benefits. 'Popularity' can sometimes be lonely and a power struggle, yet, on the other

---

5   We explore values in more detail in Chapter 8 – Screens and the Internet.

hand, 'being liked' can mean subjugating your own views to fit in with the group and not standing out from the crowd or being precious about your own needs. You may have to choose which of these you want.

## Fitting in – finding your tribe

As you go through adolescence to early adulthood, as we saw in the first chapter, the psychological task is separation and individuation from your parents. With your growing independence and freedom, you are exposed to more ways of living your life and will naturally compare and contrast. As you know, this may lead you to become critical of your parents' choices, even annoyed by them. For many of you, your peers seem more fun and exciting than your parents, they seem to understand you better and share more of your interests. This helps the separation process.

But for some of you, it is harder to find your tribe. I have seen lots of girls who feel that they don't fit into the culture in their school or society – for example, if they go to a school where lots of people are socially conservative, quiet or studious and they are not. Or it could be that lots of your peers are interested in clothes and make-up, being a 'girly girl', for example, and you aren't. It can be difficult for you if your interest is not shared by many people you know: for instance, as a girl, if you like rugby or computer programming it can sometimes feel hard to find like-minded people within your peer group at school. With the power dynamics at play, in which the 'popular' group hold the social currency, there might be times when you feel left out. Rest assured, as you get older and the pool of people you meet increases, you will find your tribe. But for now, it can be pretty tough.

Friendships inevitably go up and down. Early on in secondary school, especially if lots of you came from the same feeder primary school, it often is safer to stick to the friendships from childhood. However, as you individuate and separate, you can end up growing apart from the girls you went to primary school with. Perhaps you have nothing in common any more or they were just people with whom your mum arranged playdates, not people who share your humour or with whom you feel comfortable and relaxed. During the downs in friendships, adolescents may return to the family base to metaphorically lick their wounds. So, it is also completely normal to oscillate between arguments with your parents and times when you rely on them more and seek comfort from them.

These times when you are between friendship tribes can be emotionally awkward. You may *feel*[6] you are not liked; you may not know what to do with yourself at break or between classes. You think that everyone is noticing that you 'don't have any friends'. You might start to think there is something wrong with you – that's why nobody likes you.

*Rebecca had just turned 14 when I met her; she was the oldest in Year 9 and the oldest child in her family. She'd always been capable, mature and a natural leader, and, up to this point, her parents had rarely had any concerns about her. Her secondary transfer had been seamless and she was in a quite tight, quite intense group of three girls: studious, quite geeky, all into hockey and athletics. All three of them had taken their interest in health and fitness too far, but*

---

6    Feelings are real but not always based on reality. They are often triggered by 'unreal' thoughts, meaning we can often feel something that isn't true. It's complicated: see Chapter 4 – Emotions, Thoughts and Feelings.

Rebecca had descended into an eating disorder, her leadership qualities and self-discipline wrongly applied to food and weight.

Rebecca's eating disorder and the related mental health difficulties of her friends meant that adults had to step in to the friendships as the girls needed to separate for a bit. Rebecca had to eat her lunch with her parents or a teacher, not with her friends. Her parents both took time off work and were there for her. She took to watching movies with them in the evening rather than being on WhatsApp with her friends. Sometimes, when she felt really panicky, she would sleep in their bed and one of them would sleep in hers. It was like she was younger again. Slowly, over time, she restored her weight. She emerged from the eating disorder.

As Rebecca recovered, though, there was a rupture in this friendship group and she was left alone. In her absence, the group had closed the gap and there didn't seem to be a role for her any more. She felt bereft, humiliated, lonely. More practically, she didn't know who to eat her lunch with. She hated walking into the lunch hall as she thought everyone noticed that she was on her own, without any friends. However, Rebecca could also acknowledge her frustrations with her old group. She was extremely emotionally astute. She began to see that she wasn't really in the right social group; the girls she had previously been friends with were shyer and quieter than her, and she was more expressive. They didn't want to be conspicuous or loud or talk about their feelings, particularly. Rebecca wasn't like that: she was naturally more gregarious, outgoing and adventurous, but all the girls who were more like that seemed to be in settled groups. She didn't have a route into being friends with them. She felt as though she was useless socially, whereas actually the opposite was true and it was her enhanced social skills that meant she didn't fit into her old group.

*My advice to Rebecca was that she just needed to ride the storm. It seemed to me that she was just between friendship groups and that she was so socially and emotionally competent that she would be fine in the long run. She would find a group that was more suited. In the short term, however, every day was awful and she struggled not to think that everyone was looking at her, thinking that she was unlikeable or weird. Of course, they weren't. They were preoccupied with their own friendships and issues. During this time, she relied on her parents, who were more than happy to step up and be there for her, and friends outside of school. It took till the following year at school, when form classes were mixed up again and the girls started socialising outside of school more, that she found herself in a different group, with more similar interests, and happier. When she looked back at her old group, she could clearly see that they hadn't been the right friends for her.*

Which leads me to one of the most important skills in life of all, and another of my key messages: the art of being alone. Try not to be scared to be alone. Try to hold that inner confidence that you are OK. Find things to amuse you or pass the time during the lulls in friendships (or later, in relationships). There *will* be lulls in friendships caused by the shifting tectonic plates of friendship groups, or as friends start romantic relationships, or simply because your friends are on a school trip that you didn't go on.

Sometimes there will be arguments and falling-outs in friendships: you may feel nobody likes you and you may have no one to hang out with. You should aim to be able to tolerate that: self-worth needs to accommodate social feedback but not be dominated by it. By all means examine yourself, your motivation and your actions to others, but don't become obsessed with it.

Like many things in life, it is about balance. To not care at all or never listen to feedback from others would be to risk arrogance but to over obsess about the way people treat you or your image can also be problematic. Try to find the sweet spot between these extremes which will help you tolerate being alone.

## Problems in friendships: socially awkwardness, anxiety, Autistic Spectrum Disorder

No one gets through life without sometimes having difficulties in their friendships. There will be ups and downs, and there will be times when you are between friendship groups or you can't find people you connect with. It is also very common to sometimes feel socially awkward or socially anxious. But these both exist on a continuum, and some people experience these problems more frequently or constantly. Autistic Spectrum Disorder can also disrupt friendship.

### Social awkwardness

What do I mean by social awkwardness? I use the term in two ways: firstly, to refer to both the feeling you probably get inside when you don't feel able to understand or communicate in a social setting, and secondly, as a description of how some people get things socially wrong. Implicit social rules govern our interactions – for example, about not blurting out something rude; how close you stand to other people or how much to eye contact to make. When your feelings are running high, perhaps if you are feeling anxious or low, it can be difficult to pick up the feelings or social cues from others (e.g., how comfortable they are with you standing close). Given that female friendship is often about creating a shared mental space, this can lead to social awkwardness where you feel like you are getting it wrong.

In understanding this, it is helpful to use a simple brain model of three layers. The core brain takes care of all our basic functioning (heart beating, breathing, sleeping). It is the part of the brain that's most similar to an animal brain. One of the core functions of a mammalian brain, for example, is to attach to a caregiver when young. The middle brain layer is called the limbic system and a key player in this is the amygdala, which is important in generating and perceiving our own emotions. The top layer is called the cortex, where our higher-level human skills lie, such as language, planning and thinking.

As I described earlier, girls' friendships are often based on being in the same mental space – each girl holding in mind what their friend is thinking – and conversation or play moves on in a gradual, stepwise fashion together. In adolescence, your ability to mentalise (to understand your own and other people's mental states) becomes more crucial to maintaining both friendships and popularity. Adolescent girls typically spend a lot of time just hanging out together in awareness of each other's mental space – sharing thoughts and feelings, laughing and chatting about anything and everything. In friendship, understanding and caring about your friends' feelings is necessary for the group to work: how would anyone decide where to go or what to do if there wasn't a compromise based on each other's feelings?

However, with all girls, this closeness can create difficulties. Girls tend to hold high expectations of their friends and this can lead to guilt and disappointment on both sides. Emotions can run very strong in teenage years and are difficult to control. When your feelings are hurt or you feel really down or worried, it may make you less successful at tuning in or responding to other people's feelings and creating that sense of a shared understanding. You get caught up in your feelings and your own mental space with no ability to read the room. At these times, when you are stuck in your core and middle brain, you are experiencing high emotion, low capacity to name it or cope with it, and difficulty in reading other people's mental states, and this can contribute to problems in friendship.

Generally, in friendships, when you are having a hard time, your friend will step up and do the emotional work to understand you, but sometimes both of you are struggling. Then, through no fault your own, it can be hard to connect. It's worth noticing that when your feelings are running high, you can't necessarily be as emotionally sensitive as usual and that provides a fertile ground for things going wrong.

## Social anxiety

Again, like social awkwardness, it's normal for everyone to sometimes be shy or socially anxious. It occurs on a sliding scale: you have a natural set point but you also move up or down depending on what's going on for you at any particular moment. However, some of you are sadly at one extreme of this scale and your social anxiety occurs all the time and interferes with your day-to-day functioning. Let's understand that in a bit more detail.

Nearly all teenage girls spend quite a lot of time thinking about their friends: where they are going, who they are hanging out with. If you suffer with social anxiety, you differ in that you are not thinking about your friends but almost exclusively about what your friends are thinking *about you*. In fact, not just your friends. You will likely be wondering what everyone you meet is thinking about you: acquaintances, schoolmates, people on the bus, teachers. It is as though when you are looking at other people, you are not really seeing them at all. Everyone becomes a mirror with their perception of you reflected back. Or rather, *your assumption* of their perception of you.

You may be utterly paralysed by the belief that not only are they thinking about you but that they are doing so in the worst possible terms: that other people think that you are stupid, ugly, friendless, embarrassing. Simply put, you believe that other people are thinking about you a lot and they are thinking about you very negatively.

It is very important to separate out two very different mind states: 'thinking about other people' and 'thinking what other people think about you'. These often get confused in teenage life but they are two very different things: the former is part of being an empathic and engaged friend, while the latter can verge on egocentricity and self-obsession. Often, I see teenage girls who, in trying to be nice and likeable, end up worrying too much about what people think of them, which clouds their perception so much that they completely miss their friend's actual feelings and thoughts. They start to obsess or overthink – 'What did they mean by that?', 'Why did they turn away from me?', 'Why didn't they answer me?'

While it is natural to sometimes find your mind thinking about what other people think of you, you have to be careful that it doesn't spiral out of control in this way, as thoughts like these will likely make you self-conscious and anxious. You might even stop doing things to avoid their judgement (in actual fact, your assumption of their judgement). You can become tongue-tied or blush, or immediately convince yourself that what you have said is rubbish and they think you are stupid, rude or unkind. Feeling socially anxious inhibits humour: you can't make a joke because jokes always risk causing offense and you are very afraid of causing offence.

I often draw this out for my patients. I draw the one person, them, thinking about another person, their friend, thinking about them. That's the figure on the left, below, who is thinking that their friend's mind is thinking about them a lot, and often in the most negative terms. Then I ask them to imagine what *actually* is in their friend's mind. Is it just filled up with them? Does their friend not have any other friends or any other interests other than them? Then we draw the figure on the right, to show what their friend is really thinking about.

This is often a powerful exercise. My patients quickly realise that their friends' minds are busier than just them. More importantly, they realise that their anxiety is making them egocentric; they are actually not finding out what *is* in their friend's mind. Their preoccupation with their own image in their friend's mind is getting in the way of understanding their friend. The knowing and sharing of someone else's mental space, empathy, is paralysed by social anxiety.

So, a socially anxious young person wants nothing more than to be a good friend, yet a catch-22 has been set up in which their anxiety about people liking them is actually getting in the way of them doing that. I feel a bit harsh using the word 'egocentric' to describe this, as that is the last thing most of you would want. But, effectively, when you are in this mindset you are not thinking about anyone else, you are just thinking about yourself – yourself in other people's minds.

I think this links back to the outcome style of parenting I introduced in Chapter 2: when a child is brought up with a constant emphasis on their accomplishments, they are implicitly encouraged to be an observer of themselves. In friendship, that means you may focus less on your own experience of being a friend and more on how other people might perceive you. An outcome model of friendship would mean you are preoccupied with whether others think you are a good friend, rather than if you like someone or have fun with them.

I expect nearly all of you will have some moments of social anxiety – for example, when you experience a new situation or meet new people, or when you make a social faux pas. But if you constantly have a voice in your head critiquing what you are doing through other people's eyes, it is totally exhausting. I illustrate this to my patients by getting them to imagine a third person in my therapy room, critiquing me: why is she wearing that dress? She looks really gross. Why did she say that? That's stupid. I point out to my patient that I can't actually focus on them if I am hearing that. It is distracting me from being a good therapist.

My patients generally realise that my ability to be good at my job, to empathise and to understand them, would be inhibited if this happened. They know that the dress I'm wearing or the stupid things I say are less important than my capacity to be with them in their mental space. They understand that their inner critique, and particularly their inner critique based on assumptions of what their friends are thinking, stops them doing this for other people.

If you are worrying too much about what people think about you, it stops you really connecting and co-creating a shared experience with your friend: when you are both laughing about the same thing or catching each other's eye and knowing what each other are thinking (see the shared thought bubble illustration on page 69). Your social anxiety gets in the way of being yourself because you are scared that they might reject your true self. But without sharing yourself and risking rejection, there is no vulnerability – and vulnerability is at the heart of friendship.

I send my patients away with a task to do: to find out what is actually going on in their friend's mind. If their friend isn't thinking about them that much, what else are they thinking about? What is their friend most interested in, worried about, excited for at the moment? In this way, my patients can learn to become the good friend they so desperately want to be.

## Autistic Spectrum Disorder

As I say, our capacity to understand and use the social rules is not fixed and can vary from day to day, from situation to situation. Young women who are on the autistic spectrum are likely to feel like this in almost every social situation, and also have corresponding difficulties with social anxiety. Some of the young women I have worked with Autistic Spectrum Disorder (ASD) attach to the old diagnosis of Asperger much more than the ASD diagnosis so I use them both here.

There is a stereotype that persists that people with autism are male, quite disabled, maybe rocking back and forth, perhaps with a special talent in one area, such as drawing or maths. This stereotype is not at all true, even in boys, and in girls the condition presents very differently. Greta Thunberg has done a lot to challenge this stereotype and she illustrates beautifully how an obsessive interest in something can be a strength as well as a weakness. Girls with ASD tend to differ from boys with the same condition seemingly wanting to fit in with their peer group more. This leads to girls 'masking' or 'camouflaging' their Autism symptoms, by copying their neuro-typical[7] peers playing in primary. Often their difficulties (and strengths) go undiagnosed until teenage years, when it becomes harder to mask. Teenage years are all about the shared mental space; intuitively knowing what is going on; sarcasm and inference: all difficult for the ASD girl or young woman.

ASD could be thought of as a difficulty between the amygdala (the emotional centre) and the cortex (the thinking centre). The girls and young women I see with ASD feel the full range of emotions but they find it more difficult to think about or name their own feelings or the feelings of others. When I am working with young women with ASD, it is as though feelings are a foreign language swimming around inside of them and it takes them longer to communicate them or process what they mean. My patients with ASD struggle to think about their own or other

---

7   People with ASD often call people without it 'neuro-typical' and refer to themselves as 'neuro-diverse'. Also some people with ASD prefer the 'person-first' language where as some prefer the identity first 'autistic person' – I use both here.

people's mental states because they lack the communicative skills to 'name and tame' the emotions.

Once diagnosed with ASD, many young women feel a sense of relief of having their experience recognised. Perhaps counter-intuitively it then helps them locate the problem more externally, e.g., the world not being adaptive enough for their neurodiversity, rather than blaming themselves. They recognise the strengths of their condition, e.g., the hyper-focus on special interests, and allow work arounds for the challenges, e.g., setting boundaries around socialising so they don't feel overwhelmed.

# CHAPTER 4

# EMOTIONS, THOUGHTS AND FEELINGS

*'Mentally healthy people get upset, just like physically healthy people get sick. We only worry when a person can't recover'*

**LISA DAMOUR, *UNTANGLED***

*'I don't want to be at the mercy of my emotions. I want to use them, to enjoy them, and to dominate them'*

**OSCAR WILDE, *THE PICTURE OF DORIAN GRAY***

I write articles for an online journal about the mental health of young people and I have a reader who always comes out with a comment like 'lovey-dovey shrinks like Tara pandering to young people's feelings'. I find this quite amusing,[8] as none of my patients would ever say that I pander to their feelings. Listen, understand, re-frame, confront and challenge their feelings, yes. Pander, no. One patient told me at the end of therapy that she hadn't wanted to come to therapy as she thought it would be me asking her, 'How does that make you feel?' in a kind voice, with concerned eyes, head tilted to one side, and that she'd hate that. She needn't have feared – I'm not that sort of a therapist.

Your feelings are central to your life. But you also don't want to be a victim of them. You want to aim to have some control over them, rather than them controlling you. They are *an* important thing but they are not *the only* important thing. They are as true and real as a wave in the sea: undeniably there but also only temporary; to be respected and definitely not ignored, but not to be drowned by, either.

We live in a society now which is awash in emotion – everywhere you look, there is a high level of emotion expressed.

8 Weird how he keeps reading my work when he clearly hates it. Why would he do that to himself? Not good for his mental health, I think. Also, it was a lesson to me that not everyone will like you but the perspective of time is all important: the first time he made this criticism, it upset me. After a few, I realised it was him not me.

This is a huge contrast to a generation ago, where British people were known for their emotional reserve and stiff upper lip.

Watch, listen to or read any media now and 'How are you feeling?' is a constant refrain: on *Strictly* or *The X Factor*; daytime telly or soaps and, of course, on social media. Feelings are centre stage. The need to say something new or different, to make good media, leads to a ratcheting up of emotional content. It would be difficult under the circumstances of live TV with a microphone shoved into your face to answer the question, 'How do you feel about this person?' to answer, 'Well, they are OK, and we get on well enough, but I don't think we will keep in touch long term.' The hyperbolic language, 'She means everything to me', 'I can't thank them enough', 'He's been incredible,' trickles down into our everyday lives. It whisks up an emotional response but it also mixes up emotion with sentimentality, which is exaggerated, self-centred and self-indulgent. We will see in a later chapter how the language of absolutes ratchets up our anxiety.

We have swung so far away from traditional British repression to the unspoken assumption that expressing your emotions is always a good thing. I'm not so sure. In psychology, there is the concept of 'high expressed emotion', where a family expresses all their negative feelings openly, which is negatively associated with mental health. And what I see in the media and among some of my patients is this fuelling of an emotional fire when sometimes the flames of emotion need dousing down.

You want to aim for emotional competence. What do I mean by emotional competence? To have some semblance of control over how you feel. And, like many things in this book, this is linked to balance. The problems I see with feelings in my clinics are at the extremes of the emotional range: extremes of awareness of emotions and the choices made to manage them. So, problems seem to arise when feelings are too weak or too strong – they either are ignored or pandered to; hidden away or expressed too strongly. Ignore your feelings at your peril, of course, but it is also hazardous to listen to them too much.

My view of emotional competence is that it means you are aware of your feelings, able to identify and name them, and you manage these to your best advantage to have a happy and fulfilling life whilst being sensitive to, but not overwhelmed by, the feelings of others.

## What are feelings? Emotions? Thoughts?

Even as a psychologist, it is quite difficult to answer these questions.

A scientific definition of *emotion* involves a physical component, in that they involve a neurological, hormonal and biological response through the body reflected in facial expressions, as well as the mental component, and there is a universality about them which extends to animals too.[9] However, there are debates among psychologists about what constitutes basic, universal emotions. Traditionally, the core six were considered to be anger, happiness, sadness, fear, shock and disgust, though some psychologists would also add shame. However, more recent research on facial expressions is more suggestive of four: anger, happiness, sadness and fear.

---

9   Interestingly, this is why the scientist-psychologists (as opposed to clinical psychologists like me) would not recognise 'love' as an emotion as it doesn't have its own pattern of facial expression. They would see it as a drive (like thirst or hunger) but I'm not sure I agree with them about that.

The best analogy for this is colour: we learn early in life that there are three basic colours: red, blue and yellow, plus there are black and white for depth and tone, but after that, every colour we see is just a mix. So if there are four basic emotions, it seems to me that lots of other emotions are a mix of these four: surprise is a touch of fear with a dollop of happy. Shock would be mostly fear with a dab of sadness. These, if you like, are the green, purple and orange of the emotion world. Simple mixes of two base colours.

So, what is the difference between an emotion and a *feeling*? Well, generally, as you use them in everyday life, absolutely nothing. In this chapter I will use the words interchangeably, so don't worry too much about the technicalities. But I do think it's worth thinking about the difference for a moment because it makes an important point about your feelings. A feeling is the whole experience of emotion, incorporating your thinking, the context and your bodily response, and emotion is more the basic animalistic, physical response.

A feeling = bodily emotion + your thinking + your context

You see, lots of feelings are really only understandable if you add two other components: *thinking* and *context*. For example, you only 'feel abandoned' in the context of being left alone and minding that you are left alone. You don't 'feel abandoned' in the context of being left alone when you are totally fed up with your parents and your siblings have been driving you mad, with all the noise and nagging.

To understand feelings, I need to introduce you to the cognitive quad. When a young person comes to me with a feeling, I first try to understand the context that they were in when they got that feeling (did that situation trigger the feeling?) and then I try to understand it, to deconstruct it, at four other different levels:

1. Their physiology – what is happening in their body? E.g., is their heart beating fast? Have they got high or low energy? Are they sweating? Are they sleeping?

2. Their behaviour – what are they doing? How are they acting? Are they approaching? Avoiding? Hiding?

3. Their cognitions (commonly known as thoughts) – what are they thinking about what is going on? What internal monologue is going through their mind? What are their judgements and expectations in the situation?

4. Their emotions – what sensation are they reporting? Is it pleasant or not? Strong or weak? Can they put it into words?

These four parts of your conscious sensation of feeling are inextricably bound up together and, indeed, it is often difficult to untangle them from each other, not least because they are not in separate boxes inside of you. They are all mixed up together. I am putting them in lists and boxes as a model to help you understand yourself but of course it's not a true representation of reality. I will often draw this out for young people to help them understand how change at one level can and will influence each other level in turn, like these two I've drawn overleaf. The following cognitive quads represent two different young people both in the same situation: they were left alone in their house while the rest of the family was out. What do you notice about them?

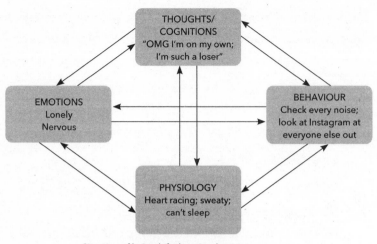

Situation of being left alone in a house on your own

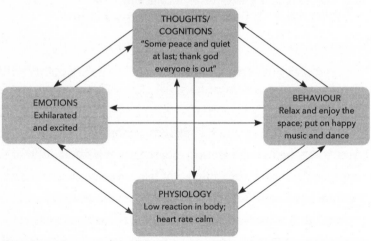

That's right, they are very different. And that is important because your feelings are sometimes innate, biological and not under your control. But sometimes they are not. Sometimes feelings are created or amplified by your physiology, thinking, behaviour or context, and these *are* things you have some control over. And if you are not going to be a victim to your feelings, you need to help yourself manage them healthily.

Expecting that you be an active participant in your feelings is not to say that you are to blame if you do feel negative emotions. Not at all. There are hundreds of situations in which it is right and appropriate to feel sad, angry or fearful – for example, if you have suffered a major loss, or been attacked or cheated on. However, it is also the case that there are plenty of situations where you do need to take responsibility for your own feelings through reining in your thoughts, the way you behave and your physical response and, if you have a choice, for the context you are putting yourself in.

## Your emotional mind and your rational mind

Your emotions are your body's early warning system for what is going on, your body's rough sketch. Are we in the realm of happiness, anger, fear or sadness? Is there shock or surprise? Fury or frustration? Your emotional reaction is wired closely into your senses: it is almost instantaneous and uncontrollable.

A millisecond later your thinking catches up. Your brain will analyse the context and your ability to cope with it, and thoughts will come into your head. And sometimes these thoughts are helpful, and sometimes they are not. At times, your thoughts will help calm the feelings down but they can also hype the feelings up. Sometimes our thoughts get hijacked by our emotions and don't let reality in. Listening to your feelings is really important but they can be influenced strongly by the things we tell ourselves.

So, for example, do you sometimes feel as if you aren't going to do well at school? Do you sometimes feel that you are going to let your teachers and parents down?

Technically, you see, feeling that you aren't going to do well isn't a feeling: it's a thought. The thought is 'I might not do well and I'm going to let people down' and the emotion that generates is worry and sadness, and the context is school. When thoughts and emotions get mixed up and baked together, it becomes hard to untangle them. And that is when you are likely to forget to let reality in. And maybe the reality is that you generally get good grades, so it is unlikely that you will do that badly, and if you do, your teachers and parents may feel momentarily disappointed for you but it is unlikely that they will care that much or that long. Let's face it, they will be busy with their other pupils/their own life. Having these thoughts in your brain is likely to be a lot less distressing than the other ones, about how you might let people down.

People feel things all the time, on the basis of their thoughts, which have no basis in reality. The power of feelings can make people believe that God wants them to hijack a plane and crash it into the World Trade Center. In other words, here's the long message made short: watch out for your feelings hijacking your brain.

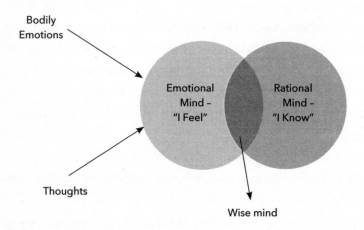

The place where your emotions get conflated with your thinking is often referred to in psychology as your 'emotional mind' – 'emotional' because it is based on your bodily emotions and 'mind' because it is your thinking about those. It is what we colloquially refer to as 'feeling'. And to be emotionally competent in this fast-paced competitive world, you need to listen to your emotional mind but not let it dominate your life. It needs to be tempered with a strong dose of reality from your 'rational mind'. Your thoughts and your feelings are one truth but the reality of the situation is a second truth. And when your feelings are really strong it's difficult to remember or look for the different truth.

To be emotionally competent, you don't ignore your emotional mind but you know to listen to it only so much. You need to listen to your rational mind as well. Sometimes talking to friends and family, sharing your thoughts and feelings, getting your emotional mind out in the open, can help you to identify the truth of the situation and get in touch with your rational mind.

The point where your feelings and reality overlap? Well, that's a really special place. That is your wise mind. When you listen to your feelings and to reality, and make a choice for yourself based on both, you develop wisdom. And to keep listening to your feelings when all the evidence says otherwise? That's not romantic, nor determined, nor committed, nor anything else you tell yourself to convince yourself that your feelings are right. In fact, that's mental illness.

*Lena believed she was fat because she 'felt fat'.*

*She felt this because everything she did (her behaviour) and her thoughts were geared towards finding evidence for this. For example, she scrutinised herself frequently in mirrors. She looked at herself from the back, front and both sides, standing and sitting. When she sat, she would look at where her thighs splayed out on the chair and call it fat. She would also body check, where she would bend over and pinch the folds in her skin and call that fat too. If she got the thought 'I ate too much' she would go to the mirror and examine if there was any change in her body. She would look in shop windows and car wing mirrors, particularly at her legs, and would compare her legs against other people who had thinner legs than her. She told herself that her friends didn't think she had anorexia, they thought she was fat, and then she found it difficult to eat in front of her friends as they might think she was greedy. Her day was taken up with body checking, looking for evidence to confirm her thoughts.*

*Lena believed her feeling that she was fat whole-heartedly, despite the evidence from reality: e.g. her diagnosis of anorexia and her treatment of that condition at an eating disorders clinic. She believed her feelings despite the evidence from her own physiology: e.g. her weight on the scale, the absence of a menstrual period, feeling cold and dizzy all the time. She allowed her feelings to guide her thinking, so she told herself that she was fatter than the other anorexic patients at the clinic and that all of us doctors and therapists had got it wrong. She would also behave in ways to keep herself underweight, e.g. constantly lying to her parents about how much she ate or making excuses as to why she couldn't join her friends for pizza.*

*She lived in a bubble of her own emotional mind, where her feeling fat caused her to fuse all her thinking to this feeling. She spent no time thinking about food, eating, weight and shape in her rational mind. She was mentally ill in relation to food, eating, weight and shape. In contrast, on nearly all other topics and issues she was completely logical and rational: a diligent student, involved in campaigning and politics, able to argue a coherent point, part of a lively group of friends.*

*Her family and friends knew she had an eating disorder but didn't know the content of her emotional mind: they didn't know how welded to her feelings her thinking had become. She hid it from them. She said she hid it from them because she was scared of reality. She was scared of the reality that she might be confirmed as 'fat' and she was also scared of the reality that she might be confirmed as 'mad', that her friends and family would see her thinking as odd or warped.*

*But without challenging her thoughts and changing her behaviour she would never recover from her eating disorder.*

So, to stay mentally well, you need to keep track of both your emotional mind and your rational mind. Keeping track of your emotional mind sometimes means trying to untangle your emotional reaction (sad, angry, worried) from your thinking ('I'm stupid/fat/ugly'). Is your internal monologue in your head telling you stuff that would make anyone feel bad? Is it telling you harsh stuff that you would never say to anyone else? Is it telling you stuff that is not true and is unhelpful? What would I hear if I could stick the jack of my headphones into your brain and listen in on your thinking?

Are you then acting in ways to back up your emotional mind? Behaving in ways that don't challenge your negative thoughts or, at worst, confirm them? Often, for example, I see young people who think no one likes them and they stay in their bed with their covers over their head, scrolling Instagram, looking at how everyone else is out and having fun, but they don't connect with anyone to start to change that. They behave in ways that confirm their hypothesis that no one likes them.

In this chapter, and the next one about anxiety, we are going to talk about how you can best manage your thoughts, your behaviour, your physiology and the situation to give you the best chance of feeling OK. While no one will ever master their feelings completely, you can give yourself the best chance of feeling differently.

In this way, emotional health is like physical health: you can't control it perfectly but you can give yourself the best odds. People who never smoke do get lung cancer and people who do all the right stuff for their mental health can get mentally ill. Stuff happens that would floor anyone emotionally. But this chapter is about giving yourself the best chance to feel happy.

To be emotionally competent, you listen to your emotions and your feelings but don't let them always dominate you. You also need to think about the reality. If you're going to make wise decisions for yourself and be emotionally available for other people, sometimes feelings need to be listened to and sometimes they need to be dampened down a bit.

## Where are you in relation to your feelings?

Before we start thinking about how to manage your own feelings, it is worth thinking about the relationship you have with them. That sounds very touchy-feely psychologist-speak, so let me explain. At any point in time, you can be in one of four places in relation to your own feelings and those of others:

- Self-absorbed

- Aware

- Understanding

- Empathic

Sometimes you can flit between any of these four places in a short space of time.

When a baby is born, it is completely **self-absorbed** and doesn't have a concept of anyone but itself. It is totally absorbed in its own feelings and sees the outside world only in relation to itself and its feelings. We can all get a bit like this when our emotions are running high and it becomes hard to think about anyone or anything else.

But when we are calmer, we can be **aware** of not only our feelings but those of the people around us: we pick up their emotions from their facial expressions, their body language, from what they say and the environment they are in. You can only do this when your own emotions are not too strong, when you are in a relatively neutral emotional gear and you are not hijacked by your own emotion. In other words: read the room, guys, read the room.

If you have a bit more time and (mental) energy, you might devote it to **understanding** emotions. In relation to other people, that involves understanding their context a little bit and what brings them to those emotions in that moment. In relation to yourself, it involves bringing in that touch of reality. It is non-judgemental.

The fourth stage of emotional functioning is being **empathic**: As you will remember, empathy is one of the most important bits in this whole book. Empathy is *being with* someone in their feelings – being aware of their feelings, understanding why they are feeling that and then being prepared to connect to that feeling in yourself. The experience is sitting in the emotions with understanding and kindness.

I wish it wasn't called empathy because it is too like the word sympathy. Empathy and sympathy are completely different and need to be separated out. The 'pathy' bit of these words is from the Greek word 'pathos', feeling, but please don't confuse the two concepts. Sympathy often places the receiver in a passive position, almost in a victim role; it implies a hierarchy – things are better for me than you and so I feel glad I'm not you. Sympathy is feeling sorry or pity *for* someone. Sympathy can be kindly meant but it can also be a patronising, hostile or superior act.

Empathy is an active state: it is hard work, really, understanding someone else's viewpoint, or even your own, in all its complexity. It is not done *to* someone else, it is done *with* someone, to share their perspective. It is also the rock on which therapy is built. Every day, I am amazed at the power of empathy in my work. It can happen in friendships, between family members and in therapy. When I'm with a patient, I am trying to tune in to the content of their mind and their patterns of thinking, so that I can finish their sentence. The power people find when I join with their mind and share their mental burden with them is incredible. I feel a recognition: 'Ah, I see, that's where you are at; I get it.' They feel validated and cared for. But crucially, empathy opens up the possibility for change. Once people truly understand themselves and feel accepted, they are ready to think about how things could be different.

Empathy can involve sharing experience – that is why you probably feel so emotionally connected to your friends – but the empathic power actually comes not from the shared experience but from the shared emotion. It is not walking in someone else's shoes but being inside someone else's mindset.

In relation to yourself, empathy can mean acknowledging your feelings and understanding them in your own context, but also understanding reality. It means resisting the pull of the emotional mind to be self-absorbed in your own mood – the victim or heroine in your own story. But it also means resisting the pull of the rational mind to dismiss or dishonour your emotions as silly or irrelevant, or, worse, beating yourself up for feeling like that. It means understanding yourself and understanding reality and *still* being kind to yourself.

And that is hard.

## Strong negative emotions: negative coping strategies

Sometimes your rational and wise minds will desert you and you will find yourself stuck in a negative place of self-absorption. When your thinking has become wedded to a negative emotional reaction you can find yourself caught in a negative cycle that causes you to behave in a way that perpetuates that feeling. I've illustrated this on the diagram overleaf: follow the arrows round. There is a trigger event which causes a physiological emotional response. Then there is a cognitive judgement of the emotional response, which leads to a feeling. This in turn causes a behavioural response. The behavioural response will, in all likelihood, lead to more negative thoughts about oneself, which will feed back into more negative feelings.

For some of you reading this book, it's likely your feelings will be overwhelming now. You may have felt sad or worried or angry for so long, or the feelings are so strong, that you feel you must do something, anything, to make the feeling stop. I am really, really sorry if that is how you are feeling right now.

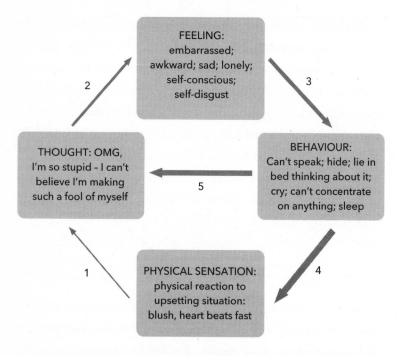

Sometimes, when you are stuck feeling like that for a long time, you can only think of punishing, unkind things to do to change it. As well as being unkind to yourself, these things are, of course, counter-productive in the longer term. They may give you some momentary relief but they make the situation worse or make you feel worse about yourself. Often that happens late at night, when a perfect storm of emotions has built up through the day, you're feeling exhausted and lack other things to distract you, or people to help you.

There are kind, wise ways to deal with your emotions and feelings and there are punitive, negative ways, and there is every shade of grey in between. All of us can get dragged into less constructive 'solutions' to our feelings, which may help in the short term but exacerbate or cause more problems in the longer term. These might include smoking, alcohol, prescription or illegal drugs, or under- or overeating.

But currently the favoured unkind way to deal with an emotional mind among teenage girls is, unfortunately, self-harm.

There is an epidemic of self-harm in the Western world – it has gone from being incredibly rare to something used by approximately 20–30 per cent of young women in the UK and America, for example. It used to be linked strongly to sadness or suicidal behaviours but now it has shockingly become an almost normalised way for lots of young people to manage a range of difficult emotions, particularly self-disgust, frustration, pressure, anxiety and depression. It is itself on a continuum of severity and intent: growing from more normal or accepted behaviours like chewing your finger or hangnails or digging your nails into your hand or arm, through scratching your arm with your nails or an object, to using an object to cut yourself. The severity of the self-harm is not necessarily a representation of how distressed you are but obviously some methods are more physically dangerous. Please don't feel that you need to use a more serious method of self-harm to show or even prove your distress: it is not a good way to show or deal with your pain. We have lots of other ways instead.

*Suzi came to see me with low mood. She was 15. She felt hopeless that anything could be better – she was regularly self-harming and didn't particularly want to be alive. She had previously done pretty well in school but now she couldn't be bothered; she often didn't go to sleep till late, then got up late and was late for school. She regularly had to leave class as she felt panicky. Her parents were super worried about her: they felt they had lost their little girl. But there was a lot of her behaviour they didn't like. They didn't like it that she was rude to them in front of her younger siblings or that her primary-aged sister had seen fresh self-harm on Suzi's arm and it had really upset her. They'd also caught her smoking weed more than once and she frequently broke her curfew and came home late and drunk.*

When I listen to young people talk about their self-harm, it reminds me of how my generation used smoking. I hope that doesn't make you feel I am trivialising self-harm? I am not. The world you live in as young people is far more complex, intense and fast-paced than it has been before. It is not surprising that your generation has had to raise the bar to express distress and to deal with overwhelming feelings. But the reliance on something for emotional release feels the same.

Currently, smoking and self-harm show similar incidence rates in surveys of teenagers. Nearly all maladaptive coping strategies contain some degree of self-harm. So, smoking hurts your lungs; alcohol your liver and your common sense; drugs have all manner of physical risks.

Can I just have a quick word about illegal drugs? I see so many teenagers who care so much about the world: they want to eat ethically; be gender inclusive; protest that Black Lives Matter and strike for climate change. Yet they take illegal drugs. The illegal drugs trade is not an ethically neutral industry, it is linked to organised crime and terrorism, violence and the exploitation of the poor and vulnerable. I know my generation has no moral authority to tell your generation what to do, given the mess we have made of all sorts of things, and we aren't living the pressures you are living that you feel you need the drugs to cope with. I also don't want to give you another thing to feel guilty about but I do want to put it out there that it might be incongruent with your other values.

But these methods do not actually sort out the problem: they just give a momentary release. At best, they maintain it and at worst, they exacerbate it. What do I mean by that? I mean that by using self-harm, or another negative coping strategy, you can get caught in a catch-22 situation. For example:

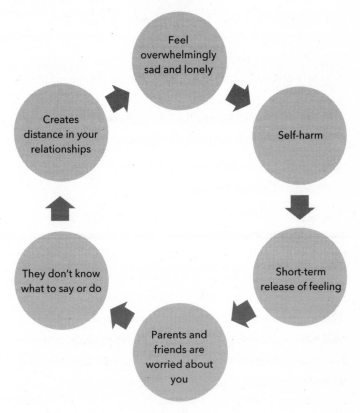

This is just an example but it is typical of what I see in my clinical work all the time: there is a difficult horrible feeling and to cope with it, a young person ends up doing something (not eating, taking drugs, smoking, self-harming, overworking, being anti-social) which actually becomes the problem: the solution to the feeling becomes the problem.

Choosing these negative or punitive or self-destructive methods to cope with difficult feelings can feel really tempting. Why?

- When you are so low you feel numb, it's better to feel something than nothing.

- It feels like it gives importance to the upsetting feeling – the importance that you feel it deserves. Being in your rational mind can feel like it's dismissing the importance of how you feel.

- You can be powerless and stuck in your situation and believe that there is no positive way out.

- You can feel as though you don't deserve the positive ways of coping with your feelings.

- When you feel unheard in your pain, you want to show people how bad it is for you.

- You may want to hurt others (parents or an ex-partner) by hurting yourself.

- There can be a drama attached to your emotional mind that makes life less boring. There can be an attraction to the victim or the tortured heroine role. Not surprisingly, as it is a version of womanhood that you are shown everywhere.

- It can somehow seem boring or wrong to be rational or wise: it seems too sensible for the strength of the pain you are in (even if it reduces it – why is that?).

I feel for you if you feel really bad and are drawn towards negative coping strategies but I want to encourage you to break that pattern. While using negative coping strategies to deal with difficult feelings is something everyone does sometimes, try not to make it your default coping mechanism over a long period of time, or take it to the extreme.

I hope, of course, that you will be able to use this next section of the book to find some positive coping strategies. You may not feel that you value yourself enough to do that. But to start to value yourself you need to use some of these, to give yourself the best chance of being emotionally competent, of being mentally well.

## The foundations of good mental health

What are the foundations of good mental health? Well, some of it is luck – a good attachment figure, genetics, the right school and friends – and some of these things are out of your control. But there *are* things you can do to maximise your mental health and cope with everyday feelings to try to give yourself the best foundation for emotional competence.

### Physical Movement
Now, look, I get it. If you are not sporty, school PE is pretty rubbish. I was put off exercise for years because I was rubbish at school sport. I just *didn't care* whether the ball went in the goal or

over the net. In my later school life, I skived off school sport to go and meet boys in town and smoke cigarettes.

This is how bad I am at sport: at the wake following my father's funeral, when I was in my thirties, I told one of my old PE teachers that I planned to run 10k to raise money for Cancer Research in his memory. My old PE teacher laughed. She laughed at the thought of me exercising *in the context of my father's funeral when the sport was in his memory*. That's pretty harsh. It tells us two things: firstly, I'm not a natural athlete; but secondly, some PE teachers believe that sport is only for natural athletes and for the rest of us, the mere idea is amusing. I am sorry, I think that attitude is fundamentally wrong and I think it's off-putting for girls.

Why off-putting? PE and sports teachers at school tend to be sporty, competitive types and good at the type of sports that are done at schools: football, athletics, netball, hockey, rugby, tennis, swimming. These sports have a privileged position in our society and those who are motivated and good at them are encouraged. And I get it. I get that lots of people do feel that and care passionately about where the ball is and who wins and loses, but that leaves the ones who don't disenfranchised from sport.

Lots of schools are dominated by traditionally male team sports, which some of you love but are not everyone's cup of tea. In fact, research shows only 23 per cent of you like school PE. You get put off by it being competitive and childish; you want to do something more grown up. Many of you feel uncomfortable in your bodies. Puberty, while taking boys more towards sporting prowess, heaps the barriers to exercise on you, as you need sports bras, to decide what to do about your body hair and to manage your periods in the changing rooms and sports outfits. Sport as a graded activity (are you in the A or B team?) becomes another area where you worry about being good enough.

Hence, in teenage years, girls' participation in sport falls off a cliff. Not as many adult women have an interest, either as a participant or spectator, in team sports in the same way as lots of men do and women tend to gravitate to more gym- and dance-based activities which are typically not offered in schools. Why not? Why is dance not offered along with football in primary school?

Is this another source of hidden sexism, that school sport has evolved to suit male rather than female preferences? Or have girls complied with social norms to be 'pretty and precious' and not sporty and strong?

Another thing that is toxic about exercise for girls is when it becomes all about how their bodies look and not about how their bodies feel. Language is interesting here as 'fit' has migrated from the latter to the former. No longer owned as a feeling inside or a quantitative reality, it has become another term to judge people. Woo-hoo! That's what we needed – more words to judge the relative attractiveness of our bodies! But how you look shouldn't be the be-all and end-all. How you feel is more important. I know, I know, you may be saying now: 'I can't feel good unless I look good.' Yes, of course, but if it is more important than being kind or smart, or you put all your time and money into it, or if it becomes the most important thing about you, well, then you need to work on that. How you look may be one thing about you but it's nowhere near the most important thing about you. I think that the person you are inside and how you show kindness to others should trump appearance in the importance stakes.

Moving your body is a crucially important thing for physical and for mental health. Indeed, I would argue that the most important thing a school can do is to find a physical activity that a young person loves that will sustain them for the rest of their life. Why? Because a massive study of over a million Americans found a surprise result that being active was the most powerful factor correlated with good mental health. Given the links between mental health on the one hand and school attainment and economic productivity on the other, this is not just a woolly psychologist, pandering-to-feelings suggestion. It is a practical economic one too. What type of activity? Any, because there are lots of pathways through which movement works its magic mental power:

- Firstly, all types of physical activity (even housework apparently) can release endorphins, which are linked to feelings of pleasure, joy, excitement.

- All physical activity reduces the stress response of cortisol and adrenaline in the body.

- Sports and team exercises show a very strong impact on mental wellbeing for some people. Being part of something bigger than yourself (a team), socialising and scratching that competitive itch, if you are that way inclined, all contribute to positive mental health.

- Yoga and walking also showed a similar impact for others, perhaps reducing aches and pains, keeping you young through flexibility and also encouraging mindfulness (see page 118).

- Cycling, going to the gym and other similar aerobic exercise, although generally more solitary, can also be great for mental health. Is this due to the impact of the aerobic function alone? Or do they have a mindful benefit? Or is about achieving goals and the self-esteem boost that brings?

There is some suggestion from the research that some people find outdoor exercise has benefits over and above that taken indoors. The benefit of the exercise might add to the separate benefit of being outside, which does seem to help you get out of your own head. When your emotional mind starts spiralling up, changing your scene can help snap you out of the escalation. It's one of those really simple things, like drinking water, that is always a surprise when it makes such a difference. A change of scene helps reset the mind and many times I have seen the impact of being outdoors on mental health.

*Suzi's parents thought they had the answers for her. They thought she'd feel better if she didn't lie in bed half the weekend and instead got up and did something with her day, like taking some exercise or going outside. They also thought she'd feel better if she ate better, as she was rarely hungry for family meals but filled up on snacks late at night. They thought her sleep was bad because she was on her phone half the night. When her parents offered this advice, Suzi felt unlistened to – that they didn't understand how bad she felt. It often ended in a row and then she felt worse about herself, as she knew that they were only trying to help. However, she was too annoyed by the advice to consider whether any of it was useful.*

## Mindfulness

Mindfulness is definitely having its moment in the sun as a way to deal with negative emotions. You have probably heard about it at school. I almost wish they wouldn't teach it in schools, as it seems to put off more of you than it engages – or maybe the ones who find it helpful don't end up in therapy. There might be a correlation that finding mindfulness helpful protects mental health. But when schools are so prescriptive, with the emphasis on breathing and meditative seriousness, they miss a chance to help you find your own mindful space.

Mindfulness at its core is about being present in the moment, rather than beating yourself up for the past or worrying about the future. Doing something physical, repetitively, can help put you in a mindful state. What can you do that makes your brain go into neutral? Where is the place where the ideas in your head start to calm down rather than spiral up? Where you are not getting off on being hyper but on being calm? Is it walking? Standing on your head? Stroking the cat? Reading? Climbing? Praying? Having a bath with candles? Knitting? It doesn't have to be you sitting cross-legged with your hands on your knees saying 'ommm'. Being in the moment can happen in different ways.

Indeed, I think lots of things might be mindful which have never been thought of or investigated as being mindful: such as watching reruns of shows you have watched a million times, reading a newspaper, sunbathing. If you can be in the moment with a neutrality towards yourself, you are being mindful.

Sadly for you, I don't think it's scrolling on your phone. Indeed, I think this is the antithesis of mindful. There is so much content that it stimulates the brain rather than helping it to stay still and often this means a spiralling up of emotion rather than allowing the brain to find a peaceful space. It is not a neutral gear for the brain. There is often an urgency and agency to social media and the content is so comparative and competitive that there is no way the brain can be in time with itself. Of course, it depends what you are doing on the phone: reading, listening to a calming podcast, gentle music – these can all be mindful. TikTok: less so. TikTok has its place as a fun distraction but not, I don't think, as mindful.

## Sleep

There are whole books devoted to why sleep is important so I'm not going to do much credit to the subject in one paragraph. A few things I want you to know, though. Firstly, circadian rhythms are in *every cell of your body*. Think about that; it really is incredible. Each cell has a natural rhythm to fall asleep at night. And yet, with the invention of the electric light, our whole society has changed so we stay up later and you probably fight this rhythm to go to bed later. Often, last thing at night is your free time and it's so nice to be not working and free to do what you want, so it's hard to give that up and go to bed. But there is a concept called 'a sleep window' – a time when you can fall asleep easily. If you miss that time, it is often actually very difficult to get to sleep and after that, you may find yourself tossing and turning. This is counter-intuitive because you think you would be more tired the later you stay up but actually you get past sleep. Being very busy on social media will give your brain too much input to process and make it harder to get to sleep. If your emotional mind is hyper alert, it will also be more difficult to sleep. As a teenager, you have a sleep window which is naturally slightly later than you will have when you are older, but not much later – 11:30pm, not 2am – and you need more sleep. As the world generally works on being up in the morning this can be a real catch-22, where tiredness contributes to you feeling sad or worried but then those feelings make it difficult to get to sleep.

## Actively managing your feelings

Finding your preferred way of moving your body, checking in with reality, finding your brain space, taking some rest and eating (so important it gets its own chapter) are the foundations to good mental health. You are unlikely to get it without these but they are not sufficient in themselves.

No life worth living is without strong emotions, so even with your foundations in place you need to take responsibility to manage, and not be dominated by, your feelings.

### Talking

As a woman, a psychologist and therapist, my first inclination was always to deal with feelings by talking about them. Generally, women and girls seem to like to talk through their feelings more than men and boys. Through my career, I have learnt that talking is not for everybody; nor is it the right solution in every situation. There are also the wrong types of talking.

The wrong types of talking? What do I mean by that? I always think *Love Island* is a particularly good place to witness the wrong sorts of talking. When you are feeling stuck in your emotional mind, you need someone who is going to listen, understand and empathise with your feelings, but not someone who is going whip up your emotions or feed you a false view of reality.

My observation of the friendships of teenage girls, and young women is that it can sometimes become too consensual and not challenging enough. You need someone to talk to who will empathise with the emotion but also help you find your wise mind, even if that means compassionately puncturing your emotional mind with a few truths from reality. You don't see that on *Love Island* or similar shows. What you see is the girls forming little groups where they back up each other's emotional minds and end up often colluding with each other on the fantasy of romance. We'll return to this in the love and relationships chapter.

So, what's the 'right' type of talking? Well, there are lots of different right types.

Sometimes we need to get things off our chest. We need to be listened to and our pain needs to be witnessed. In psychology we call this 'cathartic' and it is the basis of most counselling approaches. When your thoughts and feelings are rushing around your head, stopping to talk about them can help you understand them yourself. In other words, so much content goes in during our day-to-day lives and there is often no time to reflect except when you start talking. But you must be careful that the talking does not become self-justificatory.

*Suzi stayed up to 1am or 2am every night, talking with her friends about how bad they all felt: they could see no light; they disliked everything about themselves. They offered her reassurance about how nice/kind/funny/clever/pretty she was, how much they loved her and how valued she was to them. But these platitudes were like water off a duck's back, as were hers to them. Indeed, late at night, when tired and emotional, it did nothing to relieve the emotions nor solve the problems. In fact, to be part of their close friendship group, you had to be sad. To get better would mean not being part of the late-night sadness.*

*Sadly, one of her friends had to go to hospital because of her psychiatric risk and Suzi's feelings were really complex about this. A huge part of her was terribly sad and scared that she nearly lost her friend but another part of her felt that it should have been her. Her feelings felt diminished as not as bad or not as important as her friend's. Her parents were really freaked by this too and worried about them triggering each other, so they started taking Suzi's phone away at night. It was really stormy for a while.*

When the dark mood has taken hold of the emotional mind, talking about things, getting it out of your head, can help you to see things from a different perspective, if you let it. Sometimes when crazy stuff is going round your mind, it can seem both reasonable and totally justified. Saying it out loud gives you distance from it – like writing it down – and you then can assess your own thoughts from the position of being slightly outside them. The flaws in your logic, the inconsistencies in your feelings and the hyperbole of your emotion are easier to spot in speech or writing than in thought. I often say to my patients, 'How does that sound to you, when you say it out loud?' and they tend to reply that it sounds silly or unhelpful. It helps them to get their thoughts into perspective.

However, as I implied earlier, sometimes you still can't find your rational mind when you say it out loud. Sometimes, that emotional mind is really stuck and you need the wisdom of a good friend, parent or therapist to give you a kind little prod to challenge your thinking. You need a few friends who will be honest and open with you. You need to be brave enough to hear different views.

*After her parents had taken her phone away, Suzi started to climb out of her window at night to lie on the flat roof outside and smoke. It had started as something to do to piss off her parents but she found she actually quite liked this. She lay on her back looking at the stars or clouds. She felt better being outside than in. It seemed to blow out the negative thoughts. I didn't say it to her, as it would have put her off, but it was meditative in a way. She did end up sleeping more.*

*That enabled me to open the conversation that perhaps doing some things differently, thinking about some things differently, might make a difference in how she felt. She was resistant to the idea. I named the resistance: me being another bloody adult telling her how to feel better; another person thinking they had the answers for her. Yes, she said, and looked me in the eyes for one of the first times. I thought she was thinking, 'Yes, this strange woman seems to get me a bit, seems to understand a bit.'*

Talking about your feelings and having them understood is an incredibly powerful process for most people. Lots of young people find that it is through talking to others that they start to understand themselves. Speaking with your friends about how you feel can help you understand the causes of your own feelings and behaviour, for sure. But when this is matched by a good, honest friend sharing their feelings, it also helps you to understand that people think about the same situation very differently, and that different feelings result from taking a different view.

So, the benefits of talking are clear but what is getting in the way? There are two main barriers to talking that I hear about in my clinics. Firstly, not wanting to impose your feelings on other people and secondly, not knowing what to say.

You have to strike the right balance with your friends between talking and listening – you don't want to be emotionally incontinent – but I've found that if you are worrying about imposing on your friends, you are probably not. That you are concerned about this shows a sensitivity to the issue which indicates you are probably erring on the side of being the listener rather than the talker. But, as I mentioned in the friendship chapter, talking is the sharing of vulnerability, and sharing vulnerability builds closeness and connection. If you are not sharing your feelings with family and friends, you are curtailing your relationships with them: friendships rarely move closer or survive without some degree of vulnerability-sharing. If your inside world is completely unknown to your friends, you should probably question whether you are letting them be your friends at all?

As to what to say, there's a phrase you might have heard: name it to tame it. At the start of every session of therapy, I say, 'How are you?' and the person says, 'Fine,' and then I usually say, 'How are you really?' and then they tell me. But sometimes young people can't. They really struggle to find the right words for those abstract feelings going on inside. Yet, naming the feelings really is half the battle. In those situations, I will often use an emotional wheel and you too may find this helpful for pulling out what is going on for you.

Look at the emotional wheel opposite: start at the centre and identify roughly what core emotion you ae feeling. Then move out to the next layers and try to nail down what is going on for you exactly. When you are feeling tongue-tied and unsure what you feel, starting at the centre, identifying the rough sphere of emotion you are in and then working outwards can be really helpful.

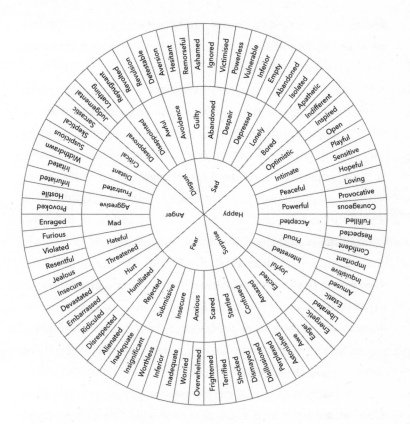

(This emotional wheel is courtesy of Laura Thomas, *Just Eat It*, 2019)

As we saw in Chapter 3 – Friends, some of you will struggle to know or express your emotions. That doesn't mean that you don't have feelings. It means that you can't notice, access or label them. At times of great emotion in your life, when you are feeling extremely sad, angry or anxious, if you can't identify or deal with it, it may come out in a million other different ways.

Knowing your own feelings requires the ability to take a meta-view of them. A meta-view is when you metaphorically stand outside of yourself and figure out what is going on inside of you. Very few people know instantaneously how they feel;

nearly everyone needs to pause and take stock: to scan body and mind, emotions and thoughts, taking in all the information then searching for the right word.

Counselling and therapy can be helpful in taking a meta-view, as you have someone there to help you. You also don't have to worry about imposing on your friends – counselling and therapy is a place you can say whatever you think and feel and don't have to consider the feelings of the other person. A good counsellor or therapist will help you find the words to express yourself. Most secondary schools now provide access to a counselling service. Counselling is giving yourself a space to talk, reflect, make sense of stuff and take a meta-view of yourself. Therapy is generally provided in health services rather than schools and may be for you if your problems have lasted that bit longer or are a bit more severe. A good counsellor or therapist should provide empathy, to understand your emotional mind, but also that little bit of difference to help you move out of it.

A final word on counselling and therapy: if you try it and don't like it or it doesn't help, it doesn't mean you shouldn't try again at a different time or with a different therapist. Finding a therapy that works for you is a bit like finding a pair of jeans: not all styles suit you.

*With no phone at night, and the shock of her friend going to hospital, and perhaps because she felt understood, something shifted in Suzi. She decided she wanted to change schools after GCSEs to go to a large sixth-form college and she knew she needed to pass her exams to do that, so she started focusing on her schoolwork. She chose A level topics that suited her and not her parents. She found different ways to express her identity and annoy her parents, dyeing her hair green and getting some extra piercings. She got a part-time job, which meant she was out more and much more active, and had to get to sleep at night. Behaviourally, things changed; emotionally, things changed. Chicken and egg.*

## Doing stuff

In psychological research, it's been shown that 'behavioural activation' is as good as anti-depressants at helping depression. What's behavioural activation? It's psychologist-language for doing stuff. When you are sad and low, or worse, depressed, you often don't feel like doing anything. You feel like sitting in a dark room, listening to sad music, eating a whole tub of ice cream, snapping at your parents for being so annoying. Do you know what? That's important . . . for a while. That's grieving whatever loss you have had that is making you sad. But, after a bit, it's time to stop because it can become self-fulfilling. It becomes one of those catch-22s again. Listening to sad music evokes sadness; you feel bad for eating all of the ice cream and not leaving some for anyone else; you really shouldn't have told Mum that her breathing was annoying, that was mean. Doing activities you like, changing your environment, going outside, connecting to your senses and some of the other things mentioned below can all be important for moving you on from the sadness.

## Doing something for someone else

Remember the four levels of feelings we discussed earlier? (See page 97 if you've forgotten.) When you are sad, you probably enter the emotional state of self-absorption. Being sad or angry takes you firmly into your own point of view: the egocentricity of misery. When thoughts about other people do puncture the bubble, they tend to do so only in relation to you, e.g. 'They don't like me', 'They were so mean to me', 'Nobody would even care if I wasn't around.' The trick of trying to truly connect to someone's thoughts, instead of thinking about their thoughts about you, as I described in relation to social anxiety in the chapter about friends, can also help drag you back from unhappiness. Then, trying to do one small thing to connect to them or help them is powerful at helping you move out of sadness. Send them a quick text: 'How did it go with your mum/boyfriend/that test you were worried about?' Show someone that you are thinking of them and *what they are feeling* rather than ruminating on your own feelings. Do something kind for them or someone else: go visit your grandma, sit with your brother and play Lego with him, make a cake for someone. These sorts of things will take you out of your self-absorbed self and also help you re-connect to the kind and good person who thinks of others that I know you are.

It is also a good idea when you are feeling sad to think about being part of something bigger than you. It's so easy when you are down to scroll on Instagram and think about how everyone has it better or is better than you. Connecting to your own values[10] by volunteering or campaigning for an organisation or cause, be it Black Lives Matter, Amnesty, the climate emergency or animal welfare, helps you feel valuable and again takes you out of your own head. Campaigning can be done from your bedroom; I am particularly fond of Amnesty's letter writing campaign on behalf of political prisoners and victims of torture.

---

10  More about values in Chapter 8 – Screens and the Internet. Sorry that this chapter has so many links to other chapters but it is a bit inevitable as emotions and feeling are at the heart of the book. They relate to every other bit.

Face-to-face working, volunteering, campaigning, protesting or helping out in some way, like reading with younger kids at an after-school club, can help move you on from the negative mindset. Often you can get caught in a comparison trap looking only at people who are seen as better than you in some way: smarter; prettier; richer and with more friends. This is even easier to do with social media. This sort of bigger-than-you work can help break that trap: it can ground you back in your strengths, your privilege, your gratitude. It also helps show that you have purpose and can make a difference.

**Ride the emotional wave**

Emotions, as discussed, are a bodily reaction. They do not last forever. Even in the strongest of negative emotions, for example the grief after someone has died, there will be moments of humour, lightness and hope as the grief comes in waves up and down. In psychology, we often talk about 'riding the wave of emotion'. Breathe, connect, talk, rest, eat, move. The feelings will go up and then they will go down. Everyone hurts sometimes. And this too shall pass.

**Connect to your senses**

When you are trying to ride out the emotional wave, connecting to your five senses can help you feel grounded again:

- What can you see? What colours, shapes? Are there things you haven't noticed before?

- What can you hear? What sounds are in your background and foreground?

- What do things feel like? Ground yourself. Feel the ground under your feet. Put your hands on your seat. Feel the support on your butt and back.

- What can you smell? Can you put something pleasant to smell in front of you?

- What can you taste? Is there a pleasant taste in your mouth? Perhaps a left over lingering taste of coffee or chocolate or mint toothpaste.

- This works really well outside and helps again to get you out of your head and connected to reality.

**Write it down**

Sometimes the feelings (the thoughts and the emotions) get really stuck. Writing them down is another good way to get them out of your head. When you write things down they become 'other' to you, slightly separate, and allow you to take a meta-view, which is also what you get in good therapy. That can help drag you back to a more helpful or accurate place and help you move on. I've noticed that writing something onto a screen, particularly on a phone, doesn't seem to give that third-person stance as strongly as writing with a pen and paper, and you need that to get a meta-view for the writing to be powerful. (I think it might be because our phones have become an extension of us, of our psyches, as we always have them with us.) There is also evidence that writing down things you are grateful for every day – sometimes called gratitude journaling – improves mood.

Finally, and most importantly, a plea from me. Please, please, please, *be kind to yourself*: In the 'Want to Know More?' section

I've put some resources for self-compassion. That means not doing unkind things to yourself to deal with your feelings. But it also means not being too self-indulgent of your feelings as well. Acknowledge your feelings to yourself, allow yourself to feel them, but don't ruminate in them. Check out reality and try to distract or move yourself on from them in a kindly way. Don't beat yourself up for feeling something but equally, don't sit with it for hours letting it dominate. Find that emotional balance; find that emotional competence. And if it's impossible to move on from it then be kind to yourself and get some help.

# CHAPTER 5

# ANXIETY AND WORRY

'The mean reds are horrible. You're afraid
and you sweat like hell, but you don't know what
you are afraid of'

**TRUMAN CAPOTE,** *BREAKFAST AT TIFFANY'S*

'There is nothing either good or bad but that
thinking makes it so.'

**WILLIAM SHAKESPEARE,** *HAMLET*

So many emotions, so little time to explore them all. So, why do anxiety, fear and worry get their own chapter? Because survey after survey indicate that anxiety is currently rife among teenage girls and young women. It seems like you are suffering from an anxiety epidemic.

What we know about this anxiety epidemic is this: we know that previous generations faced a lot of adversity, yet anxiety levels were not as high. I do not think that is because your generation is fundamentally less brave than previous generations. It seems like the stuff you worry about is similar to previous generations: school, academic work, your appearance, family and friends. But the context in which these worries exist has changed, and in the current context your worries seem to be getting whipped up into a frenzy. I see this in analogy to climate change: just as global warming has led to the weather patterns becoming stronger and more extreme, so social changes are whipping the winds of worry into an anxiety tornado. Anxiety is a spiralling force, like a whirlwind or typhoon, gaining strength and speed as it swirls around.

So, why now? What is it about society that's whipping up the anxiety? That is a tricky question. It is not simple. It is multi-factorial and to understand it we need to go back to basics.

## What is anxiety?

Anxiety is the word we use when fear or worry reach clinical levels: i.e., when they start to have a negative impact on your everyday life for too long. In this chapter, I use the words interchangeably and everything I write is applicable to the anxiety family (e.g. fear, worry, obsession, panic, phobia).

From the last chapter we need to remember there are five components to consider with any feeling – four of them are about you and the fifth is the context. Psychologists often draw the four that come from you as a 'cognitive quad' – remember the illustration on page 98?

1. Physiology – your body response

2. Behaviour – what you do

3. Cognitions – what you think

4. Emotions – your feeling

5. The context or situation within which these feelings exist.

We also saw how two of these, your thoughts and feelings, can become enmeshed into an 'emotional mind' and that when that happens it is hard to let reality (the context) in.

In the emotions chapter, we didn't focus so much on the physiology bit, by which I mean what happens in your body, but this is really important in understanding anxiety. Anxiety is experienced in the body as well as the mind. In fact, nearly every part of your body reacts as part of 'the anxious response'. Your body reacts quicker than your conscious thinking to any perceived threat to ensure your survival, to get you away from things that might harm you. This is sometimes described as the 'fight or flight' reaction: your body's attempt to fight or run away from a perceived threat.

So how does it do this? Your perceptual systems are wired to instantaneously trigger the hormones adrenaline and cortisol, which cause your heart to beat faster, your breathing to quicken, your stomach to turn over quicker and your sweat glands to activate. This reaction raises your blood sugar and oxygen because if you are going to fight or run away, your body needs that oxygen and energy. This reaction is called 'sympathetic arousal'. This all happens super quickly and is very similar to the reaction of a dog when you stand on her paw, or a cat when it sees a dog.

If we think back to more primitive times, if a cavewoman came out of her cave and confronted a sabre-toothed tiger, she needed to act pretty quickly. Her eyes saw the tiger and all the hormones flooded through her body, creating the energy she needed to fight or run away. That is what sympathetic arousal is: preparing the body for physical exertion. Similarly, now, if you are walking down the street and someone jumps out on you from behind, you need to respond fast.

And as it all happens so quickly, there is a slight time lag where your conscious thought catches up.

I think the best way to understand that time lag is when someone jumps out on you. Your instinctive response will be to jump away and that is triggered by your sympathetic arousal causing all those bodily changes. All unconscious, right? You don't decide to jump away or release hormones, it just happens as an instinctive response in the body, as it would in an animal. You might have a startle response putting your hands up to protect your chest. Your face will show shock. All unconscious.

Then your thinking system catches up and weighs in with its assessment of the situation. If you see it is your friend, joking with you, trying to give you a shock, then a message is sent to your body that it can relax. It was initially scary but the meaning you ascribe it makes it not so. Your friend's amusement comes from the time lag between your instinctive survival response and your conscious understanding a moment later.

If it's a mugger, your thinking system may catch up to decide not to fight (they may have a knife) or flee (they may be faster than you) and to reluctantly hand over your phone.

In the friendship chapter, I introduced the idea of your brain having three layers: a core animalistic-like brain where automatic things happen; a middle limbic system brain and a top layer, the cortex, that deals with rational thinking. The initial arousal happens between the core brain and the limbic system and the top layer takes a moment to catch up. It is slower but more sophisticated.

The anxious response is a useful survival mechanism in situations of physical threat. But there are two problems with that nowadays: the first, as we saw in the emotions chapter, is that when your thinking gets wedded to your emotions it doesn't let your rational mind in. The second is that the type of threats you face nowadays often don't require a fight or flight reaction.

These two factors together can create a spiral of anxiety, triggered more by your thoughts than reality.

## Internal and external triggers for anxiety

So far, we have covered a simple model of anxiety, with a threat such as a wild animal or potential mugger giving your instinctive brain a shock to release the anxiety response.

However, many of the threats you face nowadays are not immediate physical threats that require a fight or flight response – they are more complex than that. For example, if you are scared of a test or exam you get the fight or flight response, but you should neither punch the exam invigilator nor run away. Your body is left with a heightened sympathetic arousal, with blood sugar and oxygen up but no outlet to use up this energy. Similarly, as a teenage girl, you might often feel the threats in your friendships or to your social position ('Am I going to be left out or bullied?'). Again, you can't run away and fighting people is generally not 'a good plan'.

What is different about these sorts of threats is that they are either triggered or exacerbated by your own thinking. A trigger event (for example, your friends not being around) causes a worry thought to pop into your brain about the situation (that they don't like you) and it is that thought that trips the sympathetic arousal to respond with anxiety. Of course, sometimes these threats are real and are outside of you: exams are real; falling out with friends is real. Yes, but they are not universally threatening. It's the *meaning* that your thoughts give to these sorts of events that makes them scary. So, if you think the exam doesn't matter or you don't care how you do, you probably won't feel anxious about it. In contrast, if you care very deeply but haven't done enough work and you think that your teacher and parents are going to be angry if you mess up, you are likely to be more anxious. Thus, although the initial trigger is external, a test, it is *your thinking* that determines whether it is anxiety provoking to you or not.

Saying there is a 'thinking' component is not to diminish your anxiety. It is definitely not to say 'it's all in the mind'. Important fact: anxiety is never 'all in the mind', no more than it is 'all in the body'. Anxiety is a physical and mental response to feeling attacked or having concerns about your future. But it is also important to remember that your mind can trigger anxiety in the absence of any external threat: it can completely make up threats. Or, more likely, your mind can put a threatening meaning on a completely neutral event; e.g., your friends are not around because they got held back in class, not because they are leaving you out or hate you.

Just to summarise for a moment, when you feel anxious, it can be triggered in three different ways:

- **An external event:** something outside of you triggering an instinctive, unconscious reaction, e.g. a car coming at you fast; someone jumping out at you; a rottweiler barking at you; a hockey ball coming at your head; a plane you are on suffering turbulence.

- **An external event interacting with your thinking about that event:** e.g. having a test (external event) and you thinking that you haven't done enough work, or seeing that your friends are all talking in a corner (external event) and thinking that they are talking about you.

- **An internal source:** your emotional mind generating anxiety-provoking thoughts with little or no external event.

E.g. thinking that your friends might be talking about you and then that they all hate you – in fact, nobody likes you and you will never have any friends, ever.

## The spiral of anxiety

Do you remember your emotional mind? That is the combination of your body-emotions and your thinking about an event (go back to page 99 if you'd like a reminder). The thing about anxiety that makes it particularly troublesome is that the body part of the emotion can be so strong (butterflies in tummy, dry mouth, sweating, heart beating) that your thinking gets completely wedded to it. When your body is shaking or your face is going red, or your heart feels like it is beating at 100mph, it is hard not to get stuck in thinking that something is really wrong. Your thinking is responding to your body, to the internal stuff, and forgetting to look outside of itself for the rational mind stuff.

But of course, your body might be responding to some thought entirely made up in your mind. Like wondering if you are going to fail a test.

And that is why anxiety is a bit of a whirlwind. It can come from nowhere with a thought popping into your head, triggering a physical response, which itself feeds back to trigger more thinking ('I can't believe I'm getting anxious about this, I'm so ridiculous') and, before you know it, you are in a right state.

In psychological language, this is an anxiety spiral and it is where each part of the cognitive quad can potentially act as a *trigger* or a *reaction* to each of the other part. Psychologists often find it helpful to draw this out like this:

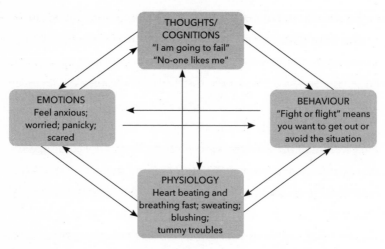

So, if, for example, this thought pops in your head: 'OMG, I hope the teacher doesn't pick on me to answer that question, I totally wasn't listening,' your heart beats fast in anticipation and then a second thought pops in your head: 'I'm so pathetic being worried that the teacher is going to pick me.' The second thought might act to increase the physiological arousal. Your core and limbic brain trigger the body responses to being under attack as someone has called you pathetic. It doesn't matter that it was you – your body responds the same whether it's your internal monologue or someone outside of yourself. Your blood sugar levels are now up and you are over-breathing and your anxiety spirals.

Sometimes young people who have physiological symptoms feel diminished by hearing that they are triggered by anxiety. They feel that people don't believe them or are saying 'it's all in their mind'. Please be reassured: your body changes are real; you are not imagining them. Whether the trigger is external, internal or a mixture of the two, the symptoms are indisputably there. It is not necessary to have an external cause to make physical symptoms. *Emily was 13 when she was referred for unexplained vomiting and weight loss. She'd had lots of physical investigations but none had found a reason for the vomiting and she wasn't dieting and she didn't want to be thin. It was a bit of a mystery but as we discussed it, we noticed Emily's breathing: it was fast, rapid and shallow. She was anxious. Emily's anxiety was coming out almost entirely in physical symptoms and mentally she didn't recognise herself as anxious. She found it hard to think about her symptoms having a psychological element at all. She felt that diminished them or made them less real, or we weren't believing her. It was hard to get her buy in to therapy.*

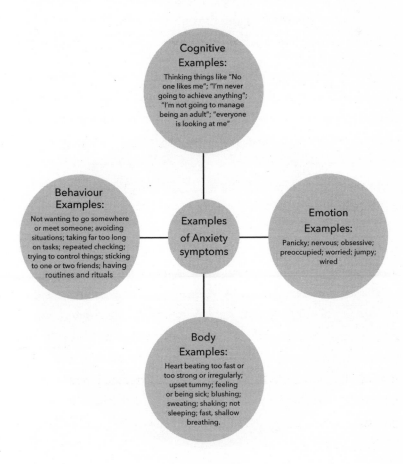

## The spiral of anxiety in a social context

So far, we have seen that anxiety is a particularly toxic emotion because it can spiral up from almost nothing with your own thoughts reacting to your bodily symptoms and vice versa.

But it has always been thus, so why is there so much anxiety around NOW?

To address that, we need to look at your social context. Do you remember the systems diagram from the chapter about family (see page 36)? You and your family do not exist in a vacuum; there is an interplay between you and the outside world. You exist in the context of a society, a school, uni or workplace, a group of your peers, your family. And there are some particular factors going on now that are contributing to the spiral of anxiety.

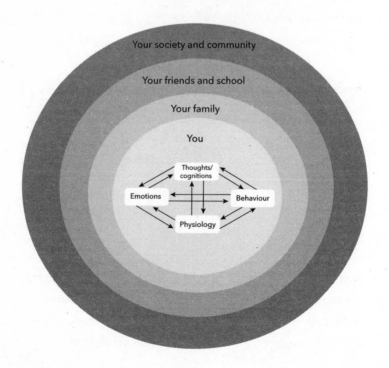

The anxiety spiral is whipped up when:

- Things are moving very quickly and there isn't time to stop and think – your bodily emotions are pulling you this way and that, and there isn't time to catch up with your rational brain. Is it a sabre-toothed tiger? Is it a mugger? Or is it just a friend jumping out at you?

- Things are uncertain and there is a perceived lack of control. Uncertainty fans the winds of anxiety by giving an infinite number of possibilities to get your head around.

- There is a lot of comparison going on or a sense of competition: 'Am I going to be good enough? Am I going to make the grade/get the place?'

- The situation is extreme, such as finals, loss, death, break-ups.

## Why is *now* so stressful?

So, looking at the levels of social context we can think about why now is so stressful for young people.

- **Society:** The society people live in has always impacted on their mental health: the personal experience of racism or misogyny, for example. Today's global, hyperconnected society makes you much more aware of the range of life possibilities and other people's successes. It is easy to believe you have failed compared to others ('She has 20,000 Instagram followers and I have 200' or 'She won the US Open at 18'). The pace of communication puts pressure on you to keep up, like there is a constant race on. It also overloads the brain with too much stimulation. Consumerism is based on creating dissatisfaction, to try to pressure you to buy more with hyperbolic language: you must have this. There is a sense of always chasing and never arriving, which is anxiety provoking. You might think of this as an 'always more and better' attitude. It's never enough.

- **Community:** As global connectedness increases, the sense of a local community has diminished. The rise of the two-income family and economic migration (people moving away from where they grew up for work) means you see fewer people each day who know you well. This is not necessarily a wholly bad thing. I, for one, would not want to go back to a village community. But it does mean your everyday world is likely less predictable than your mother's or grandmother's: bigger, more freedom, more exciting, more vibrant, more opportunity – but all of that means more uncertainty.

- **Your school, college or university:** There has been an increased scrutiny on how good educational settings are over the last generation. The quality of a school is defined largely by the scores you get in your SATs, your GCSEs and your A levels. This inevitably influences how schools and teachers relate to you, their pupils. They have less time for pastoral care (getting to know you and looking after you). They are judged by your results, which leads to kids being put under pressure to get top grades – for yourself, yes, but also for that school's league tables.

- **Friends:** The anxiety about fitting in, which has always been a normal part of every adolescent girl's life, is heightened in this visual, social media-driven society where there is constant comparison across all the different domains of your life: appearance, size, coolness, sporting prowess, academic achievement, etc. A sense of comparison, or even competing, for limited jobs, places at uni or getting 'likes' decreases social connectedness, which, in turn, decreases the sense of belonging and increases anxiety.

- **Family:** Anxiety is triggered by so many aspects of family life, including family breakdown, homelessness, ill health and money worries. These may not be under your parents' control and many families are in anxiety-provoking situations through no fault of their own. In those circumstances, a good attachment bond between child and parent can help mitigate the stress as parents try their best for their children. Other parents create situations which are both uncertain and threatening, such as situations of domestic abuse or drug addiction. It is inevitable in those situations to be in a heightened sense of alert.

- Parents can also trigger or add to anxiety by exacerbating the pressure from other sources, particularly that from schools. Academic pressure from family can be explicit or implicit. Explicit pressure is apparent in the proliferation of tutoring, Kumon clubs and helicopter parents micro-managing homework. Yours is the first generation likely to be poorer than their parents, which is another 'climate change' factor which intensifies this pressure.

- **You:** And at the centre of this is you and your anxiety, impacted on by these systems around you and made up of your combined experience in your brain and body and the way you act. But – and it is a very important 'but' – you should not see yourself as a passive victim of external or internal forces: you have the capacity to change your thoughts, behaviour and physiology so that your anxiety is reduced. You will also, as you get older, have more and more choice about what systems you put yourself in and your response to them. Choose wisely.

## Anxiety management

When you want to reduce or manage your anxiety, you can act on yourself (your thoughts, physiology and behaviour) or you can act on your systems (society, community, school, friends and family). In Chapter 4 – Emotions, Thoughts and Feelings, I introduced lots of things that are generally good for mental health, and that includes reducing anxiety. So revisit this if you feel you need to. In the rest of this chapter, we will be particularly focusing on the three broad ways to change your anxiety from inside:

- Changing your physiological response
- Changing your thinking
- Changing your behaviour

*When we unpicked Emily's symptoms, it seemed that the vomiting had started with a tummy bug, which had caused her to be sick in school. She had felt so embarrassed and then worried that she was going to be sick again, or that she was going to be humiliated in some other way. She had started cutting out various foods and avoiding certain situations but it seemed that when she worried, her stomach began to turn over very quickly, she 'got butterflies', she felt nauseous and like she needed the toilet urgently. While initially she couldn't identify a cognitive component, it seemed that this started a spiral and the physical symptoms increased. Vomiting was almost a relief for her in this situation as it stopped her tummy turning over and the sense of nausea that accompanied her nerves.*

## Physiological management of anxiety

When you feel anxious and your sympathetic arousal system is kicking into place, lots of this is automatic and not under your conscious control. It impacts nearly every system and organ in the body. Only two of these systems can be easily brought under your conscious control. Those two systems are your breathing and your muscle tension.

So, while you can't bring down your heart rate, nor get rid of the butterflies in your tummy, nor stop sweating or blushing, you can bring the tension in your muscles and the rate and depth of your breathing under your control.

And that is a little bit magic.

It is a little bit magic because through taking charge of our breathing and muscle tension, we can trick our body into thinking it's NOT so anxious and start to reverse our sympathetic arousal. If your cortical (rational) brain consciously decides to breathe slower and more calmly, this will be feedback into the core brain, which, in turn, will kickstart the calming down system (called the parasympathetic response). That acts on the other organs, like your heart, your stomach and your sweat system, all of which you can't otherwise consciously control.

## Breathing

When you are anxious, you are likely to breathe faster and shallower than usual, and breathe in more than you breathe out. If this extra oxygen is not used up by fighting or fleeing, it changes the respiratory balance in the body: if there is too little carbon dioxide in the lungs, it increases the pH balance of the blood, making it too alkaline. This can spiral into hyperventilation, which can cause shaking, dizziness, headaches and make you feel like you can't breathe. It can be very scary if it gets that far.

See, I told you anxiety is not all in your mind: it may be triggered by something in your mind but its effects are real and definitely in your body.

By slowing your breathing down, breathing deeply and fully breathing out, you can regain the correct balance of carbon dioxide in your body and reverse this process. You can trick your body into thinking it's not under threat. The action of breathing out also relaxes the chest muscles and the diaphragm.

There are lots of different tricks for helping yourself breathe out and relax more. I sometimes advise young people to breathe in and out to the count of ten, where the inbreath takes you to three or four, then the outbreath is much longer and takes you up to nine or ten. And there can be a small relaxation pause before breathing in again. Nailing the exact speed of the counting isn't that important – it's just to help you focus on breathing out for longer than you breathed in. You are trying to structure your breathing and gain some sense of control over it.

Another popular method is to run your finger up and down the fingers of the other hand. Breathe in – up the side of one finger; breathe out – down the other. This doesn't focus on making the outbreath longer than the inbreath but has the advantage of being something simple and physical you can do, rather than putting an extra burden on your mind to count. It also has the advantage that it is easy to do under your desk at school.

Or you can place your hand on your tummy to focus on breathing deeply. If your tummy goes up and down that means you are using your diaphragm to breathe deeply, rather than just the top of your chest.

We also have a natural inclination to pick up the breathing speed of those close to us, and so if you have family or a friend who will sit and breathe slowly with you, you can peg your rate to theirs.

If the breathing has tipped into hyperventilation you may find it easier to breathe into a paper bag. By re-breathing the same air you can raise the level of $CO_2$ in the body again.[11]

*While Emily didn't buy into the 'anxiety' explanation for her vomiting, she began to make the connection that when she thought about this stuff, her breathing would change, her stomach would tighten and her face would feel flushed. She liked having something to practical to do to help manage the vomiting, so she practised breathing slowly and breathing out, and found meditations online that helped her. Emily also practised progressive muscle relaxation and positive imagery every night before she went to bed. Eventually, she could use this before meals to calm herself down. She breathed slowly, relaxed her muscles and thought about other things.*

---

11  CO2 levels in the air run at 0.04 per cent – it's a trace gas but a crucial one. The body's respiratory response is linked to levels of CO2 and not oxygen. Our outbreath contains 100 times that amount.

## Muscle tension

As part of the fight or flight reaction, blood sugar and blood move away from the brain into the limbs, which tighten to prepare for fight or flight: to punch someone or run away.

If you decide not to run away from your exam, nor punch the exam invigilator (which is probably best), your muscle tension doesn't go anywhere. However, as with breathing, you can take the tension in your muscles under your own conscious control and trick your body into a parasympathetic calming down response. This is the second tool in your anxiety-management toolbox.

If I say, 'relax your body now', what happens? Do you notice your body sink down? Your shoulders fall? Your legs relax into the chair or bed? The muscles in your face drop? You may find you hold a lot of tension in your body all the time.

One way to address this is through progressive muscle relaxation. Start at your feet: tense the muscles in your feet and then relax them; then move up to your calf muscles and do the same, followed by thighs and bottom, fists and arms, and face. Then take a deep breath in and hold and tense your shoulders to your ears. Then release and let your whole body sink into relaxation.

I've put a couple of links relating to progressive muscle relaxation in the 'Want to Know More?' section at the end. Practise relaxation at bedtime – it is definitely a skill and you need to practise it, if you want it to be ready to use when you need it.

## Cognitive management of anxiety

OK, this is the nub. Anxiety is not 'all in your mind' but it is 'in your mind' and your mind is an important tool to combat it. Your brain, like breathing and muscle tension, acts unconsciously most of the time but you can bring some of your brain under your conscious control.

You do not want to be a victim to anxiety – you have to fight it. As I described earlier, your mind can spiral actual worries ('I haven't done enough work . . . I am going to do badly in this test') and create fantastical worries in your mind ('I got a B . . . I'm going to fail my GCSEs'). You have to fight this part of your brain, and then you have to fight it again. And again. And again.

Why so many times? Because the brain sets up neural pathways and the pathways it fires frequently become the default. Your brain gets so used to going down them as they are easy, quick and very well trodden. It becomes natural and habitual to think in that way.

Everyone has a genetic predisposition to be more or less anxious but we've seen how the different systems you live in (your society, your community, your school, your friends, your family) as well as your own personality may have contributed to wiring your brain into an anxious response. So if you are naturally quite an anxious person and like to work hard and hope to do well, the snippets of overheard conversation from parents about getting you into a 'good' school; the increasing crescendo of SATs as you go through to Year 6; the constant harping on about GCSEs from the start of Year 7 and the proliferation of after-school tutoring, will, over years, set up anxious pathways in your brain. 'I must do well, work hard, get good grades – it's so important.'

With my patients, I make an analogy between their brains and a field of grass. They need to walk over it all the time and they have trampled down a section of the grass to get across easily. That pathway might sound like, 'What if I don't do well? My teachers will be so disappointed; I might not get into sixth form or university.' As you use that pathway in your brain over and over it becomes the easiest pathway to use.

You might have lots of different metaphorical anxiety fields and pathways in your head. Another might be, 'What if everyone looks at me as I go in the classroom? What if there's nowhere to sit and everyone stares at me; it will be so embarrassing.' Or, 'My tummy sticks out in this dress; I look fat. I am fat; no one will ever love me and I'm going to spend my life alone.'

And up around you the grass grows tall and you forget there is even another way across the field.

*Emily made the connection that the thought 'what if I am sick?' was driving the bodily symptoms. While she didn't think the cause was anxiety, she could recognise that saying mantras to herself such as, 'It's OK; I'm going to be OK, I can do this' did help her manage to eat more and made it less likely that she was sick. We talked about while it was unpleasant to be sick, awful for her, she could manage it and no one thought the worse of her for it. It certainly wasn't the humiliating disaster she had made in her head. When it was really bad, she used audio books and favourite videos to distract herself. Her family had to drop their standard 'we all eat at the table and talk to each other' as we began to understand that her parents' attempts at chitchat were actually making the situation worse, because she would often interpret their remarks as criticism. So if they asked her if she'd done her homework, she'd hear it as 'they don't think I've done my homework; they think I'm lazy'.*

## Catastrophising

These short-cut pathways in your head are your 'negative automatic thoughts' (NATs) and these are a big thing in psychology. Negative automatic thoughts are heuristics – shortcuts to thinking – that often involve a catastrophic kind of unchallenged logic. In your mind, it is easily to leap from each small semi-logical statement to the next, but overall the logic is flawed.

If I said to you, this girl I know, she got a D in a test, and so she'll probably end up jobless, homeless on the streets, you'd laugh, right? It's ridiculous. One test doesn't matter, you'd say. Most people who have jobs have also failed a test or two at some point in their life.

But in your mind it might sound like, 'I failed the test – what if I fail my GCSEs? I'll never get a job. What will become of me? I might end up homeless.' By breaking it up into smaller steps, the gap between each step reduces. It seems more plausible. Of course, it isn't actually more likely to happen, it still is equally impossible. It just seems less impossible due to the way your mind has framed it to itself.

This is a well-known marketing, sales or interviewing trick, where you get someone to agree to something bland and non-controversial then add a series of small seemingly logical steps or questions to reach something that they would have never agreed to if you'd asked them straight out in the first place. In this case, your anxiety-wired brain is fooling itself by jumping down a series of quasi-logical steps to a fantastical position.

However, your brain ends up in the worst place with you unloved, unwashed and on the street, and therefore the fight-or-flight response is triggered (remember: anxiety can be triggered internally as well as externally). This response was much more useful to your cave-girl facing a sabre-toothed tiger than it is for you facing an exam. When's evolution going to kick in and sort this out for us? Our sympathetic arousal system is not fit for twenty-first-century living!

*I began to understand that Emily saw disaster everywhere. For example, she had always got the bus to school with another girl but that girl no longer wanted to go as early as her and that upset her, but she didn't change the time to go later ('what if the bus was late – we might be late for school'). She found her friends' fluid arrangements difficult and triggered her 'what if...' thinking. For example, timings or what they were doing would change at the last minute ('what if people ate? I might be sick') and other people might join in unexpectedly ('what if they don't like me'). It all felt so uncertain to Emily.*

## Black and white, all-or-nothing thinking

This is another NAT pattern. For humans, categorising things is a useful shortcut in thinking: we quickly recognise things as part of a category and know what to do. Boy/girl, cat/dog, friend or foe. Useful as this system is, it falls down when things are more complex and nuanced. And life now is a lot more complex and nuanced.

In a stressful situation, we rely more on shortcuts for thinking, as our instinctive brain takes over. We think in a less thorough way: self-judgements become that you are either bad or good; fat or thin; clever or stupid. And if you got a D on a test, your shortcut, categorical thinking might be 'I'm stupid'. Your more nuanced thinking might be that you are not very good at that subject and aren't going to take it for GCSE anyway, that it was only a stupid little test, and you had cramps and couldn't concentrate. If your stomach sticks out, your short-cut categorical thinking might be 'I'm fat'. Your more nuanced thinking might be that you have just had an enormous meal and so of course your stomach sticks out temporarily while your body digests the food and, in any case, that is your bigger area of your body but your legs are beautifully slender. Trying to avoid negative, categorical labels for yourself will reduce your anxiety.

## Absolutes: shoulds, musts and oughts

A different type of categorical label is the absolutes for behaviour: shoulds, oughts and musts. These words often lead to a standard or expectation on yourself and setting too many of these is likely to contribute to anxiety. For example, you may be told (or tell yourself) that you should eat five portions of fruit and veg; your food should be ethically sourced and have low food miles; you ought to floss your teeth; you must exercise for at least an hour; you have to do your piano practice and homework; you need to get your friend a present; you ought not fly or use plastic bags or aerosols.

While the shoulds, oughts and musts pattern of thinking was first identified by psychologists almost 100 years ago, it seems to me that the current pace of life, consumerism and competition has exacerbated the tendency to think this way. I see the language of absolutes everywhere now, much more than just the shoulds, oughts and musts. I see it in the language of 'essentials' – in the 'everyone else is', in the 'always', in the 'have to', the 'need to', 'I'll die if I don't' and even 'literally'. Exaggerated language creates endless standards that you can never live up to. The sheer number of life expectations is unachievable, leading to an endless feeling of not having enough, not being good enough, not being enough. Absolutes become a stick to beat yourself with and that harms your mental health.

Good mental health is more often based on balance. Replace some of those absolutes with the tentatives when you speak and, crucially, when you think, and don't let your mind go to the absolutes. It's probably best to eat fruit and veg and to exercise. You'd rather get your homework in on time but, hey, things happen. Most people are going to the party and it's sad that you are not, but not everyone is. You want to go to that university but there will be lots of good applicants and some of it will be just luck. See how much kinder it sounds when you substitute the absolutes with more realistic expectations?

I believe the increase in unrealistic expectations that the world imposes is contributing to the increase in mental health problems with young people. If you take too many standards to heart, life just ends up feeling like a checklist to complete. We are back to the assembly line of childhood again where, as adolescence hits, you start checking off that the product (you) is good enough against society's expectations. The effect is to make life miserable and anxiety provoking – overwhelming and unbearable, in fact, if you are constantly berating yourself for not meeting an infinite cacophony of standards. There is no room for fun nor spontaneity.

Having good expectations for yourself does not mean more and higher expectations but generous, kinder and compassionate expectations. It means prioritising certain key expectations and letting other things go. The only absolute is that you need to ditch the absolutes.

*Emily's life was governed by absolute, exacting standards – she must always be on time for school; she always had to go over her notes of every class; she wanted everyone to like her. When she was in primary school and, at first, at secondary school, she had managed to keep her self-imposed standards by being super organised. She had a rigid evening routine: she always did her homework as soon as she got in; she had her dinner at 6.30 (she was more likely to be sick if it was late); she had a shower; tidied her room and packed her bag three times.*

*Her routine was so organised, in fact, that she hadn't realised she even was anxious. This rigid structure protected her from it. But as she got older, it wasn't possible to keep control like this. For example, homework was sometimes set over a week or two, not finished on one night. With more subjects to cover, she couldn't keep up with the time-consuming level of note making, flashcard making and revision she had developed for each test or exam.*

*And that was the fundamental fear we had to address: teenage life is complex; you can't always have everything in control and perfect; there are messy compromises to be made. You can be with your friend (feels safe and nice to be with someone who's part of your group) or you can be on the earlier bus (feels good not to worry about being late). There is no squaring that circle.*

### Other types of negative automatic thoughts

I haven't got space to go into all the different negative automatic thoughts that might pop into your mind. If you are interested, there's a lot of stuff on the internet about them. Some of the other types include:[12]

---

12  Don't get too bogged down in the categories, as they aren't perfectly discrete! Sometimes a thought can be in several different categories.

- **'Personalisation'** – when you think that everything is about you, when generally it isn't. E.g. that everyone is looking at you or talking about you.

- **'Mind reading'** – when you think that you know what people are thinking. E.g. they didn't like your post and so they hate you.

- **'Magnification and minimisation'** – when we highlight some aspects of the situation – e.g. that we failed one test – and ignore the other aspects – e.g. that we passed all the other tests.

How do you know if your thought is an NAT? Is it negative? Has it popped into your head quickly? Does it reflect an extreme position? That's probably an NAT.

### The Ah Ha test: accurate and helpful

We all get NATs, moments of doubt, uncertainty and illogical thinking. The Ah Ha test is a way to check out whether the NAT is true or not and challenge it so it doesn't make you anxious. The Ah Ha test helps turn NATs into background noise in your head or to dismiss them quickly from your mind. Ah Ha is a mnemonic for 'Accurate and Helpful'.[13]

- Is the thought in your brain **accurate**? What is your evidence that it is true?

- If it is true, is it really **helpful** to be thinking about right now?

---

13 OK, OK, the perfectionists among you will have noticed that Ah isn't a shortening of accurate and Ha isn't a shortening of helpful. It's an imperfect mnemonic.

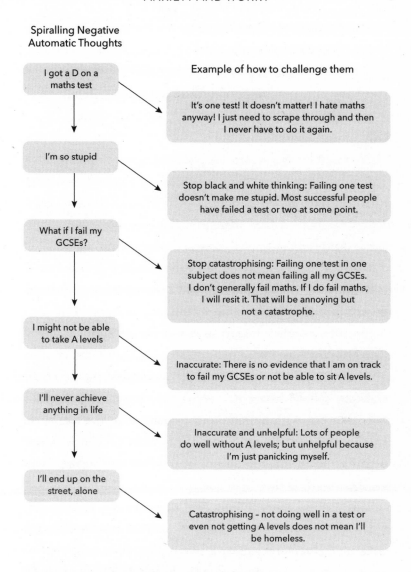

Spiralling Negative
Automatic Thoughts

I got a D on a maths test

Example of how to challenge them

It's one test! It doesn't matter! I hate maths anyway! I just need to scrape through and then I never have to do it again.

I'm so stupid

Stop black and white thinking: Failing one test doesn't make me stupid. Most successful people have failed a test or two at some point.

What if I fail my GCSEs?

Stop catastrophising: Failing one test in one subject does not mean failing all my GCSEs. I don't generally fail maths. If I do fail maths, I will resit it. That will be annoying but not a catastrophe.

I might not be able to take A levels

Inaccurate: There is no evidence that I am on track to fail my GCSEs or not be able to sit A levels.

I'll never achieve anything in life

Inaccurate and unhelpful: Lots of people do well without A levels; but unhelpful because I'm just panicking myself.

I'll end up on the street, alone

Catastrophising - not doing well in a test or even not getting A levels does not mean I'll be homeless.

## Behavioural management of anxiety

And to our final category of anxiety management: behaviour. The way you behave before, during and after you are anxious will impact your anxiety then and in the future.

Some people try to avoid anxiety;
some try to control it;
some people feed it.
None of these responses are helpful...

## AAA – Avoid anxiety avoidance

No life worth living has zero anxiety. It is impossible to eliminate anxiety but sometimes young people try to by avoiding certain situations. This often spectacularly backfires. Trying to avoid anxiety tends to reduce anxiety in the short term but nearly always makes anxiety much worse in the long term.

A story I often tell my patients about myself is that I used to be scared of public speaking and tried to avoid it. I think, in part, that is why I became a therapist, as I got to sit one-to-one with people rather than face a crowd. Burnt into my memory is the time I tried to do a debate in sixth form. I ended up reading my argument, stumbling over my words, sweating, while my fellow debater (a very dorky guy generally) spoke without notes, with humour and responded to the audience. Another time, in the early part of my career, I had to speak to parents about sleep problems in toddlers and, again, I was stuck for words as they fired questions at me, while in my head I thought, 'You are making a fool of yourself – look at you stumbling over your words! Everyone can see how ridiculously anxious you are.' I remember I used to have to brace myself to speak in our team ward round at the hospital, in front of 10–15 people. What if I stumbled over my words? What if someone laughs at me? I hated it.

Do you think, over that time of my life, I got over my fear? No, of course I didn't. Because to get over your fears, you have to face them, and, with these few occasions burnt into my psyche, I was largely avoiding them.

Unfortunately, or fortunately depending how you look at it, public speaking then became a key part of my job. Our team started to run teaching groups for parents of our newly diagnosed patients and I was shifted onto the schedule. No one on my team would have had the least clue that I was scared of public speaking: I'd avoided it so successfully and my fear was hidden.

I can still remember the first group I ran – what I was wearing, which parents were in it, where it was, who I ran it with. Most of all, I can remember the sweat dripping down inside my dress.

But the circumstances were right, in lots of different ways. Firstly, while I didn't have confidence in public speaking, I did have confidence in my topic. I was prepared and I knew what I was doing. Secondly, my colleague had the expectation that I was going to do it and was confident in me and was there to back me up. He had no clue that I was nervous. Not being able to speak would have been embarrassing in front of him. Thirdly, I had the audience on my side. They all had a seriously ill child and they knew I knew about that illness – they weren't there to harangue me or argue with me. They wanted to know what I knew. It was the perfect situation in which to face my fear.

And perhaps most importantly, I had to keep going. Do you think I got over the fear after that? Yes. Now I give talks all the time. People who've met me in the last 15 years would be astonished to hear that I once was scared to do so.

So, while in theory it would seem a good thing to reduce the anxiety in your life, in reality there is a very thin line between reducing your anxiety and avoiding your anxiety. You have to be very honest with yourself about which you are doing. On the one hand, you could say I reduced my anxiety in the short term, on numerous occasions, over 15 years, by not speaking to an audience. On the other hand, if you actually totalled the anxiety I felt having to avoid public speaking, hiding my fear of it, over all of those years it would probably come to more than I would have experienced had I just tackled the problem in the first place. In addition, I probably missed out on all sorts of career opportunities.

*Katie consulted me in her early twenties. She was in her second year at a top university but was suffering crippling anxiety. Katie felt constantly anxious: when she woke up in the morning, she worried about what the day would bring; when she got into bed at night, she worried about what she had done and said that day.*

*Katie had always found school easy. She'd been well enough liked though quite a quiet girl – studious, with a photographic memory, she didn't need to work too hard to stay at the top of the class. Other people competed with her but that didn't trouble her too much. She went to a relatively small all-girls school and it wasn't a surprise that she got into a top university. Life had been good except for one thing: blushing. She hated that. Of course, kids had always pointed and said 'you're blushing' when she was younger but as she had got older, she had been very comfortable in her school and didn't blush much, nor worry if her close-knit group of girls had noticed, knowing they wouldn't care or judge her.*

*When she went to university she started to feel more anxious. She found her course harder than she thought she would and was aware of how smart her fellow students were. She started to feel self-conscious about putting her hand up in class for fear of blushing and so she stopped doing it. She began to feel that she was a fraud, that she wasn't smart at all, and she was going to be caught out as not good enough. She felt gauche and unsophisticated compared to many of the other students and so she often would sit in the lecture hall at lunch or go to the library. While she was attracted to boys and girls, as soon as she liked someone she found that she'd blush when she spoke to them, and she avoided it so she'd never had a relationship.*

In the 1980s, a book was published called *Feel the Fear and Do it Anyway*. It is hard to sum it up better than the title does, really. When it comes down to it, when we avoid things, we fear them more. Instead, we need to find the circumstances in which we can confront our fears, overcome them and allow our confidence to grow.

**Anxiety and control**

For many of the girls and young women I see, their anxiety is more abstract than a fear of public speaking. Our society has offered them more opportunity and choice than at any time in history and that is exciting, but excitement has tipped into fear as the pace is so fast. They feel relentlessly scrutinised and judged, particularly at school and on the internet (issues I explore in later chapters). The anxiety I see in these patients is linked to a belief they hold about not being good enough/thin enough/clever enough/popular enough. Their response to this anxiety is to seek control.

In an uncertain, changing, high-stakes world they seek certainty by attempting to control their studies, their exam results, their physical environment, their weight, their appearance and their parents. They have strived to be beyond any fault, to be the very best they possibly can be, in an attempt to lessen their anxiety. Psychologists call this perfectionism.

Let me tell you some important secrets about perfection: perfection is a myth – there is no such thing. Every single thing is just a matter of opinion. And the relentless pursuit of perfection does not reduce anxiety. It fuels it. The endless striving, dieting, studying, revising is actually a type of avoidance. It is preventing you facing the fear of uncertainty, of not doing your best or getting your best results. Short-term anxiety reduction through seeking perfection is actually you avoiding the fear of failure and, as we've seen, in the long term, anxiety avoidance doesn't help. By working hard, by dieting, by practising your dance over and over, by training every day, by relentlessly keeping all the shoulds, oughts and musts, you may gain the illusion of control over your situation and reduce your anxiety for a while. But in fact, you are avoiding something: the anxiety of not being in control and of being vulnerable, that is the biggest fear of all. And as time goes by, without facing the fear of your own vulnerability, without having the experience of failing and it being fine, the fear just increases and your perfectionistic or controlling standards mushroom. Perfectionism is really toxic for mental health and for connection, and we will return to it in the chapters about the internet and relationships.

Don't get me wrong, there will be situations when it is best to reduce your anxiety but this is rarely by raising the pressure you put yourself under or setting higher standards for yourself. You may, for example, be feeling overwhelmed with your GCSEs and want to reduce your anxiety. Dropping one subject that you don't like, aren't that good at or don't need for your future life, might be a sensible plan. What is not sensible is to get up at 5:45am to start working six months before your exams. The former is anxiety reduction, the latter is anxiety avoidance, which will work in the short term but will make you more stressed, more wired, more driven in the long term.

| Anxiety reduction | Anxiety avoidance |
|---|---|
| Telling yourself that you look fine and, anyway, your looks are the least important thing about you | Avoiding carbs and getting up to do cardio training at 6:30am |
| Working solidly and steadily, but also taking time out to have fun, exercise, be with your family and dog | Working every waking moment. Having revision posters in the bathroom. Eating, breathing, sleeping exams 24/7 for six months |
| Being yourself | Being the best |
| Living your life according to your values | Living life according to output or achievement |

So, it's complex: sometimes stopping activities can be avoidance in disguise (like me refusing to speak publicly to avoid anxiety) and sometimes not stopping activities can also be avoidance (e.g. trying to be perfect and do everything). Generally, reducing anxiety happens by reducing the pressure, pace and stimulation on yourself, but not avoiding specific (e.g. public speaking; carbs) or generic (being vulnerable or out of control) fears. But, in truth, only you know in your heart whether your actions are sensible actions to reduce some of the overwhelming pressure in your life or, in fact, you are trying to avoid something because you are scared of your own vulnerability or of failing.

## Feeding or starving your anxiety

Seeking control or perfection can fuel your anxiety but it's not the only way; another way is to seek out more information. Again, if you think of an animal disturbed by a predator in the wild, even before the animal fights or flees, we get a startled response: ears prick up; eyes widen, watching and gathering information. When we feel startled or worried, we want more information. But now we live in a world full of information and we have to learn when to stop, when the information flow is feeding the anxiety.

As I write this book, coronavirus is spreading around the world. It can be very tempting to search for more and more information about it. Two generations ago, when my mother was a baby in the Second World War, there would have been a news report on the radio every few hours and a newspaper delivered once a day. Now, we have multiple sources of news, giving the illusion of more information to gather. Everything gets analysed and built up to a crescendo of anxiety, and that is before you start on your own Snapchats or WhatsApp groups. The traditional and social media uses the 'absolute' definitive language that fuels the anxiety cycle: 'The government NEEDS to act now', 'Something 'MUST' be done'. Shades of grey are ignored and nuance papered over because they make quite dull stories.[14]

Neither overfeeding (with the relentless pursuit of information)

---

14 If there was a newspaper headline on this it would be, 'Psychologist claims media CAUSES anxiety', rather than 'Psychologist thinks media using inflammatory language may contribute to a culture of anxiety'. See, nuance just doesn't make good headlines but we live in a hyped-up world, which risks exacerbating anxiety.

nor starving (with avoidance or perfection) your anxiety is a good approach. A balanced approach would have you face your fears in a managed, controlled environment, and then spread your wings and fly.

*Katie's course had a lot of lectures compared to other courses and she had to study really hard to keep up. Her flatmates had fewer lectures and were much more raucous than her, and she constantly felt that she was the boring one going off to bed early. One morning, when she had been kept up late by them drinking, she had overslept and run late for a lecture. Sitting at the back of the lecture hall, she had her first panic attack. She lay down across the benches and, luckily, she didn't think that anyone had noticed, but felt mortified. She was terrified that it would happen again and so she started always sitting at the back, or sometimes just doing the work online and not going in. She also worried about oversleeping again, but then often lay awake worrying about this, or worrying that she'd be too tired tomorrow, which ironically kept her awake. She found reasons to go back home at the weekends as it was easier to study, she could sleep better and it was less anxiety provoking.*

*Halfway through the year, she discovered that her flatmates had all started to look for second-year accommodation without involving her: Three of them were in one group with others from outside her flat and two of them were in another group. It seemed they had left her out more by oversight than by design, as they'd all talked about it one weekend when she was away. There had been lots of uncertainty as they tried to find the right size houses and, in the end, she joined one of the groups as they needed one more person.*

*Starting back in second year, she'd been well aware that she was the 'extra' person in the flat and was super careful not to upset* anyone. She started second guessing what she said, often apologising for herself or repeatedly asking if people minded. She did this so much she annoyed herself. She'd always been attracted to one of the girls in her new flat, but she was so conscious of blushing that she didn't dare talk to her. Katie found herself avoiding the kitchen at times when she was there, and spending more time in her room. Often, when she did go into the common spaces, she felt that she was a downer or that people were thinking she was boring. So she tended to stay in her room more. Her world closed down. She was thinking of deferring a year as she really couldn't face going back. But that made her feel like a failure.

With Katie, we had to track how avoidance had led to her anxiety spiralling. She was so scared of being noticed, of blushing, of being seen panicking and of being a nuisance, that she had retreated away from any situations where these things happened, or could happen. It had started with her not being able to put her hand up in a lecture, which became wanting to avoid being in a lecture, then she didn't want to be in her flat. She catastrophised that people seeing her blushing would be hideous, that seeing her panicking would be mortifying, that finding the course hard meant she was a fraud. Were those thoughts accurate? Were they helpful? Or was avoiding all these situations allowing her anxiety to dictate her life to the point that she was thinking of leaving university?

She needed to face her fears. In therapy, once this was understood, she, with my support, started to face some of these fears and not limit her life. She had to confront situations she had previously avoided and ignore thoughts that undermined her confidence. She had to let go of her wish to always be in control and allow herself to be vulnerable.

## Don't do your best, don't be the best – live your best life

Anxiety is complex and it doesn't look like one thing. This might make your own feelings difficult to recognise or understand, particularly when you hide it too well with avoidance or control. Anxiety rises up in a spiral, with symptoms at one level, causing more symptoms in another, and the whole thing ends up like a tangled ball of wool.

However, on the positive side, it means that there are three different levels within yourself at which you can try to reduce or manage it (physiological, cognitive and behavioural). There is also the option to try to change your surrounding systems, such as your friends, your school or your activities. You may want to think about whether all that pressure is good for you or whether you want to lead a less anxiety provoking life. Breathe, relax, think accurately and helpfully. Neither avoid things nor try to control them. Look for balance.

# CHAPTER 6

# EDUCATION AND QUALIFICATIONS

*'Many highly talented, brilliant, creative people think they're not because the thing that they were good at, at school wasn't valued.'*

**KEN ROBINSON**

*'And we won't forget the day we fought for the right To be a little bit naughty.'*

**TIM MINCHIN, 'NAUGHTY', FROM THE MUSICAL *MATILDA***

In Western economies, young women are outperforming their male contemporaries in terms of exam results. This chapter is going to be a breeze, right? It seems as though you girls have nailed this education thing. But have you? You get better qualifications than boys, that's a fact. But I want to ask you a few questions about it: what's education like for you? And what is the cost on you?

Because this book isn't about grades – it's about mental health and emotional survival. And what I notice, sitting with my patients, is the enormous impact that the education system has on them, often at the cost of all else, including a sense of sanity. I see that a lot of my patients have become swept up in a belief that going to school, college or university is all about getting qualifications, and that they are only worthwhile if they get good exam results. Every other part of their life and their experience is sacrificed on the altar of 'doing well', or on that of its even more insidiously toxic cousin, 'doing their best'.

I don't think their thoughts and feelings about education have developed in isolation. I believe they feel or think this because it is a reflection of how education is often talked about in their families, among their friends, in their education settings, in this society and in the world as a whole. The pressure cascades down as internationally, countries are compared on exam grades and achievement; nationally, governments rank schools on outcomes; schools, mindful of this, analyse their teachers' capacity to get these results; parents, wanting the best for their child, compete for places at these highly rated schools and question teachers about how their child is going to do compared to others.

Do you know the tale of 'The Emperor's New Clothes'? Where the whole of society banded together in the king's delusion that he was actually wearing something? Well that, to me, is what has happened in our society in relation to qualifications. These qualifications have become the centre of everyone's attention and we talk about them all the time. They are given enormous importance: in primary school leading up to the SATs and in secondary to the GCSEs and A levels. A mass hysteria descends on the country.

And yet . . . when I talk to parents they say they don't care about exam results, they just want their child to be happy. When I talk to teachers and heads, they just want children to achieve their potential and that exam results are less important than a child's pastoral needs and wellbeing. Governments know that, to function, society requires children with all different interests and achievement levels, and yet they talk about getting good qualifications as the only route to future life chances. They talk about missing learning, hiring tutors, essay plans and study clubs over the holidays, implicitly and explicitly giving the message that qualifications are very, very important.

But meanwhile, there you are at the centre of this mass delusion, indoctrinated into this madness, which puts enormous pressure on you and all the other children around you – worn down and wound up to believe that these mythical good qualifications are the path to happiness and a sense of being good enough. In fact, many girls often believe that their academic achievement is the most important thing about them.

And that belief is incredibly bad for you. Sometimes fatally bad for you.

But there is another way. With the candour of youth, perhaps you need to call the adults out on this madness. Perhaps you look around at the constantly-striving-for-better-for-more adults and, like the child blurting out that the emperor is wearing nothing at all, perhaps you should question, 'Really? Is this it?'

*Frankie came to see me in the summer after her GCSEs suffering with low mood, panic and anxiety. She had always worked hard and been near the top of the class, and had been predicted good grades. But she had almost broken down during her GCSEs. She had often barely slept and couldn't focus or study at all. She had just felt wired. As a result, she thought her GCSEs had gone really badly and hadn't been able to relax over the summer holidays. She was dreading results day – even more than that, she was dreading starting her A levels. She couldn't bear the thought of all that pressure and worry all over again*

## Education and mental health

It seems, nowadays, that education usually gets discussed in terms of what your output is – that is, how you do in your exams. The qualifications are increasingly seen as a measurement of your and a school's success. This wasn't true a generation ago. I think of talking to a receptionist at a primary school. She reminisced about the old days, 40 years previously, when there was no national curriculum or SATs and teachers were left to pretty much teach what they liked. She remembered fondly one teacher who spent half of each day strumming on a guitar, ostensibly teaching them music. And whilst just learning the guitar for a year is probably less than ideal, what we have now, this 'output model' of education, like the outcome model of parenting, has major disadvantages, primarily in your mental health. And ignoring mental health is crazy because it is in any case intrinsically bound up together with your achievement at school, as we know that, on average, kids who are happy generally and like their school at 11, get better results.

So, let's try to understand what the relationship is between school achievement and mental health.

### For those of you who struggle more with schoolwork

For some of you, well, it's likely that academics – that is, learning stuff for the purpose of passing exams – isn't your thing. In the long term, that is completely OK. The world is broad and academic study is just one part of it. There will be something for you. But for years and years you are in a situation (school) where it is the major focus and you are graded and judged on your academic ability.

If you think back to your primary school and you and all your little classmates joining at four or five years old, there were kids who were tall and kids who were short. Kids who ran fast, and kids who dawdled. Kids who wet their pants and kids who didn't. Kids who spoke several languages and kids who rarely spoke. Kids who were noisy or outgoing and kids who were quiet or shy. Kids who were funny and kids who were serious. Kids who were caring and kids who were pushy. Kids who were creative and kids who did as they were told. Kids who could concentrate and kids who daydreamed. Kids who poured the counting beads on the floor and turned the book upside down and put it on their head and kids who understood counting and could read intuitively.

Now, any of those characteristics (except perhaps wetting your pants) might be important in the scheme of anyone's life, but of them, only counting and reading are the major focus of school life. Arriving at school, children quickly get the message that academics are the currency in that setting, they are what matter to the folks at school and are the centre of how you are being judged and divided. However adults dress it up (e.g. calling the top table 'squirrels' and the bottom table 'rabbits'), they fool no one and everyone instinctively knows that you are being graded on your ability, or lack of ability, to do those random academic things.

*I heard how Frankie had always done well in school all her life and she thought that was how everyone saw her. Over the years, she had often felt competitive with her friends over her marks and worked hard to be near the top, but then hated herself for doing so. They were her friends! She wasn't meant to want to beat them. What did that mean about her? She clearly wasn't a very nice person. As she worked harder and harder, she found other parts of her life closing down. She thought her friends thought she was a bit dull. But that kept her stuck working hard too: it felt like her hard work defined her and was all she had. She couldn't work any less hard because if she didn't get good grades then who would she be?*

Of course, in the long run, your other characteristics may be more important in what you want to do or who you become. You may become a basketball player, a comedian, work in PR or be a librarian. You may want to be in a hierarchical work structure like the police or army, or you may want to have your own business and be your own boss. You may want to have a job where you are creative and think outside the (counting beads) box. You may want to do something practical with your hands or make things, like a plumber or a tailor. You may want to care for people, in a paid way, or you may wish to raise a family and find a part-time job. Many different skills and talents are important in who you are and what you become but school increasingly focuses on a very narrow band of academic subjects.

This gives you the idea that academic subjects are the key skills you need to achieve in life. An idea which I, and lots of people who know much more about education than me, believe is fundamentally wrong (see Ken Robinson in the 'Want to Know More?' section). For many people, the stuff they learn at GCSE, past a very rudimentary level of maths and English, have almost nothing to do with most people's future work and day-to-day life.

The assumption that everything we learn in school is important and we remember it all is endemic in society and is fundamentally untrue. We see it reflected in the talk about 'missed learning' during the pandemic, as though you will be permanently short of that knowledge. I did maths, physics and chemistry for A levels, and I do not remember anything of differential equations, mechanics or the periodic table, except the fact that once I knew something about them. Even in my doctorate, I didn't have one single lecture on therapy with children and adolescents with eating disorders, which is now my day-to-day work. I had to learn that on the job. Some of the learning I did to get those qualifications I then built on in the next stage of my education – e.g. a smattering of maths was useful for the statistics involved in psychology. But the vast majority of those qualifications were just a hoop I had to jump through.

But if you aren't good at jumping through those academic hoops, school can be a bit miserable. Say you are below average at maths and English, perhaps you have dyslexia or dyscalculia, or perhaps you just find it all a bit boring. This means that for you, school may be a bit off-putting. You can see how that might make you a bit sad or worried. It might make you feel a bit crap about yourself.

And if you are already a bit sad – perhaps because your parents are mean and so home is pretty miserable; or perhaps they are lovely but haven't been well or have lost their job; or if you suffer from social disadvantage such as poverty – it is going to be harder still for you. And in your head, that might become, 'I'm rubbish, everyone is smarter than me, I'll never do well.'

It is also often difficult to talk to adults about this. I imagine if you said, 'I don't like school. I don't like lots of the subjects and I'm not very good at it,' most adults' natural response to that would be, 'Well, everyone has to go to school, you just need to get on with it, and why don't you try actually getting down to your work?' (You can picture it, can't you? Slightly sarcastic tone, pursed lips, disapproving face.)

But there are risks from you not liking school, or thinking you are not good at it, and the main one is it becomes irrelevant to your life; you become disenfranchised from it. Lots of young people who, as we psychologists would say, 'don't get self-esteem from their academic work and school' turn to other pursuits to feel good about themselves. Ideally, you would turn to pro-social and constructive things like art, exercise, drama, dance, sport, charity, social justice, advocacy, politics, helping others.

However, teenagers are often not so pro-social when coping with being disenfranchised from school and, as they get older, instead use drugs, alcohol or cigarettes to numb the pain, or turn to crime and gangs to get status. Girls can be pushed to rely too much on external appearances (being fashionable, skinny or pretty) or using their sexuality to get attention or status. We call that objectification: when a person is only judged on their looks and not on what's inside. It can lead to young women thinking their appearance is all they have to offer, rather than their personality, their brains, their warmth, humour and their general kick-ass-ness. And while most of those pursuits are acceptable to some extent – except crime and gangs – problems will arise if you start using them not for fun but for self-esteem, because you hate school, or for coping with difficult feelings, like being angry, anxious or sad.

So, if you aren't so great at academics, I say this to you: school shouldn't be just about qualifications and I'm sorry if the adults around you have forgotten that. Education should spark interest and passion in you and give richness and depth to your life. It should help you to understand the society you live in and give you a sense of purpose and worth. School should be a gateway for you to become a well-functioning, reasonably, happy, adult member of a society. If it isn't and you are not great at it then hang on in there; life is long and you can make a success of it.

### For those of you who do better at schoolwork

But what about those of you who like school and do OK, or even well, in the academic subjects? Surely, the logic is that then school will be a place where you will enjoy lots of success and build good mental health? Well, it doesn't seem so. The evidence is that you are struggling, too.

The increase in anxiety and self-harm in young women is a

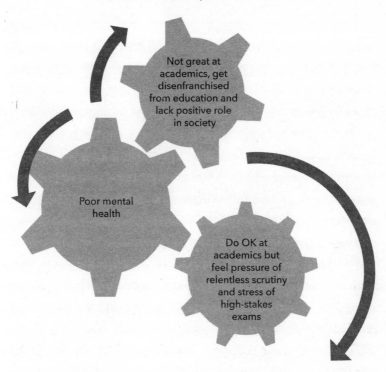

huge problem, and school is often the area where young people rate themselves as most unhappy. Test anxiety is much higher among girls than boys. If you do well in school or university, it may feel that you are on an uphill path to the gold at the end of the rainbow . . . good qualifications. You work for years for something that is abstract, never feels good enough and often is completely irrelevant the day after you get them.

### Education – missing the pleasure of now?

Let's think about qualifications in analogy to something concrete to make this clearer. Imagine you are making a car (your GCSEs). You have to learn to make an engine, weld metal together and paint the body work. People keep coming in and giving you advice. They teach you how to do certain tasks and tell you how to improve. But they never once say, 'This car is good enough. You can stop working now. Go rest, have fun!' Instead, they say, 'Excellent work on the car but you'd better pump up the tyres a bit more just in case and keep polishing the interior upholstery.'

The car is only done when the time is up, when it is submitted for scrutiny. They say, 'Wait two months and we will tell you whether it is good enough.' You get to relax and have some fun – maybe you go to a festival, get drunk, kiss some people you shouldn't. And then way-hey! What do you know? The car passes the assessment (but it's never perfect) and so for a day or so you feel really happy and get to drive the car around. But then they say, 'That car was good enough for then but now you are going into a Formula 1 race and you need a racing car – your A levels. Leave it behind and come to work on this.' And, as you do, you realise your old car was so slow and simple, and whilst you occasionally use some of the skills you learnt making it, it is basically irrelevant. Everyone's forgotten about it.

And when that is done you will get pushed to enter a different context where both cars are irrelevant – perhaps because the task is moving across water or flying and you will need to make a speed boat or a plane – your degree.

It's perhaps obvious to you that this would be dispiriting and depressing and anxiety provoking, but let me spell it out.

At any point in time, we can be thinking about the present, the past or the future. If we look to the past with regret or embarrassment, it is likely to make us sad. As we've already talked about, if you don't do well in school and you are the type to look back, you might think, 'I didn't do very well on that, I'm not very good at that.' Your mood might get a bit low and people with low mood tend to feel less motivated. That can lead to a negative spiral down, where young people can feel a sense of learnt helplessness, that nothing they do makes any difference. That they are not good enough. That they won't ever be good enough and have no meaningful future, and this sort of mental state can cause depression.

However, if you do OK at school or uni, or even really well, you may constantly feel as though you have to look forward in time to the next test, coursework or the seemingly all-important formal exams. It induces feelings of constantly having to keep up or of competition. For some young people, there is a sense of always having to do more and to do better, striving for the next thing, never able to relax. And if you think (or are told) there are very few places at the next stage or it's very important to be at the top, or that 'your whole future depends on it', the stakes are very high indeed, and that is a true recipe for anxiety.

> Recipe for anxiety: Take 1 part relentless high pressure and competition, add 1 part high stakes, keep brewing for years and create an anxiety disorder.

If you are constantly sacrificing the present for your future, you miss out on the happiness of now. We know from mindfulness and meditation that being mentally in the present is key for a sense of wellbeing; being at school can mean you are constantly looking forward to the next assignment, essay or end-of-unit test. Not only can that feel depressing and anxiety provoking, it also means you miss out on the mental wellbeing benefits of being you, you in that moment in time.

*Frankie and I thought together about how for years, she had felt a building pressure on her: her parents were so proud of her; the teachers would praise her work; her friends said to her all the time that she didn't need to worry as she always got high marks. Rather than reassuring her, when they all said that it had made her feel the weight of everyone's expectations and she worried about disappointing them. She was constantly second guessing herself: 'What if I get a low mark? They might think I didn't work hard. They might think I'm lazy.' Then, if she got a good mark, it was never enough because there was always another essay, test or exam looming on the horizon, and now they would be disappointed if she didn't do as well as before.*

*I got her to predict what her exam marks would be: she predicted mainly 5s or 6s – she had definitely failed history and she may have scraped a 7 in biology.*

**Qualifications are not an identity**

It feels to me when I listen to a whole heap of young people that they mainly think about themselves in terms of doing well at school. They think this is the most important thing, or worse, *the only* thing, about them. They've lost any sense of themselves – their own pleasure and joy, their own preferences and wishes have all been sacrificed to keep their work output to a good standard. It seems that if something can't be graded or ranked or marked, it just doesn't matter.

And in this way, the education system contributes its part to your whole growing up being focused on your outcomes, about your final achievements. It seems for many of you academic types, for a lot of your childhood, other people are working hard on the assembly line to create the-product-which-is-you, to reach some arbitrary standard of 'best'. Right from those educational toys your parents gave you, teachers and tutors, sports and swimming coaches, music and drama teachers have been focused on you doing your best and fulfilling your potential. By the time you get to the last few years of school, you have totally internalised this mindset and taken over creating the product-which-is-you. Not from the inside out, which would be about your true self blossoming. But, instead, totally based on meeting the infinite standards endemic in society: chasing a concept of perfect. It can mean you spend years trained to look at yourself in the third person, depersonalised from *being* you, instead *doing* stuff to achieve more and better.

So it seems for many young people, the product isn't a metaphorical car or even their GCSEs. They look at themselves as a product: a product and also the producer of that product. And quite frankly, thinking of yourself like that is a total headfuck, and has a terrible impact on your relationships and your mental health.

## There is another way: setting realistic expectations

Your education should not be a relentless slog to you. You should not be metaphorically, as well as literally, weighed down by a heavy backpack of work and demands. Education should not feel like a race to a mythical top.

If education does feel like that for you, we need to change that.

How? Good question.

You have no control over lots of things about school, college and university. Education policy is set by government; school policy is set by your schools; your parents will have their views.

Education as it feels for many of you ... That is, it feels like a weeding out of people and you are competing against your fellow pupils for a narrow definition of success.

Very few achieve success of best

Teenagers are 'weeded out' by GCSE and A levels

Lots of children enter school and are graded and placed in hierarchies of achievement

But there are things you can do. You might need to remember quite a lot of what we've talked about before to do so. You can do your best to promote your mental health in all those ways I outlined in the emotions chapter: sleep, eat, stay in the present. You can try to stay in your wise mind, keeping hold of the whole picture in relation to school, and not just be pulled into your emotional mind. You can say, 'Hang on a minute . . . is the emperor wearing clothes? Are qualifications worth the sacrifice of my mental health?'

It is not going to be easy. In raising these questions, you will be going against a tsunami of opposite pressure hitting you from those multiple other sources. You will need to summon every ounce of teenage rebellion in you to fight for the right to be a little bit naughty. The right to be more than the sum of your output. You are a person not a production line.

You might need to bear in mind the stuff from the anxiety chapter about the spiralling up of anxiety. You need to remember that any piece of homework, or test, or exam, is just, well, a bit of homework or a test or exam. In the scheme of things, it doesn't mean much. It needs to be done, for sure, but it doesn't need to be done perfectly. It doesn't all need to be done to the best of your ability; it needs to be done to the best of your ability *within a limited time period so you can get on with the rest of your life and stay mentally well.*

You also might need to remember the bit about social anxiety in the friendship chapter, where you think about what your friends think about you. Because that doesn't just happen in relation to friends – I see many of you spending a lot of time thinking about what your teachers think of you. Teachers' views of you often feature very loudly in your mind. That sounds like 'I don't want them to be disappointed in me.' There is an egocentricity attached to this which assumes that you might feature a lot in your teachers' minds. Long story short: you don't. Of course, you feature in their minds a bit. When they are in class with you; when they mark your homework; when they are at a parents' evening. You may pop into their mind at another time, as something occurs to them about you.

But, according to a friend of mine who is a teacher, in British secondary schools, teachers might have about 175 pupils each. And, they have their own lives, with their own combination of mothers, fathers, husbands, wives, boyfriends, girlfriends, friends, flatmates, children, grandchildren. Like anyone, they have their own stuff going on. So, let's assume that they think about their work for about 40 hours a week. And let's also assume that their thoughts are divided into thoughts about their pupils, thoughts about the subject and thoughts about the practicalities of the work (staff meetings, timetabling, career progression). That's about four minutes per pupil per week. So no, they are really not thinking about you that much. Not enough to justify you worrying about it for hours. If you do less well than usual, and if they notice, and if they feel disappointed, it will be a fleeting thought that will disappear in the thousands of other thoughts they get each day. They are also likely to feel disappointed *for* you and not *at* you.

You also need to remember that every teacher thinks their subject is important and some of them are indoctrinated into the false belief that qualifications are of crucial importance, so they will inadvertently say things that cause you pressure, such as, 'I want you all to work really hard on this because it's important for your GCSEs.' You need to ask yourself, are they talking to you? Or is the pressure a clumsy attempt at motivating some of the lazy-arses[15] at the back?

*When Frankie came in for her session after her exam results, it turned out she hadn't got 5s and 6s but mainly 7s or 8s and she hadn't failed any.*

*'How did you feel?' I asked. 'Relief,' she said. 'Not joy? Not happiness?' I asked. 'No, no joy. Just relief and slightly numb.' She had gone out with her friends that evening and had some fun, but again, felt slightly disconnected when they congratulated her on her results. It was like someone else had got them. The next morning, she had woken up and not even felt relieved any more. Yesterday's results felt irrelevant. She just felt dread and fear. It was all starting again in two weeks.*

*However, she could see now that it would never be enough. She wanted to change.*

'But,' I can hear you protest, 'even if I don't let myself get worked up about exams, or worry about what my teachers or

---

15  No disrespect to the lazy-arses at the back. Many of my favourite people are lazy-arses and I believe there would be fewer mental health difficulties with a bit more lazy-arsing.

tutors think, you can't tell me exams aren't important. Even if I don't think I'll end up on the street, they are quite important.' Well, yes, but of course the key word is *quite*. Are you acting as if your exams are *quite* important or are you acting as if they are the *be-all and end-all*? Exams and qualifications, in this current world, are things where the worry can spiral out of control if you don't keep an eye on it.

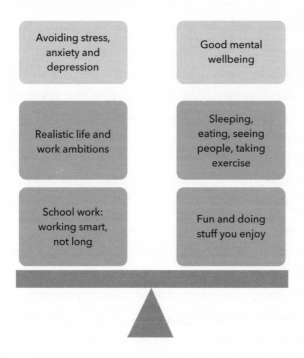

Education, at its worst, can be a competitive race to the finish line of exam results. But truths about education that you need to keep in mind to keep the pressure in perspective are:

- Life is long and few people end up doing anything directly related to what they learnt at school.

- Going with the race analogy again: there is more than one type of race. There are marathons and there are sprints. There are hurdles and cross country, too. There are tortoises and hares. They are all good.

- The exams are just to open a door to a certain type of academic job and it's OK if you don't want one of those.

- Other sorts of jobs are not second class and do not mean you are failing at life.

- If finances are really important to you, academic jobs *on average* have better salaries but there are lots that don't and lots of people who are mega-successful never passed their GCSEs. And I don't just mean footballers and popstars, but entrepreneurs, builders and hairdressers. They work hard at something they are good at and build their own business or businesses and financially overtake lots of us graduates.

- University isn't the be-all and end-all of life, or the guaranteed path to a good life. A generation ago, a goal was set that 50 per cent of young people should go to university in UK without any analysis of whether there were graduate jobs for that 50 per cent. Lots of graduates are doing un-graduate jobs and lots of non-graduates lead happy, professionally successful and fulfilling lives.

So, set academic expectations for yourself that are challenging but not mentally or physically exhausting for you. That goes for those of you who are thinking about university, too. Try to think of your education as a blossoming of your opportunities rather than a narrowing of your options towards the goal of a mythical,

unobtainable best. A broadening of experience, knowledge, skills
... now that's an education for you.

As adults, they have a wide and broad
range of different interests and jobs
available

Teenagers pick a favoured
mix of academic topics
and practical skills

Education as it
should be - a broadening
of opportunity and
celebration of individuality.

All children enter
school and learn
their ABCs and
maths

*I worked with Frankie on identifying her negative automatic
thoughts: she made the thinking error of mind-reading her teachers
all the time. She learnt to challenge this: her teachers didn't
spend that much time thinking about her; they had 100 pupils to
worry about and probably wouldn't even remember what she got.
In any case, so what if momentarily a teacher thought that she
hadn't worked as hard as usual? If that thought passed through a
teacher's mind, it really wouldn't impact on the rest of her life. She
began to realise that she couldn't control what everyone thought of
her all the time.*

*She also began to think about her core beliefs and saw how being
such a high achiever felt competitive, rather than collaborative, with
her friends. That made her less part of the group as it set her aside.
She didn't like that. She challenged herself to join in more and be top
less. She found going out with her friends gave her more focus when
she was working because she wasn't working all the time and needed
to get it done by a deadline. She felt more relaxed and confident*

*in class because she was more sure of her friendships. She worked hard at not minding if people beat her rather than using it as a stick to beat herself.*

## The truth about university

If university is for you, I want to help you set realistic expectations about it, despite all the hyperbole that exists out there about it.

Over the years I have been listening to young people, I have noticed a change in the way you talk about university. When the young people I met in my therapy room used to talk about where they wanted to go to university, they would say they wanted a campus university, or a city university, or a university with a good nightlife or one close to home, or one where they did a particular course. But now, more often than not, the young people I talk to say they want to go to a 'good' university. When I ask what they mean by that, it generally seems to mean that they want to get the one that requires *the highest grades that they can possibly get.*

Why? Listening to you, it seems that universities that require you to get higher A level grades are seen as *better* than those that have lower grade requirements. Somehow, an invisible hierarchy of universities has become embedded into your brains, along with a belief that there is an unequivocally best university, measured by how hard it is to get in. Also, the assumption is that you should want that (arguable) best, even if that pushes you to your absolute limit in getting in – or *you don't like it.*

Universities are businesses and have become very good at promoting their exclusivity and telling you they are the best with scant evidence provided. For example, what does a 'Russell Group' or 'Ivy League' university actually mean, objectively? Do you know? They are terms that get bandied about all the time but who actually knows what they mean?

Russell Group means a group of universities who met at the Russell Hotel in London in 1994 to form a group to represent their interests and promote themselves. Effectively, it is a group of universities who decided to make themselves exclusive: it's like an old boys' club but for universities, with all that means for social diversity and equality of opportunity. They do get lots of research money and their graduates often get good graduate jobs, but that is a chicken-and-egg situation.

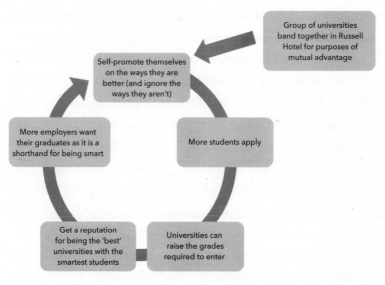

There is no external validation of their Russell Group status. No university is thrown out if they don't make a particular standard – e.g. on the calibre of student accommodation, the mental health of their students or even on the standard of teaching. In fact, less than half of them have gold standard teaching, according to an independent assessment by the government called the Teaching Excellence Framework.

The Ivy League status in the USA is based on old universities who used to compete with each other at athletics. All existed in the colonial period and are therefore founded on white, male, moneyed privilege. This is a case of the powerful setting themselves up as the best. Then everyone applies, wanting the best, and they become the best funded, most competitive, 'brightest' universities.

If you are aiming for uni, whether you get AAA or AAB will matter little in the scale of life. There are very few courses where you can't do them at all if your grades are one or two points off where you want them to be. But putting yourself under unbearable pressure to get to a particular university or group of universities has a touch of Groucho Marx to it: 'I don't want to be a member of any club that will accept me.' Especially when that club is a self-selecting one and is based on traditional privilege.

The most important thing is to decide what YOU want out of a university – and, indeed, if you are not going to university, out of your job and where you are going to live. Once you have a shortlist, surely there is an argument for aiming for one with a realistic grade entry requirement and not one with the highest?

This push and pull for the so-called best without any consideration what is best for you seems insidious in society generally and is hard to resist at a time in your life when you are genetically programmed to look to the views of others. It's like you wanted a new pair of trainers, you found some that you like that weren't the cheapest or the most expensive but then someone makes a face of disgust at them and says, 'Don't get those ones,

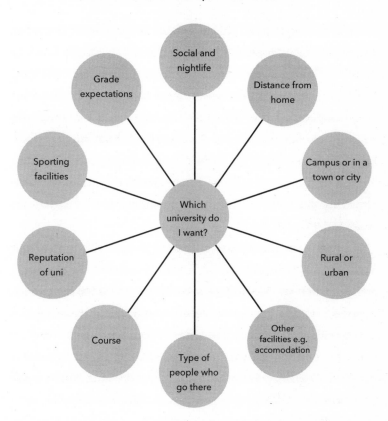

they're rubbish, these more expensive ones are better – they are a designer brand, they are cooler and they're the ones that everyone wants.' Would you say you wanted the more expensive ones even if they didn't suit you? Or would you think that was rubbish and just get the ones that you choose, you liked, and you could afford?

In universities, do not assume because they have set their grade entry requirements higher than somewhere else that they are either a better university, per se, or a better university *for you*. Remember the main thing the high-grade offer from a particular university reflects is that lots of other people want that university. It's like you are all bidding on the same thing on eBay and the entrance grades/cost has gone up. Other people may have wanted it for reasons that might not be important to you, like snobbery or tradition. Other people are entirely different from you and want different things out of life. I mean, if you want to be a Conservative prime minister of the UK or love tradition, old buildings and punting, you might want to try to go to the University of Oxford. But if you're aiming to be a clinical psychologist and love urban life and nightclubs, it will make not one iota of difference which university you went to and in the meantime you won't have as much fun.[16]

If you choose a university at the top of your ability level and have to push yourself beyond reason to achieve the necessary grades, all that you are doing is signing yourself to having to push yourself beyond reason at university too. Or being at the bottom of your cohort at university in terms of your academic ability.

So, I would suggest that you think what you want from your years at university and not what other people want. Ask yourself what is realistic for you and how you can keep a reasonable work-life balance and not stress yourself out.

*When it became time to choose a university, Frankie struggled against the pressure of her family, friends and teachers to not think she should go to the best university that she could get into and instead to think about what she wanted from university. Her family lived in London but she thought she was happier in a more rural setting: she wanted to be a vet and get a dog. She thought hard about what was best for her, rather than what was 'the best' university.*

---

16  A completely random example here, said a clinical psychologist who didn't go to Oxford and loves urban life.

## Study smart not long

Up until now in this chapter I have been mainly focused on popping the bubble that holds that exams and qualifications are the be-all and end-all. I have warned against doing your best at the cost of your mental health . You might be surprised that, after saying all of that, I am now writing advice about study skills and passing exams. Well, don't be. I am not 'against' working hard, what I am against is working so hard that you risk mental ill health. I am for you setting realistic expectations for yourself and working smart within those.

Also, let's not forget that mental health problems at 11 years old correlate on average with poorer grades five years later, and I suspect that one of the reasons for that is that it interrupts studying. Mental ill-health can get in the way of studying smart. It can create problems including procrastination (getting started with your work), stopping work and working for too long.

*Nia came to see me in late November of her first term at university. She felt overwhelmed, out of control and panicky. She had always worked hard at school, done her best and had been well supported by her teachers and parents. Set loose from the strictures of school and family, she had felt free for the first time in her life and had really enjoyed the social side of university in the first month or so, with plenty of drink and parties and a couple of romantic flings. For the first time in her life, she had missed some lectures, sleeping in late, and was now behind on her coursework. When she tried to catch up she felt anxious about being behind – that had never happened before – and she hated being alone with those feelings. So she would go and be with friends again. As time passed, she felt overwhelmed by how much she had to do.*

## Procrastination

Getting started with your work, procrastination, is a huge problem for lots of people. Now, you may be thinking I'm a hypocrite, banging on about how much of a problem it is working too hard and then giving you tips to get over procrastination.

Well, actually, no. While it might seem counter-intuitive, some girls procrastinate because they are perfectionists. They avoid starting because they are worried it won't be good enough when they finish it or because deep down, they know if they start it at the right time, they will be utterly obsessed on it until the deadline. The only way they 'allow' themselves to have some fun is through procrastinating . . . Except the fun you get when you are procrastinating generally isn't that much fun, is it? It's usually tinged with guilt and dread. You don't actually do something fun or relaxing that you want to do, like see a friend or a film, because then you'd be officially not working. And so you pretend to yourself that you are about to start . . . And end up watching end-to-end *Buffy* episodes.

## Enough is enough

Knowing when to start is one problem, and that is intrinsically bound up with the second problem which is knowing when to stop. Have you heard of the pareto principle? That states that 20 per cent of your efforts account for 80 per cent of your marks and working late into the night re-writing something messy, repeatedly editing an essay or working on the final problem that you are stuck on is unlikely to be studying smart. It's likely to make very little difference to your mark. It may even make you hate your course and want to give up or drive you into the type of poor mental health that means you have to give up.

Academic work follows the law of diminishing returns: you will get most reward from covering most of the essential stuff reasonably well. Not from trying to know all of it inside out and back to front. That will simply stress you out and put you at risk of burnout. Or stop you wanting to even start.

As we've seen, the key message to staying sane and surviving the flawed education system you find yourself in is to set yourself realistic, mentally healthy expectations for yourself. Once you've done that, learn to start *and stop* your work in a timely and sensible way. The mantra 'better done than perfect' should always apply and you should never be aiming for 100 per cent. ('Better done than perfect' is the motto of Sheryl Sandberg, COO of Facebook, and arguably one of the most successful women in the world, and it's worked well enough for her, it will do for the rest of us.) And, just for the record, to those whose perfectionism doesn't let them think they are perfectionists because they don't always get 100 per cent, it is the striving for 100 per cent that is perfectionism and not the getting 100 per cent. And it's also worth remembering that perfectionism is strongly linked with mental illness (see page 166 in Chapter 5 – Anxiety and Worry).

Even if you don't start your tasks in good time, the stopping is just as important. Don't become overwhelmed by the enormity of what you have to do because then you will procrastinate and not start. Set yourself a time limit, say one hour, that you will sit there for and study. There is nothing magical or scientific about an hour, it's just a handy unit of time. If 45 minutes or 70 minutes or whatever is easier for you, that's fine. After that time block, the best thing you can do for your mental wellbeing and your learning is to stop and have a break. All you have to do then is repeat. As we will see, this pattern will let the material consolidate in your brain and will allow you to assess whether you are still being effective in your learning.

## Studying for too long

It's really important for your mental health that you have downtime: not downtime when you are procrastinating, with the work hanging over you, but genuine downtime, when you've done some work and you know you need a break. Nobody passed exams because they had the neatest, most colour-coded revision cards. You don't get top marks by putting in the most hours. Work smart not long. And smart work means having breaks, not because of your mental wellbeing but because of the way memory works. *Memory works best when you have breaks.*

*Nia came to see me one week after pulling an all-nighter on Sunday night to revise for an exam. She'd had increasing panic and dread the week before as she thought about the exam but couldn't bear to start, to even look at the task. Previously, when she sat exams, she'd had all the notes, revision timetables and neat flashcards. She didn't know how to start revising without all that. She finally started work on Saturday lunchtime and continued until 2am with no proper breaks, and then woke up at 7am on Sunday and worked all day and most of the night. When I said that there must have been a tipping point when she knew that the work she was doing was making little difference to her potential scores, she laughed ruefully. She had realised late at night that she was taking in little of the information and yet she had felt powerless to stop. We reflected on how it had become self-punishing for her to carry on working on account of her perceived laziness before.*

To understand this, it's helpful to think of your memory as a big walk-in cupboard – a cupboard where you have to store everything you own. In fact, you don't have any other cupboards, or drawers, or bags, or anything else.

So, what would you keep at the front of the cupboard? Probably the stuff you use every day, right? Your keys and bus pass, a hairbrush and mascara, this year's schoolbooks. And each day, when you are out, you pick up new stuff that all has to go in the cupboard. Some of it is important and you need it tomorrow; some of it is important but you don't need it for a year and some of it you don't know if you need it or whether it's rubbish. This is like your short-term working memory in your brain, which consists of the new stuff or the stuff we need right now, or regularly.

But suddenly, it gets really cold and snows and you need some boots and a warm jacket. They are somewhere at the back and you need to find them. This is like your long-term memory in your brain.

So how easily can you find them? That depends on a few things.

1. Remembering that you have them.

2. Where and how well you stored them in the first place.

3. Whether there is a clear pathway to that place from the front of the cupboard.

OK, so to find things you don't use very often, what do you think you needed to have done when you got the new stuff? Do you think you will be able to find or reach the old stuff if you have just thrown the new stuff in at the front and let it all pile up, getting muddled together, broken, lost and pushed back? Or do you think you would have needed to take breaks from getting new stuff to sort and organise your things in a way that makes sense – i.e. snow boots and a winter coat stored together – and check there are paths through to the back of the cupboard?

That's what your memory is like. Doing your homework or work in class is like using the stuff at the front of the cupboard – it's right there and easy to take in and out. You can pop into the front of the cupboard – your short-term memory – and easily find something you had an hour or day ago. It feels very efficient and like you are working hard: dump some stuff in at the front, get some stuff out from there, never venture further back.

But learning something more long term, accessing what you studied at the beginning of the year for a test at the end of the year, well, that's different. To make sure that happens you need to do three things:

1. You need to use the stuff at the back regularly – that will make sure that you remember that you have it and where it is.

2. You need to regularly take a break from putting new stuff in so you have time to store it appropriately.

3. You need to make sure the route back and forth to it is clear – so it's easy to get in and out.

In order to store the new stuff effectively and avoid dumping it at the front of the cupboard in a tangled heap, the best thing you can do is have a break. This gives your brain time to integrate the new information into your other knowledge. Then, if you keep going back to it, getting it out and using it again, you'll always know where it is. That way it makes a great memory.

So, when you just want to get some homework done, it might *be possible* to work solidly for a few hours but it's unlikely to be beneficial to your long-term memory. During the breaks you give your brain, it mulls over the new information, integrates it into your memories of daily life and other stuff you already have stored there. If, after the break, you go back and look at it again, reminding yourself of it before moving on, that is like refreshing yourself about where you put it and how you get there.

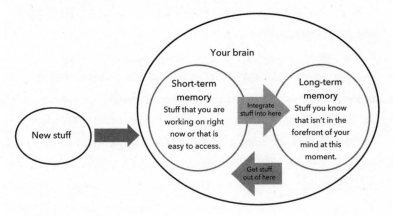

There is another reason why breaks work well for learning stuff and that is the primacy and recency effect. Your brain is better at remembering the first information you get and the last information you get in any study period or lesson. Breaking up your study takes advantage of this phenomenon and maximises learning. The first and last stuff of the study period will be more likely to make it to the back of the memory cupboard and stored in a retrievable place. The middle stuff? Nah! It's more likely to get lost or trampled on the floor.

Finally, always remember the difference between recognition and recall. Recognition is the sense of familiarity you feel when you read over something and think, 'Yes, I recognise this. We studied this once.' And nobody ever passed an exam by *only* thinking that. Recall is when you remember it, can find it quickly in your brain and use it – and that only happens when you get it out of your memory cupboard again and again and use it so you remember you have it and what it's for. Then, in a test situation, you will be able to find it really easily. Again, to do this, you need to have breaks, so the information gets integrated. And to be able to have breaks, you need to be able to start your work promptly and stop before it's perfect.

*Nia got through the exam with a 2:2 and went back to her family home for the winter holidays. It was probably the lowest score she had ever got. In therapy, we thought about her independence and her separation from her family. Without the structure of home and school it was difficult for her to motivate herself. It seemed like this might be something of a teenage rebellion after all the years of being on an educational conveyor belt. She realised that the perfect standards she had set herself in that first term had actually got in the way of doing her work rather than helping her. For example, if she thought she was going to be late for a lecture, she just hadn't gone.*

*Nia was surprised that her parents didn't seem disappointed with her 2:2. They had laughed and said they were glad she was having some fun. She began to wonder if her course was even for her. She knew if she applied herself to it, she would be able to do it – but did she want to? Just because you are capable of something doesn't mean you have to do it. She began to think about what she might want to do instead.*

## The right to be a little bit naughty

It is likely that your school, college and university is full of kind, brilliant, well-meaning teachers, lecturers and heads whose job it is to get you some qualifications within a system they know to be flawed. The best teachers do the best they can within it and also try to put some interest and passion into your education, while not placing undue pressure on you. In primary years, they try to squeeze a bit of dancing, baking and candlestick making in between the SATs and progress measures. In secondary school, they try to find time to introduce you to their favourite books before they teach you the standard, pre-analysed answers of the set exam text.

I think most of us would like a different education system. One that teaches you to think for yourself and dream big. One that values potential plumbers and politicians equally. One that tests what you do know rather than what you don't know and celebrates the differences between us rather than forces us to toe the line.

But this is the one we have and, one day soon, you will be out of the other side of it. So, in the meantime, play the academic game if you want to: set some achievable objectives; work smart, not long; continue to have fun and learn to start and stop your work in a timely way. But whatever you do, don't invest *too much* into it emotionally. And if it is making you so unhappy that you want to kill yourself, or hurt yourself, or you are having panic attacks regularly, or are revolving your whole day around a punishing work schedule, then STOP.

Because if those things are happening, whatever it is meant to be leading to is *probably not for you*. If you have to push yourself so hard to get it or the work takes that much toll on you, it's honestly not worth it and that's not a problem. There will be something else for you.

Remember, there are many routes in life, not all academic and not all 'the best', but many of them are good. Life is long and there are different ways to succeed and, more importantly, to be happy.

# CHAPTER 7

# FOOD, EATING, WEIGHT AND SHAPE

*'I was brought up in taffeta dresses, taught taught to be pretty
and precious, and spending my playtime with plastic princesses,
who all had these bodies just utterly ludicrous, minuscule waists and
huge boobs, and it's all nipple-less and no pubes, and no creases
I mean, Jesus it's pretty confusing, especially at 6.'*

**TIM MINCHIN, 'ONE DAY', FROM *GROUNDHOG DAY: THE MUSICAL***

*'Grant me the serenity to accept the things I cannot change;
Courage to change the things I can;
And wisdom to know the difference.'*

**REINHOLD NIEBUHR, 'THE SERENITY PRAYER'**

I'm not sure there is any topic where you are subject to more contradictory messages than you are with food, eating, weight and shape, and the relationship between them. For previous generations, this was exemplified in magazines that all kept to a paradoxical formula of pages of glamorous but extraordinarily thin models, followed by pages of cream- and sugar-laden recipes, followed by a new fad diet. For your generation, the internet has intensified the madness. Analysis of social media content suggests it is dominated by a mix of appearance-driven content: selfies, fitspiration, fashion and also food. You are sold (and sell yourselves) the fantasy of a perfect body, by stylised, doctored photos side-by-side with stories of decadent eating and extravagant recipes, and an endless stream of new fad diets and healthy eating plans. The message: be slim, be indulgent and treat yourself, eat in a restrained way. It is a no-win situation.

Silent scream.

I'm not sure whether this is a misogynist plot. Or whether it's something that women do to each other, in some sort of perfectionistic competition. What you eat, how you look and what size you are often seem to be the things you feel most judged about and perhaps consequentially most judge about yourselves.

Let's try to understand this a bit more and see if we can find you a different way.

## Beware the healthy eating messages

What does 'healthy eating' mean? This concept is drilled into you from an early age, often by your parents, your school and society in general. And, like many other issues in this book, food has become infinitely more complex for your generation, due to the proliferation of choice and availability, and, of course, the internet.

Perhaps your parents said you could have certain 'unhealthy' foods 'as a treat' but 'not too much, now'. Perhaps you heard them say they were trying to be 'good' or 'they couldn't have biscuits in the house'. Certainly, for your generation, healthy eating is part of the school curriculum and primary schools often have rules about which foods are allowed in packed lunch boxes or for snacks. You need a 'healthy' snack.

*I met Orla in the autumn when she started Year 8, presenting with anorexia. I asked her to tell me when it all started and she said that it had started in primary school. She had always been the tallest and in Year 6 had gone through puberty, which meant she had to wear a bra and manage her period. At that time, they had covered healthy eating in school and the message she got was not to eat sweets, cakes, chocolates or biscuits, and to exercise solidly for one hour a day. She'd started cutting down on these food types and made sure she jumped on her trampoline for an hour a day.*

As you get into your teen years, your friends and internet health influencers may contribute to the 'healthy eating' cacophony of voices. You may find your friends start dieting or talking about a wonder diet or health plan. New diets and health plans seem to pop up every week. They often promote the qualities of one particular type of food, such as kale, chia seeds or nut butters. Or ban certain foods, like carbs, sugar or fats. Different healthy eating programmes can be inconsistent or contradictory. Often these come from an 'it works for me, so it will work for you' methodology. Some suggest raw, or vegan, or grain-free, or gluten-free. Others fat-free, or unprocessed, or sugar-free, ethical or organic.

Often 'healthy' is confused with 'low calorie' and is used to describe food which is either low sugar or low fat. It is rarely mentioned that calories are crucially important when you are a teenager. Calories aren't the enemy. They are necessary to grow and develop, to have energy, to be warm enough, to sleep well and to be able to concentrate. In any case, low-sugar food can be poor for health if it is jammed full of trans-fats or artificial sugars, and the health (as opposed to weight) benefits of these are questionable.

Fats too are often presented in a very negative light, seen as almost toxic. In part, I think that is because of a conflagration of the multiple meanings of the word 'fat'. We have more words to describe the subcategories of 'chair' than we do different types of fats. 'Fat' can refer to nutrients in food (lipids), the part of the body that provides cushioning, warmth and energy stores (adipose tissue) and a large-sized body (obesity). Lipids (fats) include some of the most crucial nutrients for health, as well as the most toxic, and adipose tissue (fat) is as important in the body as skin or bones: we can't live without it. Many high-fat foods are actually super healthy for you, like nuts, fish and avocado.

So, food isn't as simple as 'healthy' and 'unhealthy', but, also, your bodies aren't all going to react exactly the same to the food either. Your weight, shape, height, size and biology are all different. You will all be genetically at risk from different diseases, have different blood groups and blood pressures. You all move a different amount: from organised sport to fidgeting. Your hunger, thirst, satiety, food preferences and allergies are all different.

In addition to your bodies all being different, the psychology of your eating and your socio-cultural backgrounds are also all different. What do I mean by this? How the food tastes to you and your preferences for certain foods or patterns of eating, your individuality about variety and regularity, and for balance over the day, week, month and year. Food and eating occur in a social context and food has meaning in that context. Every family, religion and culture uses food for more purposes than simple hunger: it is used to celebrate, to mark the passing of time and to connect you to those relationships. As you go in teenage years, food may become symbolic of your independence. There are certain foods that you eat with your friends and mark that you are part of the gang, fitting in. And it's likely there are foods you eat when you don't want to think about food too much and just get on with living your life.

*For Orla, it was only after she transferred to secondary school that the eating disorder had really taken hold of her. Her secondary school was enormous and she wasn't in the same classes as her old friends. She felt big, awkward and clumsy when she went to the canteen. She wasn't sure whether people wanted her there. She found herself skipping lunch and joining sports clubs instead. She felt good at dieting.*

In much of the way we talk about food this diversity is lost. Too often, food seems to live in one of only two categories: good and healthy, or bad and unhealthy.

Healthy eating is also held up as morally superior; such eaters are judged to be better people. They get told 'you are so good'; 'you have great willpower'. But such eating can come at a cost; it can also mean treating your body as something 'pretty and precious' rather than accepting its role in your busy, normal, everyday life. Sweets can be exactly what you need if you haven't got any energy and you need a quick boost. Crisps and cake are a perfect snack for a teenager, particularly when you are moving a lot, and fruit or rice cakes would simply not contain enough energy (calories) to offset the movement. While obesity is a problem in society, it is still the case that most kids medically don't need to lose weight.

So, while it might be true that some foods are linked to some illnesses in some people, and some foods have particular health benefits for other people, you should try to remember that some foods are also more palatable and desirable to you, and some foods are cheaper or more available. Also, some foods make you feel fuller or satisfy you more. Some foods are linked in your mind to comfort or family. Sometimes food and eating means you are part of a group or joining in a social event. Some foods are more likely to make you gain weight as they are easier to eat to excess and high in calories; other foods are less calorie dense and so are less likely to be eaten in bulk or contribute to weight gain. No food should be exclusively seen as healthy or unhealthy, or good or bad. Food is simply not that simple.

As you will have seen throughout this book, it is black-and-white categories like these that often impact negatively on your emotional wellbeing. Categorising food, or eating, into healthy and good, or unhealthy and bad is a black-and-white categorisation. It is both inaccurate and unhelpful. In this chapter, I will show how such a schematic way of thinking can contribute to having a disordered relationship with food and eating, and, in turn, how having a disordered relationship with food and eating puts you at risk of both eating disorders and obesity. This simplification can stop you leading the life you want to live: being with friends, travel, fun. It risks instead tying you up in psychological knots.

So, the first key thing I have learnt about food, eating, weight and shape that I want to share with you is that it's not as simple as healthy or unhealthy. It's more complicated than that, with lots of diversity and shades of grey. It's tied up with friends, family, culture, society. And probably, but unhelpfully, it's tied up with your relationship to your own body – and that is perhaps most complex of all.

## Your body shape

In adolescence, as you move along to independence, your parents have probably stopped monitoring your food intake as much as they used to. You have more freedom and choice about what you eat. At this time, girls tend to look more to their peers for what is normal to eat and begin to think about the link between this and their body shape.

As you begin puberty, your body develops curves and the percentage of your body which is adipose tissue (fat) increases. You may start to feel self-conscious about your changing body. It's new – you haven't got used to it yet. You likely compare yourself to others – which can also make you feel self-conscious, especially if you are one of the first or one of the last to go through puberty, or one of the tallest, shortest, biggest or thinnest.

But on top of that, nearly all the millions of images of beauty you have seen over your life are bodies with low percentages of adipose tissue and suddenly puberty is taking all of you away from this societal 'ideal' body. The indoctrination into the thin-ideal starts early. The Disney princesses, with their unrealistic thinness, are always defined as beautiful, and that beauty is linked with being good and kind and someone loving you. As you get older, the number of ideal bodies you see on media outlets proliferates and most of those images of women will have bodies more similar to a prepubertal, flat-breasted and small-bottomed girl than they do to an average-sized woman.

There are literally hundreds of research studies that show that these images of thin bodies and the constant talking about body shape do impact on body dissatisfaction. There is evidence that even when you don't consciously see the thin bodies – i.e. when they are glimpsed too quickly for your conscious brain – they will still increase your body dissatisfaction. It makes no difference whether the images are on Instagram or whether they are in magazines, they will make you dissatisfied. If these images are posed in active #fitspiration, rather than in a more usual fashion shot, they will make you feel inadequate. If they are labelled as photoshopped, that will still increase your body dissatisfaction. Indeed, there is some evidence that if images are labelled as altered it makes them *more* likely rather than *less* likely to increase your body dissatisfaction. It's as if your unconscious says to you, well, if they are taking the trouble to alter it, that's clearly what thighs are meant to look like, and my thighs don't and so they are clearly fat.

*In secondary school, Orla had also become even more self-conscious about her boobs, which she thought were huge. In her first few weeks in Year 7, some older boys had made some comment about them as she walked into school with her friends. She was mortified and blushed and had to run to the loos to calm down. She crossed her arms over them. She didn't want to have a grown-up woman's body, she didn't want the older boys to cat-call her, or worse. She just wanted to be the same as everyone else and fit in. By starving herself and running all the time, she had reduced her boobs but she thought they still were bigger than anyone else's. She wanted to be smaller, more invisible.*

In the teenage years, as we have seen, it is part of your psychological profile to compare yourself to others, and yet your body gets bigger and further away from the societal body-ideal. Thus, the disparity between your image of yourself and your image of others is likely to increase. And you might feel pretty rubbish about that.

Under those circumstances, it is hard to accept that mostly your body shape and size is as genetic as your eye or hair colour, and actually rather more difficult to change or hide.

I know that might be hard and upsetting to hear. I also know that there are lots of people trying to tell you (or, perhaps more accurately, sell you) something different. We are constantly sold the idea that we can change our bodies. The whole diet and fitness industry depends on it. Societal messaging creates an insecurity with thousands of doctored, unachievable images and then there's a whole industry waiting to sell you a (false) solution to it almost seamlessly.

For you, unsure or uncomfortable in your changing body, you want to believe the internet-vlogger-exercise-guru who is trying to sell you the belief that you could look like her. What we know, of course, is that even she doesn't look like that. She is presenting an image of her best side and you are comparing your worst side to that, and then thinking that if you follow her advice you could look more like her image – something that doesn't even really exist.

But, of course, part of her image is lighting, make-up, staging, costume, and part of her image is genetic – what she was born with. Only a very small part of what you see she's achieved through diet and exercise. You may have chosen to follow her because she has a particular attribute that you don't – a flat tummy, for example – but it's likely that that attribute is largely genetic and her exercise and fitness has only enhanced it. In addition, if you met her in real life, she would likely envy you some other part of your appearance: your height or how thick your hair is, or something else that you dismiss in your mind as you focus on what you don't like about your own appearance.

Many of the young people I've met in therapy obsess about a certain part of their body. I really hope you don't do this. It might sound in your head like 'I hate my thunder thighs/big breasts/sticky-out tummy/big bum.' You may feel that you look out of proportion. It is likely that, in reality, you are not as out of proportion as you think, as focusing on that area is likely to mean it's bigger in your mind than it is really (more on this later in the chapter).

But it is also true that that proportion is unlikely to change. I have met so many girls with anorexia, sometimes on a ward, or with an NG feeding tube, or eating so little they are cold, energy-less and their hair is falling out, who *still* hate the 'fact' that their thighs are too big. Or their stomach sticks out. Now, thinking that way when you are clinically underweight is obviously a mental illness but this reflects something fundamental: what they are actually unhappy with is the proportion of parts of their body in relation to other parts. They are skeletal but when they scrutinise their own body in the mirror or look down on that part of their body, it looks big compared to the other parts.

So, the second key thing I want you to know about food and eating and its relationship to your body: your body proportions are pre-determined and barely alterable at all. I wish for you the wisdom to know this and the serenity to accept it. You have a basic body shape: you don't get to pick it and you can't do much about it. All the dieting or exercising in the world isn't going to change it much. If you think your thighs are too big, it is likely that you are judging that they are too big in relation to the rest of your body, rather than 'too big' per se. If you did manage to lose some weight (which, as we will see later in the chapter, is a big if), you might know they were smaller but you'd likely be smaller all over your body. Proportion-wise, they would probably still look too big to you.

I think you might not like what I'm saying here but I think also you might recognise it's true.

## Your inaccurate body image

But there is some good news. The good news is that you do not hold an accurate image of yourself in your head. That's right: the mental image you have of yourself is unlikely to be how other people see you, or the size you are actually. Your body image is likely to be bigger than the image other people hold of you.

How do I know this? Because research has shown it.

Why does it happen? Your image of yourself is mediated by

your senses. Everything you see, hear, taste, touch and smell has to go through your central processing, through your brain, where you hold pre-existing categories, previous experiences and expectations. Some neural connections are eager to fire, while others need to grow to accommodate new impressions.

To do this, our brain takes lots of shortcuts and makes lots of assumptions in putting together the image. What we 'see' on a photo or in a mirror is a 2D representation of a 3D reality based on the brain's previous experience and assumptions it makes from perspective and context. Visual shortcuts are (not surprisingly) hard to sum up in words and best experienced, so please see the 'Want to Know More?' section for some examples. But in summary, all of this research points to one thing: our visual system remains too limited to tackle all of the information our eyes take in. As one famous neuroscientist said, 'For that, our brain would need to be bigger than a building, and still then it wouldn't be enough.' Psychologists call this top-down processing.

So the image you hold of your body was created in your mind and mediated by your senses. You are likely to be viewing your body in one of three different ways, either by looking down at it, using a mirror or in a photograph, and each of these three ways is subject to its own biases, which can lead you to judge your body inaccurately.

*Orla believed she was fat. She sought out confirmatory evidence for this all the time, scrutinising herself frequently in mirrors. She looked at herself from the back, front and both sides, standing and sitting. I explained that 'normally' people didn't use mirrors like that and it was usual to glance in mirrors to check aspects of our dress or appearance, but not to use mirrors for hours, naked, to examine size. She would bend over and pinch her stomach 'fat' (actually her stomach skin, muscle, ligaments and adipose tissue). I explained how everyone's stomach needed to concertina in because otherwise we would not be able to stand up straight. She thought everyone was 'skinnier' than her (often they had smaller boobs) or 'smaller' than her (often they were shorter). Meanwhile, she never glanced at anyone else's legs as she was relatively happy with her own. I challenged her to swap her negative, unkind glasses that she used on herself and we did an exercise where she had to compare herself to every third person and not just the ones who were shorter and smaller chested. I challenged her to empathise with them, about what part of their body they might struggle with.*

Let's take looking down at your body first. When you do this, you are looking at it from a distance and angle from which you are unlikely to see any other body. Because your body is closer, it is going to look bigger than other people's bodies, as perspective dictates that things further away look smaller. In addition, you are likely to see your body much more than other people's bodies and in the least flattering poses, as you go to the toilet or shave your legs. You may even focus on the areas of your body you don't like and scrutinise them from a close distance. You certainly don't do this to anyone else. You are always seeing your body from a different angle and context than anyone else's body.

Yet we need context to help us judge size accurately. We constantly use the relative size of surrounding objects to judge size as the Ebbinghaus illusion opposite shows, but if you are ever staring down at your tummy or thighs, that's pretty difficult to do.

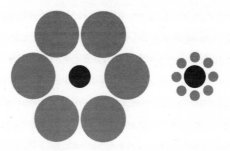

The middle circles are the same size but look different due to the impact of the surrounding objects.

Which brings me to mirrors. Let me ask you a question: what size is your body in the mirror?

I have asked this question to lots of people and they always say, 'It will be the size of me.' But it's not. Your image in the mirror is an image of you from a focal point behind the mirror. Your image will be shorter than you. If you don't believe me go and try it out with a lipstick and a full-length mirror. Stand an arm's length away from the mirror and draw a line at the top of your head, the bottom of your chin, at your feet and both sides of your waist.

Now stand aside and measure or look at those marks. Your image in the mirror will be much shorter than you and the width will be a bit narrower. Similarly, your head will be smaller.

Now experiment with walking towards and away from the mirror. As you walk away, your length will get shorter and as you walk nearer your length will get longer. Your width? It barely changes. Your head also barely changes.

Weird, huh? Why the difference? Because it is where the image (behind the mirror) enters your eyes.

You might be saying now, 'So I am bigger than my reflection, that it is even worse.' But no, because what you have learnt is that mirrors distort things: they are an illusion. And you have also learnt that in your whole life, up until this moment, you hadn't noticed that. And that means every single time you have looked in the mirror up to now, your brain has been secretly making that image bigger and you have never noticed. If we put that together with all the photos you have seen of photoshopped bodies and your bird's eye view of your own body, what do you think your brain does as it looks at your mirror image? It makes it bigger than it is. And that is what the research shows.

So, you know how some days you think you look fat and some days you think you look thin? That shouldn't be a surprise now, not because your size does change dramatically but because your **image constancy** is nothing to do with an accurate representation and everything to do with **top-down processing and expectations**. Your brain is creating the image along with your expectations – you are not seeing what is actually happening in the mirror (i.e. your body does not appear to grow and shrink as you walk backwards and forwards). And, if you are telling yourself for most of the day that you've eaten too much and you are too fat, that is the image your brain will produce.

Added to which, if you are obsessed with one key part of your body, you will notice it more and will see it as bigger than it is. If you look in the mirror and look straight at your self-defined worst bit to see how it looks, it will look bigger because you are focusing on it, without any context. It will be more noticeable. What that is likely to mean for you in practice is that all the millions of images you have seen throughout your childhood – from Barbie, to Elsa, to Katy Perry, to Kim Kardashian – and all the discussions you have had at school, with your friends and with your family about eating healthily and body size have affected the way you view your own body. They are likely to make you think it is bigger than it is because society has given you an unrealistic image of how women's bodies are meant to be, and lots of you look at yourself with critical, negative judgements about how you don't meet these societal standards.

I often think when I talk to young people that before they look at their bodies they put on a pair of magic 'negative and unkind' glasses. They look for the worst and not their best, and they think they are being vain if they are happy with their appearance. When they look at their friends they take these glasses off and put on a pair of 'positive and kind' glasses, where they look for the best.

And this is particularly true of photos. The phone camera has increased the opportunity for that self-directed negative unkindness, not least because there are simply more photos, but also particularly because of the use of filters and the ability to photoshop photos before sharing. The young women I see have always used photos to focus on the bits of themselves they like the least but that used to be one or two photos. Now having access to an immediate, potentially endless album of images of yourself and others can intensify that process and increase perfectionism. You take the worst 2D image of your 3D body taken from an unflattering angle and in a bad light and see it as real. Yet the good photos of yourself are also dismissed, for the exact the same reason – 'It's just the angle/light/make-up; I had to take hundreds to get one good one.' So many young people I meet obsess about how beautiful their friends look in their Instagram photos and mentally compare those photos to the ones of themselves that they deleted and didn't post (i.e. comparing their friend's best side to their worst side – we'll look at this in Chapter 8 – Screens and the Internet).

Online or in real life, you do not see your friends in the same unflattering, up-close situations as you see your own self. You probably don't squeeze anyone else's blackheads, or deal with anyone else's toenails, or see their thighs when they sit on the loo. Because you are kind, you look at their best features with positive-tinted glasses and you scrutinise your own disliked-parts with a critical frame of mind.

## Dieting

For many women and girls, the disparity between their own body image and the ideal image leaves them feeling too big, too fat, obese, even. They feel that they take up too much space. They are too tall. Too gawky. Too awkward. The proliferation of female images of beauty makes them self-conscious about their body, and that it is too . . . much. And they are sold the idea that dieting is the answer.

Or, to quote Marika Tiggemann, a prolific researcher in this area, the media presents women with 'a constant barrage of idealized images of extremely thin women . . . that are nearly impossible for most women to achieve' and this is linked to 'excessive dieting practices and the emergence of . . . eating disorders'. Women strive for a fat-free body, a concept that is warped – it's as nonsensical as being a skin-free body or a bone-free body.

There is a famous quote: 'Try everything once except folk dancing and incest.' To update that quote for a female, teenage generation in the twenty-first century: 'Try everything once except dieting and hard drugs.'

I pair dieting with hard drugs because, like hard drugs, some of you will flirt with it and escape unharmed. Others of you will find your food, eating, weight and shape is influenced for life by a brush with dieting in your youth from which it is hard to recover.

Why am I keen that you avoid dieting? Because research shows that dieting is predictive of both eating disorders (probably not surprising) and obesity (more surprising). Dieting is generally seen as the way to avoid obesity but actually the opposite is true: it is predictive of future obesity. Dieting gives you a disordered relationship with food and, for a whole heap of physiological, psychological and societal reasons, that may lead to gaining or losing too much weight in the longer term.

Let's understand how that happens.

*Being on a diet had initially helped Orla feel more comfortable in her body, but also more able to manage her life. Because she was thinking about calories and not eating all the time, she didn't worry about her schoolwork or her friends, or anything really. She just thought numbers – numbers of calories and the number on the scale. But now she felt she was losing control – she couldn't stop. She felt kind of cut off from everyone and everything. She didn't have any energy, she always felt cold, she wasn't interested in anything except dieting and her body. And she still thought she was too big.*

We'll start with the physiology of reducing your food intake. The best way to understand the physiology of dieting is by thinking about the impact of restricting food on an animal. So, if you have a pet, imagine if you reduced your pet's food by half every day for a month or so. Let's imagine that pet is put on a crash 'diet'. How would your pet react?

You remember my dog, Suki, right? I introduced her in the family chapter. So, for example, say I stopped feeding Suki morning and night and just fed her in the evening. And I didn't let her out to eat fox poo (why do you do this, Suki, why?). What would she do?

Well, I think on the first morning, she would bound up to me as usual and sit with pleading eyes as I had my Weetabix (or whine and jump up if it were a bacon sandwich) but she knows the routine, her food comes next. But if I started to leave, she would bark and run back and forth to her bowl. And I think when I came in that evening, she would be barking and going bonkers, and she'd wolf down her food.

The next morning I think she would be more insistent with her whining and jumping; she might even try to give me a friendly nip. In in dog language, she'd be saying, 'Just to remind you, Mum, feed me before you go, you forgot yesterday and I was hungry.' By the third day, she'd be watching me warily. But over time, I think she'd give up. Indeed, psychological experiments on learned helplessness indicate that she would give up. She'd lie sadly, energy-less in her basket and wouldn't jump up to greet me nor wag her tail. She'd be thinner and sadder, and spend less time trying to eat tennis balls, chasing-and-never-catching squirrels, and stop leaping into my lap every time I sit down.

Remember the three layers of the brain that we talked about in previous chapters? Eating is wired into all three layers. Eating is in the core brain, the part of the brain that is most like an animal's brain. It's there because it is necessary for survival, like breathing and your heartbeat. But eating is one of those core-brain functions that can be controlled by the top layer, your thinking brain, the cortex. In fact, civilisation has brought eating firmly into that planning, organising part of the brain.

Thus, our core brain picks up our hunger cues, such as low

blood sugar level or an empty stomach, and the cortex makes a plan about what to eat. But, when you are starving, the core brain overrides everything else and makes you eat. Grass, if you are in a famine, or whatever you can find in an emergency. In 1975, after a plane crash, the survivors ate the dead fellow passengers to survive. That is how strong the drive to eat and the survival instinct is.

The core brain will also try to get you to eat more when you diet. It doesn't understand 'diet'. It understands low blood sugar level, empty stomach, low reserves of glycogen in the liver. It is there to protect against famine and thinks this is a famine, and knows what to do. It sends messages to the conscious brain – EAT! It sends out an animalistic drive so strong that it will likely overpower all your good intentions, all your willpower, your promises to yourself. Your core brain isn't verbal, so it won't reason or argue. You will find yourself wanting to eat more while another part of you argues against the impulse. That's your cortex offering up some resistance, through its reasonable plans and arguments. But it's a losing battle against the biological survival instinct of the core brain.

And that is why 80 per cent or more of diets fail to result in significant weight loss over two years, and indeed usually result in weight gain over four. Because once your core brain kicks in, it wants to prepare for the next famine and so sends your appetite up sky high. By driving your satiety (fullness) hormones down and your hunger hormones up, it lowers your metabolism a bit, stops spontaneous physical activity (i.e. you fidget and move less) and generally stocks up its food store, the adipose tissue, with spare energy for the next famine.

Core brain – one; cortex – nil.

So, whatever random diet you go on, be it the cabbage-soup diet or the Keto diet or the only-eating-foods-beginning-with-b diet,[17] while you might lose a bit of weight, the core brain will fight back with it's full 'famine alert' and send a strong drive against dieting, which makes it very hard to keep to the diet.

And that's before we even factor in the psychology of eating and dieting.

While we do that, let's imagine you are on the 'b' foods diet, and it is very important that in this next section you don't think of carrots. In fact, try to avoid thinking about anything orange or pointy or vegetably at all, to help. Absolutely no carrots, ignore carrots, you definitely don't want to think about them.

How are you doing on that?

Being told not to think about something makes you think about it and being told you can't have it makes you want it.

Think about how the brain works. You are on the 'b' food diet and you go down for your lunch of bread and butter, thinking what a good diet this is and how you are definitely not going to have carrots, cake, curry. But the thinking of banning any food type means that you are putting it in your brain and all the carrot neurons are firing. The effort of not doing something makes it alive in your brain.

In some legendary experiments in the 1950s, Ancel Keys studied the effect of starvation on healthy young men by reducing their calorie intake by a half for six months. Do you know what happened? They got obsessed by food and eating. They all got obsessed in very different ways. They talked about food all the time. Some of them started reading cookbooks. Some obsessed

17  I made up this diet but it is likely to be as 'successful' as any other diet. So, knock yourself out – bread, bananas, bacon, beef, bolognaise, butter are all sounding great to me.

over the details of their meals. Some were very particular about the seasoning. Some cut their food up into very tiny little bits and ate it very slowly. They also got sad, lonely and anxious. They stopped wanting to socialise, or have sex, or go out, etc.

So, psychologically, the very act of saying 'I'm on a diet – I can have this, I can't have that' puts food in your mind. It wakes up the neurons associated with them, the nice memories of having them, and puts your brain at odds with itself. If it goes on too long, you can become obsessed with the very things you are trying to resist. And, of course, that won't make much difference to your weight if that obsession is carrot, but you can be damned sure that your food obsession won't be. It will be chocolate or cake as they are foods designed to be appealing to the human desire for sugar and lipids.

*Orla found herself thinking about food and eating all the time, and her body and shape. She scrolled the internet all the time for thinspiration – she followed a whole heap of health and fitness influencers on Instagram and several 'recovery' blogs, where people often seemed to be flaunting their restrictive diets and their thinness. She looked at food and recipes. She had several fitness and calorie-counting apps. It was a chicken-and-egg situation – her mind wandered onto food so she channelled it into looking at stuff on her phone. Then all the algorithms on her phone offered her more of the same, so every time she picked up her phone there was stuff related to food, eating, weight and shape, and that took her mind back to it again.*

*We thought if she wanted that. Did she want to be thinking about food 24/7? What else was she interested in that was squeezed out of her thinking by the preoccupation with food, eating, weight and shape? How could she protect herself from the societal pressures that were intensifying her mental health condition?*

There are also societal factors that push against the diet working. As we discussed earlier, in books, TV shows, TikTok and YouTube videos, magazines and films, there are two main, contradictory narratives about food. There is a narrative about 'healthy', 'clean', 'ethical', 'being good' eating and then there is a narrative about 'baking', 'indulgent', 'treat' and 'being naughty' eating. Think about that for a moment. It's a bit weird, isn't it? I think if an alien arrived and looked to the media to learn about how to eat on this planet, they'd think that the way to eat would be to oscillate between periods of indulgent overeating, with all the cookery shows and food advertising, and then undereating and restriction, with all the diet books and health blogs. Society reinforces the concepts of both restrictive dieting and indulgent overeating all the time.

Why does that happen? The industrialisation and commercialisation of the food industry has also contributed to creating a polarity between restrictive dieting and gluttonous overeating. It's a perfect business model. Sell high fat, high sugar foods in large quantities, making people gain weight. Then, also sell diet products to apparently solve this problem.

This representation of food has seeped into every corner of society and has become embedded in the meaning of food, so that if you saw a girl crying and eating ice cream out of the tub, you would likely assume she'd had a romantic break-up and was 'treating' herself. High calorie food is presented as the solution to emotional pain.

And there is almost no one selling the idea of just eating enough, balancing your intuitive needs and your nutrition needs, regularly. Where's the money in that?

## How dieting leads to overeating: the 'what the hell?' effect

*Yasmin came to me worried that she had bulimia. She was one of two children of a single mum, and her mum was always on some new-fangled diet or fitness plan. She had never said it to her mum, but Yasmin couldn't help but notice that none of these had resulted in significant weight loss or lasting change. Her mum had remained roughly the same shape for as long as Yasmin could remember. Yasmin's shape was similar to her mum's, while her brother was taller and skinnier. Her mum's dieting had impacted on Yasmin's beliefs about foods. But Yasmin was clear, she didn't want the same relationship with food as her mum.*

Dieting fails because of a combination of these physiological, psychological and societal factors. How it fails is best illustrated by some classic experiments by Polivy and Herman. They are a bit complicated to explain but worth looking at in order to understand the psychology of eating.

These experimenters took two groups of people – dieters and non-dieters – and told them all they were doing a taste test. They then gave them a snack to keep them going before the taste test but they didn't give them all the same snack. In each group, they gave half of the participants a seemingly 'unhealthy' filling snack and the other half a cracker, making four groups in all. Actually, they weren't interested in the participants' views on taste but instead, they secretly measured how much they ate in the taste test.

Among the non-dieting group, they found that when they had a small snack, they ate more later in the taste test and when they had a big snack, they ate less. That makes sense, right? When they weren't full they ate a bit more; when they were, they ate a bit less.

However, where it gets interesting is with the dieters. The dieters ate counter-intuitively. When they had a small snack, they only had a little bit later but when they had a big, 'unhealthy' snack, they ate the most afterwards. They ate to extremes.

|  |  | Before the taste test | In the taste test |
|---|---|---|---|
| Non-dieters | Small snack | Ate more |
|  | Big snack | Ate less |
| Dieters | Small snack | Ate the least |
|  | Big snack | Ate the most |

It is like the brain of dieters is saying, 'No, no, don't listen to your hunger, eat less,' until a certain point is reached when it says, 'Oh no, you've ruined it now, what the hell, just eat what you want. In fact, you'd better eat more than you want or need as the diet will start again soon and you will be hungry and deprived, so stock up now.'

*Yasmin was determined to have a different relationship with food than her mother had … she had seen the failure of yo-yo dieting with her own eyes. And yet, she struggled to break free from the dieting, healthy–unhealthy, good–bad eating mentality. Currently, her mum wasn't eating carbs and while she and her brother were served carbs for dinner, Yasmin struggled not to see carbs as fattening and dieting as the answer to her discomfort in her body. Thus, she rarely ate breakfast on a regular school day when she was being 'good' but if there was some excuse, like a birthday or something, she would happily eat several croissants or muffins. It wasn't that she didn't like breakfast or wasn't a breakfast person, she was trying to eat like someone else rather than listening to her own body. During the day, she aligned her eating to her friends, often ordering what they ordered, or had a salad so they couldn't judge her for being fat or greedy. She was often starving when she got in from school and couldn't resist any more – so she'd eat all the biscuits and crisps in the house. She then felt wretched – ugly, fat, stupid – and would make herself sick.*

Most dieters recognise this 'what the hell' effect, yet the logic underneath this mentality is false. It is based on the logic that food and eating is either 'good or bad', 'healthy or unhealthy', that you are 'on a diet' or 'indulging yourself'. But food and eating do not fall into neat categories – they should be seen on a continuum. In fact, they fall on multiple continua, such as fat content, fibre content, chemical content, sugar content, fullness, preference, etc.

However, when you hear and see food reduced to simple concepts everywhere, when high fat and high sugar foods have been sold to us as indulgent treats, and low fat and low sugar food has been sold to us as good and healthy, it sets up a dichotomy in your mind. You are either being good with food or bad with food – it's an all-or-nothing concept. If you can't be good and healthy and keep to your diet, you may as well be bad, bad, bad.

But food and eating don't actually work like that – they are a matter of degree and graduation. So embedded are notions of healthy and unhealthy, good and bad, it becomes difficult to see, so let's look at that concept in analogy to money.

Say you are saving up for a gap-year trip or something and you need £1,000. And for weeks you go without socialising. You don't buy any clothes, no frappuccinos. You do extra babysitting and iron all your mum's shirts for £10, and get yourself up to £300. You are feeling pretty pleased with yourself – but also pretty bored by being so sensible with no fun. And then you see the shoes you've lusted over for weeks are on sale at £50 and you have a moment of weakness and buy them, and then you feel really bad because they pinch, you've got loads of shoes and you don't really need them.

So, what do you do? Do you go, 'Oh, what the hell, I've ruined saving now, I might as well give up for today and spend all the £300 on rubbish stuff I don't really want and don't need and start again saving tomorrow?'

NO, of course you don't. That would be daft. You think, 'Oh, never mind, I'll iron Dad's shirts too and do extra babysitting, and it will be fine. I've got to have some fun and luxury, so I've had it now and I'll knuckle down. I'll make it up and it won't make much difference in the long run.'

And yet, that all-or-nothing attitude impacts people's eating all the time. If you start telling yourself that you are on a diet and you shouldn't eat that, you are creating categories of food and eating in your mind, rather than seeing food and eating as a continuum. And therefore, if you 'fail' (and you probably will because of all those physiological, psychological and societal factors we discussed earlier) to be 'good', you may feel you have 'ruined your healthy eating' and jump all the shades of grey of moderation and balance straight to the bad banned food. You can then end up feeling compelled to eat all the so-called 'bad' foods to excess before they are banned again tomorrow.

We fail to recognise that, like with saving money, food, eating, weight and shape are a matter of degree, of small graduations, and are not all-or-nothing, good-or-bad, separate categories.


## A perfect storm: willpower and dieting

Baumeister and Tierney, in their seminal 2011 book *Willpower: Why Self Control is the Secret to Success*, call dieting 'the nutritional catch-22'. That is:

1. In order not to eat, a dieter needs willpower

2. In order to have willpower, a dieter needs to eat

The best way to think about willpower is as a resource that we have a limited supply of: every morning, we wake up with one pot of willpower for the day. Each time we are called up to control ourselves and do the right thing, we use a little bit up. Thus, when you force yourself out of bed so you are not late for school or do your homework rather than laze on the sofa; when you bite your tongue to stop yourself answering a teacher back or keep your feelings hidden in your friendship group, all of these 'use up' your self-restraint, your willpower.

As soon as you go on a diet, you are using up some of your limited daily supply of willpower in resisting all those chocolates and cake that are appearing in your brain. But willpower is not just used up by resisting things during the day, it is also destroyed by two other things: tiredness and hunger. As the day goes on, your willpower supply dwindles because you've used it up 'being good' but also because you are getting tireder and *because you're on a diet* your blood sugar is low. So, just at the point when you need your willpower the most, it is not there, because your blood sugar is low and you are tired.

It is not that you have 'no willpower', it is just you have used it all up and the rest was destroyed through hunger. And then, because you ate stuff you told yourself that you'd forbidden, you may get into the whole 'what the hell' mentality and end up eating to excess because of the 'may-as-well now you've broken the diet'.

Willpower comes from your brain but your brain needs blood sugar to create it. In fact, your brains use about 20 per cent of your daily calorie intake, even before you move at all (this is your 'resting metabolic state'). It's a funny thought that your brain needs calories, but it does. If you have only eaten an egg-white omelette or have skipped your lunch, your brain isn't going to be able to function properly and you won't be able to do certain cognitive tasks. Our brains need blood sugar for memory, word fluency – all sorts of things – and kids perform worse at tasks when they are not fed. One of the tasks they do much less well is willpower. Willpower needs blood sugar to work.

In an added twist, if you have made it a rule to resist things, e.g. 'I love chocolate but I mustn't eat it as it is unhealthy/bad/fattening' then 'not eating chocolate' requires willpower and will be hard to do. Of course, if you don't have any dietary rules about chocolate, it's not hard to resist it at all. You might have some if you fancy it or you might not. If you have some you will probably stop when you have a sense inside that you've had enough. You barely consciously think about it at all and it doesn't tax the brain for its willpower store at all. It takes minimal mental effort.

*Yasmin and I worked on regular eating first. I explained how eating regularly would help her avoid the feelings of deprivation and starvation that triggered the bingeing. It was hard to do – hard to plan to eat – that felt greedy. So indoctrinated had she been in the dieting mentality, she found it difficult to let go of it, e.g. that doing without breakfasts would make her thinner. Over time, she learnt that she was more likely to overeat or binge when she skipped meals or ate too little earlier in the day. Also, she noticed that her brother ate what he wanted and stopped when he was full, and never gained weight.*

Long story, short. The relationship between willpower and blood sugar is another reason why dieting doesn't work.

I say this as someone who works with seemingly the most successful dieters – young people with anorexia. I wonder if you are thinking, well, how can you say that? Your patients stay thin, so surely it is possible? That is not about willpower, that is about being mentally ill. Thinness becomes an overwhelming obsession and it feels physically almost impossible to eat more. They stay thin because they generally think about food and eating nearly a third of the time they are awake, and they think about weight and shape another third of the time. Then they spend most of the rest of the time thinking about their academic studies or work. I know this because I have asked all my patients with anorexia over 20 years, 'How much time do you spend thinking about food and eating?' 'What about weight and shape?' 'And how much time do you spend thinking about your friends? Your family? Your interests?' The only way to stay in the really, really thin demographic if you are not naturally in that group is by making your day *only* about food, eating, weight and shape, at the expense of any other interests, fun, your family, your friends. You must, in fact, abandon the rest of your whole world. And when I draw out this pie chart with my young anorexic patients, even they don't think it's worth it. They feel sad that they are not really connecting to their friends and family and other interests: they recognise that being really thin is not worth the sacrifice of everything else.

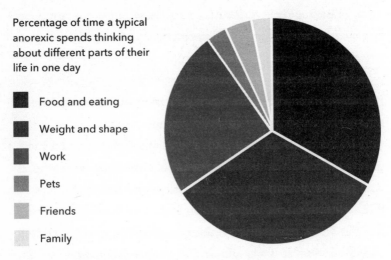

Percentage of time a typical anorexic spends thinking about different parts of their life in one day

- Food and eating
- Weight and shape
- Work
- Pets
- Friends
- Family

## All-or-nothing eating and yo-yo dieting

The idea of dieting is embedded into our culture as the cure for obesity but actually, through all the processes outlined above, it can be a route to overeating and bingeing, which of course, in turn, contribute to obesity.

Dieting and then periods of overeating or bingeing is a route by which many people become overweight over the course of their lifetimes. In fact, for about a third of people who are obese, binge eating is thought to be a factor. Their weight goes down during periods of dieting but also their body adjusts to having less food. The core brain responds as though it is in another famine and therefore it must make the body more efficient – burn fewer calories, send more hunger cues. Thus, when the diet slips or ends, it becomes easier to put on weight and also eat to excess, due to the psychological obsession and sense of deprivation they have suffered.

Ancel Key's experiments also show us the after-effects of dieting, as when they started feeding these men normally again 'many participants reported maintaining a higher than normal weight and had abnormal eating habits for many months and even years before returning to "normal" state.' Thus, after a diet, our brains want us to eat more and move less, and the psychological obsession elicited by the diet is slow to fade.

So it seems that if you do go on a diet and lose some weight, you risk developing a strong urge to eat and a bit of an obsession with food. Which is probably not what you want.

The dimension of time is important here too. The diets I see girls start in their teens are generally designed for older, overweight people with health conditions, *whose daily calorie needs are considerably less than yours*. Avoid starting down the dieting path as a young woman as it risks tying you in for life and puts you at risk for obesity.

*The second part of Yasmin's treatment focused on her tuning in to her hunger and satiety, preferences and choices for all her meals, and not just when she binged. She had no confidence that if she ate 'banned foods' – carbs, sweet things, pizza – that she wouldn't eat them to excess and then have to vomit. We tried with chocolate first – just having one portion a day. She started the week with the right amount, so she felt in control. Then she practised*

*eating something 'she fancied' each day from the school canteen.*
*She listened to her own hunger, fullness and sense of satisfaction*
*with the food, rather than eating to try to control what other people*
*thought of her.*

## Body satisfaction

So far, we have seen that your body shape is largely pre-determined:
some of you are shorter with bigger boobs; some taller with bigger
hips; some of you have big boobs and small hips, or small boobs
and big hips; some of you are curvy all over. All of these body
shapes can be beautiful and will be attractive to some people. It is
not the case that if your body does not match the prescribed ideal,
you just need to work harder at it, or have better willpower. That
is a myth, often pedalled by people trying to sell you something.
The thin-myth.

How come it's so hard to accept your body and be satisfied
with it as you might do other aspects of yourself? I hear young
people say all the time 'that's just who I am' about all aspects of
themselves – except, that is, their bodies. With that phrase they
show that they *accept themselves* or are even *proud of themselves* for
all the different parts of their personality, even when these are not
necessarily wholly positive things.

Do you do this? Do you show a greater acceptance of yourself
in other areas than you do for your body or appearance? You
might say, for example, 'I'm not a morning person' or 'I'm no good
at maths' or 'I'm a cat person' and accept this is an individual
difference about yourself. You might try to get up earlier or study
harder at maths but you accept the pros and cons of these
you, and probably don't spend hours agonising over

why it is or how you can change it. You might know that you find languages easy and envy the maths kids their ease in that area but don't think they are overall better people than you – they are just better than you at maths and that's OK. You natural cat-lovers don't spend hours gazing at your cat saying, 'I wish I loved dogs.' Yet we find it so difficult to do this with different body shapes.

Why? Because society dictates that one body shape is more socially acceptable and morally superior and sells you a belief that if you are dedicated enough you can achieve it.

The misery caused by people trying to be something that they are not is untold.

*Yasmin was bright, clever, funny, kind and stylish but she didn't think anyone would find her attractive as she was bigger than many of her friends. She pretended she wasn't interested in boys. It seemed like she had consigned herself to playing the smart best friend in life. So, for example, she felt so much shame about her appearance she never posted photos of herself on Instagram. She would never put herself centre stage in that way. We thought about how that needed to change and how she could live her best life, dress as she wanted, own her own eating and try to listen to her body, rather than trying to mind-read what her friends thought of her eating. To help with this she sought out body positivity and health at any size on social media.*

There are glimmers of change: we see stars such as Lizzo, Billie Eilish and Camila Cabello representing something different for you in this next generation. They refuse to be defined by body shape. They know the most important thing about themselves is not what body they were given but the person they became. The internet has allowed movements such as health at every size and body positivity to flourish.

The size of your body is only one thing about your general appearance but it is often the thing teenage girls ascribe the most importance. You forget the other parts of your appearance that you like more, such as your skin, face, hair and eyes. But your overall appearance is only one thing about you along with your personality, your intelligence, your achievements. Do not give it more importance than that in your life. You do not choose your friends nor judge your family on their body size, you value them for their loyalty, humour, kindness and joy. Try to treat yourself with the same respect.

## How to eat

Dieting is a strange concept when we think of it in terms of other bodily functions. I mean, you wouldn't think of trying to pee less, would you? You wouldn't try to breathe less? If you did these things your core brain would similarly take charge and you'd wet your pants or, as one of the most famous yo-yo dieters Oprah Winfrey puts it, 'For most of us, diets are a temporary solution at best. They hold as long as our willpower holds out. But how long can any of us hold our breath before we need a gulp of air?' The same is true of eating: the core brain will kick in when the body needs more food.

I hope that I have convinced you to give up on the idea of dieting for weight management. My wish for your generation is a move to body acceptance, for a wide range of bodies to be represented to you in magazines, on TV, in your internet content. We need to understand that people can be healthy at a range of different sizes, rather than being an obesity-shaming society. Giving up on dieting also forces people to give up justifying overeating to themselves by saying they will diet later. But what am I suggesting instead?

Whether you are of a larger or smaller body shape, I think you should be aiming for a balanced approach to food and eating, where no foods are banned but moderation is encouraged. You need to try to listen to your body and your hunger cues, to understand that foods have a spectrum of relative costs and benefits. You should untangle the concept of healthy from low fat and low calorie but not forget the benefits and pleasures of having a cheap, plentiful supply of delicious food. You should be thinking about the multiple meanings of food, how you might use it to connect or celebrate, and its relationship to your mood and emotions. Try not to reduce all food to binary concepts of good and bad.

I think that food and eating should be taught in school – though not in terms of healthy or unhealthy foods, obviously; you know that I think that's a gross simplification that does more harm than good. Instead, the more complicated stuff, like stopping when you are approaching fullness, eating slowly enough so that fullness comes in the mealtime, noticing the tipping point where you are eating with little pleasure and should probably stop and why dieting is dangerous. These are all useful things to understand in order to have a comfortable relationship with food, to avoid the risk of tipping into obesity or into an eating disorder. Most of all, schools should teach a long-term planning approach to food, eating, weight and shape, while acknowledging the short-term motivations and pulls.

I am not going to fully explore the concept of intuitive eating here, not least because it's already been done brilliantly for a female teenage/young adult audience by Laura Thomas in *Just Eat It*, as well as by Rick Kausman, in *If Not Dieting, Then What?*, but I would encourage you to look at these books. Kausman makes an analogy between eating and a rowing boat with two oars: intuition and nutrition. Do you know what happens if you row with one oar? You go around in circles. Similarly, if you eat with either intuition alone or nutrition alone you get stuck in one place. You need to use both.

Nutrition is more than what food is good for you. It's about what food you need in order to accomplish what you need to do. It is thinking about what breakfast will give you the energy you need to get to lunch and what lunch will stop you being hangry after school. It's about knowing about carbs, protein, fats, fruits and veg, etc., and checking in that you have had about the right amount, not in any particular meal, or day, but over a week or a month. It is listening to your body, your hunger cues, your satiety and your energy levels, and putting it all together. That is nutrition.

Intuition, on the other hand, is thinking about what food you fancy to eat, what you are craving and what will satisfy you. If you really fancy a pasta salad for your lunch but instead decide to 'be good' and have some lettuce and protein, no carbs, you do not satisfy your intuition. It is more likely later that you will obsess about food and overeat. Intuition also covers the other meanings of food. The Friday night takeaway, the birthday cake, the first date. They are the occasions that you will connect with people by eating with them or eating the food they make.

Problems come when we use one 'oar' too much, as my patients with anorexia show in their obsession with nutrition and their neglect of intuition. They spend their lives thinking about calories and little else. Alternatively, people who listen to their intuition too much can become disordered in their eating and eat too much 'junk' food and end up overweight. It's a delicate balance.

*Yasmin wanted to practise eating intuitively. She made an analogy between eating and clothes to me. She said when she got up in the morning, she looked at the weather, she thought what she was doing that day (was she going clubbing? To school? To visit her granny?) and then she thought about what she wanted to wear. She sometimes wanted to wear leggings, sometimes a pretty dress and sometimes jeans. She didn't overthink it; she considered the practicalities (what was she doing? With whom? What was the weather like?) but after that, she wore what she fancied and accepted that every day she wanted to wear different things. She learnt to do the same with her food: she thought about what she was doing and the day ahead, what she needed out of the food in terms of energy, warmth, timing, availability, and then she thought about what she fancied. Sometimes that might be a hot, filling stew and other days a cool ice cream. Sometimes she wanted a salad and sometimes a sandwich stuffed with ham and cheese. Food became about nutrition, yes, what she needed, but also intuition, what she fancied. Like how she was with clothes – she just accepted that she just fancied things sometimes and learnt not to overthink it or judge herself as healthy or unhealthy.*

## Food, eating, weight and shape: how to get sanity in an insane world

So, what have I learnt about food, eating, weight and shape by talking and listening to hundreds of girls?

1. Weight and shape are things we have limited control over, and the control we do have is to make them bigger. Because of the physiology of the body and the strong brain urge to eat, weight goes on easily and comes off torturously. And much of your body shape is pre-decided.

2. Therefore, you need to work hard to accept your basic body shape. Know that you won't see it accurately or the way other people do, so try to minimise this self-scrutiny. I try not to be directive but if you are spending more than 10 minutes a day looking in the mirror, it's probably too much. It's likely to leave you with a distorted image of yourself by looking at your body out of context and for too long.

3. Put on your 'positive and kind' glasses before you view any image of yourself. Don't save these glasses just for others. Counter the negative (and inaccurate) self-evaluation with some positive self-talk. But also keep your appearance in perspective. You wouldn't want it to be the most important thing about you. You want people to like you for yourself, not your looks. Focus on being the person you want to be, rather than looking a particular way.

4. Rail against the relentless presentation of women's bodies as one size and shape and do your bit by avoiding supporting the promotion of idealised body types on social media. Don't post stuff that plays that game. Try not to judge other people on their size. Nor yourself.

5. Eat for general health but not obsessive health, which means following the basic advice of the medical community rather than any self-appointed health expert on the internet. Listen to your body and figure out what works for you. But do not negate the role of food as communication and a way of connection. If you are too pretty and precious about food, it puts you outside rather than part of your social group.

6. Eat intuitively. Kausman again: 'You can eat anything you want, you just have to really, really want it.' If you want chocolate, chips and crisps all the time, you need to turn down your want-o-meter and use your nutritional oar a bit more, or come to terms with a larger body. But don't deprive yourself of these things completely.

7. And, of course, move your body regularly in a way you enjoy.

So, as I said, it's not as simple as good and bad, or healthy and unhealthy, but nor do I think it's more complicated than these seven points.

# CHAPTER 8

# SCREENS AND THE INTERNET

*'It's not enough; I've had enough; I'm not enough'*

TIM MINCHIN, 'IT'S NOT ENOUGH', FROM
*GROUNDHOG DAY: THE MUSICAL*

*'The difference between technology and slavery is
that slaves are fully aware that they are not free'*

NASSIM NICHOLAS TALEB, *THE BED OF PROCRUSTES:
PHILOSOPHICAL AND PRACTICAL APHORISMS*

The internet reminds me of *The Wizard of Oz*. In Kansas, everything was grey and dull but Dorothy's house got pulled up into a twister typhoon and crashed in the Land of Oz. Here, everything was in Technicolor; it was bright, light and things worked differently than they did back in Kansas. Like the internet, Oz was sometimes exciting and thrilling, but sometimes it was overwhelming and scary. And, like Dorothy, you are exploring this new land without maps or knowledge about what lies ahead. The adults are stuck back in Kansas, and online, as in Oz, you might meet some new people who, perhaps, aren't all they seem.

The smartphone is only 20 years old. It really is uncharted territory and nobody knows what impact it will have on you. You are the digital natives, the first generation born in this new world, and in some ways that's a huge social experiment. Your parents and I are digital immigrants; we weren't born into the digital world and have had to learn it like a foreign language. Many adults are, somewhat hypocritically, attached to the cultures and virtues of the old world while fully enjoying the freedoms and benefits of the new one.

Life before the internet now seems a bit hazy. How did it work? How did anyone make a group plan? Or keep in touch with their friends? Or take photos? How did people find out information? The internet arriving has fundamentally changed the way you live now.

Working with young people, it's clear to me that there are

lots of great things about the digital revolution but there may be psychological risks too. As Dorothy passed down the yellow brick road, along with the excitement of discovery and new friends, there were also unforeseen dangers and downsides. In any tale of progress there are winners and losers. What are the risks with screens and the internet? Who will get hurt? Really, no one knows yet; the jury is out. So, I can't give you the definitive answers but I do want to share some of the preliminary research pointers and some of my patients' stories to help you navigate your own way through the Land of the Internet.

I qualified as a psychologist in 1997, just at the cusp of the digital revolution, so I've had a front row seat to the changes young people have faced over that time. This is what I've observed: the content of young people's worries and distress has stayed the same. All the young people I've seen over the last 20-plus years have worried about belonging, the future, their friends, their bodies and their studies. But since the digital revolution, their worry and distress has intensified. This has pushed more young people over that metaphorical line between normal upset and mental illness.

The intensifying of this distress has happened at the same time as the digital revolution, but of course there have been many other changes in society too and correlation does not equal causality. I do not think that the internet and proliferation of screens have caused the mental health crisis among teenagers and young women, but I do think they may have contributed. Like friendship itself, screen culture can be wonderful or it can be toxic. I want to share with you my observations of this and how to make it work for you.

This chapter is not about e-safety, cyberbullying, identity fraud and stuff like that; I know they cover that at school. This is about how screens and the internet may impact on you personally and psychologically, and how it whips up ordinary, everyday emotion into a typhoon of mental distress. I want you to be prepared for what you may find down the yellow brick road.

*Maria presented with depression in her late teens. We tried to unpick why she was so low. Maria knew her parents cared for her but they did so in very practical or formal ways. They were not particularly warm, worked long hours and were rarely around in the evening. There was a bit of a mismatch between her parents' style and her own, as she craved affection. Luckily, she had a close-knit group of friends; they provided the affection she needed and she felt understood by them. In the absence of warmth and companionship at home, Maria had used her phone and social media to distract her from the sense of loneliness in the evening. She so relied on it that she had not noticed when it had stopped being a support and started to be a stress.*

## 24/7 culture

One of the big changes I've noticed working with young people over these years is the 24/7 culture that the internet and smart-phones has created. What has been the impact on mental distress of having this available?

Well, I am sure that phones and the internet do help some people who are feeling lonely and anxious in the middle of the night to connect to other people and not feel so alone. I expect that is particularly true for young people who are in marginalised groups or difficult situations.

I genuinely believe that happens but, TBH, I don't hear about that a lot when I am talking with young people.

What I do hear is that having a phone with you 24/7 can exaggerate and exacerbate different negative social situations and emotions. It means that as a young person you can't escape bullying and are all too aware of when you are being left out or excluded. It also means that there is always an opportunity to negatively compare yourself to others.

Prior to our digital age, teenage drama or conflict had time to blow over or dissipate overnight before the next school day, but I've noticed that now, often young people do not get an opportunity to calm down, sleep on it or take a step back. It's easier to say mean things digitally than it is face to face too, which, when combined with tiredness, can create a perfect storm in which mean things can escalate. Your smartphone turns up the volume and the frequency of the issues and consequently increases the distress.

When you are feeling anxious or sad it can be hard to sleep – sometimes thoughts go whizzing around your head and you can't let go of them – but I'm not sure much good is done by then going online. Nearly all negative emotions are exacerbated by tiredness: things get said, hurts get cemented, poor decisions get made. And once it's out there on social media, it can be very hard to take back.

But, what I see most of all, is the unrealistic expectations that the 24/7 culture places on friendships. It becomes another stick with which to beat yourself for being not good enough, particularly in relation to your friends. Before screens, the expectation of 'being there' for your friends was limited by the social conventions of a landline, in a shared space in the home, which could, in any case, only be used in the early evening. Nobody could 'be there' for their friends at 10pm, let alone 1am.

Having a smartphone ramps up the expectation of what being a 'good friend' means and it becomes harder and harder to meet those expectations. It creates a situation that previously wouldn't have existed (being able to phone a friend late at night) and then makes it easier for the negative automatic thoughts to kick in when you can't meet an impossible standard (can't be there 24/7 for your friend so therefore feel you do not meet the standard of being a 'good friend').

No one can be 'on' all the time, even with friendship. We all need time out to eat, sleep, rest, exercise and think our own thoughts, even when things are going well. And when things start to go wrong . . . Well, when your friends are unhappy or worried, or awful things are happening in their lives, of course you want to support them, but time out is key to emotional survival. Even saint-like figures such as Mother Teresa or the Dalai Lama take time out for themselves to eat and sleep, and for prayer or meditation so they can recharge. As a therapist, I have had years of training and clinical practice and yet I still get distressed hearing people's pain and need time off to recuperate.

So, before screens, the expectation of the girls I met was 'to be there for their friends', but now teenage girls seem to hold the expectation 'to *always* be there for their friends'. Those absolute expectations again. That you would be able to stay up all night messaging with a friend who is sad, talking them down from a panic attack or listening to them cry hour after hour, or, worst of all, witness their self-harm or suicide attempts? I don't think that is a very realistic or helpful expectation to have of yourself, do you? I don't believe it will help you or your friends and it's the path to you all getting worse. You will end up feeling overwhelmed and guilty, and in this way, mental ill health becomes contagious as, tired and emotional, you may find your mood gets worse or your anxiety goes up.

I often make an analogy to my young patients that, like during an emergency on a plane, you need to put on your own (emotional) oxygen mask before you help your friends with theirs. Sometimes that might mean putting your phone away and taking a break.

*Many of Maria's friends were also suffering with low mood and anxiety, and some of them were managing that by deliberate self-harm, alcohol and drugs. She relied so much on her friends that their low moods destabilised her. Some evenings, when she wasn't feeling so good, she found her friends' distress increasingly difficult to be around. It was a catch-22, where either Maria answered her friend's call, knowing that it would bring her down further and she may be triggered to self-harm, or she avoided the call and then felt horribly guilty, like she was an awful friend, because they might need her. Either could trigger a spiral down of mood and anxiety. She found it hard to stay up late as it made her wired and crazy the next day. She wasn't someone who found it easy to lie in, like her friends, so it was doubly difficult if they wanted to talk until the early morning. She found that if she took their calls her mood plummeted through tiredness and despair, but if she ignored the call, her mood plummeted through thinking she was a selfish, bad friend, a horrible person and that no one would ever love her.*

It's hard to do, taking care of yourself and not giving into the urge to try to save others. It can *feel* selfish but we have to or else risk both of us not surviving. As we saw in Chapter 4

– Emotions, Thoughts and Feelings, feelings are not always accurate guides. Just because it would *feel* selfish does not mean it *is* selfish – on the contrary, having boundaries is best for your friends too. The unrealistic expectation that 'friends should always be there for each other' can also backfire: it can lead you (or your friend) spiralling quickly into the negative automatic thought that 'nobody cares for me' when no one is available. That expectation heightens the sense of loneliness. You can quickly start fantasising that they don't like you, or nobody likes you, that you are an unlikeable person, that no one would even miss you if you were gone. That spiral can feel rational and real when you are distressed but is a myth at every level. People have other stuff to do, like homework, having a shower, spending time with their family, eating, visits to Grandma. They cannot be on call all the time but that doesn't mean they don't like you, love you and want you around. In contrast, if you and your friends regularly say to each other, 'I have to go to bed now' or 'Mum says I need to be off my phone' even if you are upset, it sets up a boundary or expectation for both of you that you won't be there at 1am.

Also, the illusion of friend-therapy stops young people seeking out other sources of help and support from their parents, teachers, youth workers, relatives or, when necessary, professional treatment.

## The impact of stimulation on mental wellbeing

Being able to sleep is key in mental wellbeing. When we are tired, emotions get heightened and normal distress can tip over into mental ill health. Most of the young people I work with are smart enough to have a blue light filter on their phone so that the light doesn't disturb their circadian rhythms but they are less concerned about how the overwhelming amount of information that they are subject to, and subjecting themselves to, impacts on their brains and their sleep.

I think you are probably exposed to more images, more information, more people, more stories in one day than your contemporaries from 100 years ago would have been in one year. No one wants to go back to a time when women's lives were so limited, tied to hearth and home, with few opportunities for excitement or self-fulfilment. But nor do I think your brain has yet evolved to cope with the sheer volume of ideas, conversations, interactions and videos that the internet throws at you in the digital day. Your brain has neither evolved to work 24/7 nor has it evolved to process so much information at such a speed.

In Chapter 6, I compared your brain to a cupboard where you have to store everything you want to save from the day. When you have been scrolling a lot, it is like you have a whole skip load of stuff, most of it discardable, dumped at the brain-cupboard door and you need to go through it and find what you need. Do you sometimes lie awake, feeling wired, your body tired, but your mind racing with everything you've seen, heard, done and scrolled in the day? That's your brain trying to sort through it all before it shuts down. It is trying to figure out whether it needs to keep it or whether it can be thrown away.

As we have seen, the teenage and young adult years are all about separating from your parents and fitting in with your peers. These days, that means keeping up to date with Instagram feeds, Snapchat streaks, the latest TikToks or favourite influencers – it's a huge amount of information for your brain to scan for the stuff you need to know, the information you need to be attached in your peer group. But you are not a computer and you can't expect to take in this much info, and even computers can overload if there is too much information too fast. Computers get glitches and need re-charging. So does your brain.

Your brain's attempts to make sense of and file all the information you see online can leave it feeling overloaded. It leaves your brain agitated and hyper, but also craving more: the information never stops and the urge to look at it is never satisfied. The brain also has an annoying habit of working at stuff that isn't finished, like an earworm in your mind, trying to create closure so it can store or discard the information. The constant push notifications of new content mean that the internet is never done and finished. That can make you twitchy or even anxious when you are not on it. Rather than streaks, memes, likes and messages giving you a sense of connection, they can become a tyranny.

*Maria often would miss her sleep window through being on the phone with her friends and would find it hard to get to sleep. While awake, she scrolled through TikTok or watched Netflix. She did online quizzes and had a secret Hay Day habit. She'd sleep fitfully, dream vividly and wake up tired.*

Because the internet is never finished, it is never *over*. You can never put it away and think 'that's done now'. That can lead to a compulsion to check it and you then may find yourself struggling to leave your phone alone, finding excuses to yourself or others about why you need to be online.

It starts to look and feel a bit like an addiction.

## Addicted to your screen?

Phones, gaming and screens can be addictive because they provide another partial reinforcement schedule. Do you remember this from the friendship chapter? A phone is a bit like the on/off friend, in that it provides a positive reward occasionally but not every time you use it, but, crucially, often enough that you keep going back in the hope of more. A partial reinforcement schedule is a psychological theory of addiction: you get a positive (praise, money, joy, excitement) frequently enough that you keep going back for more. Sometimes you get a negative but that doesn't stop you seeking the positive – in fact, it makes you more likely to try again to get the positive. This is why people gamble: betting shops and casinos manage their odds very carefully so the punters get a reward often enough to keep them hooked. If no one ever got any money, no one would come, but if the casinos gave a reward every time, they wouldn't make any money.

Phone use, as I'm sure many adults have told you, is linked to dopamine, one of the 'addiction neurotransmitters' in the brain. They may indeed have shown you the research, scrolling through their own phones. I know, we adults are hypocrites when it comes to phones! When you use your phone or screen you often get that little bit of pleasure: a message from a friend or someone you like; a sense of connection or of mattering if someone likes your post; or a feeling of achievement when you reach the next level of a game. That little bit of pleasure means you are more likely to pick up the screen again. For similar reasons, it can also be addictive when you are anxious and down as you check your messages over and over to see if you have one from someone important or to reassure yourself that the catastrophe hasn't happened yet.

This addictiveness isn't accidental: the brightest minds of Silicon Valley have worked to make the apps, games and internet sites partially reinforcing so that you stay on for longer: they tried, and succeeded, to make them addictive so they hook you in. They continue to analyse all the data they get about your use of their platforms; they will study your timings, in light of the content and behavioural psychology, to manipulate you into staying on for hours. This is how they make money, by making their products as magnetic as possible. This means you are at risk of over-stimulating yourself and getting whipped up in the internet typhoon.

While we are talking about screen use and addiction, we need to digress into gaming. Generally, statistics show that, on average, there is a bit of a gender split on what young people use their screens for and girls game less than boys. However, gaming is on the increase among girls, and I'm sure there are whole departments of computer-geniuses whose sole purpose is how to hook girls in more. Many computer games are structured so they have no end and as our brains tend to return to unfinished things, they keep you coming back for more. Or there is always another level, with more rewards. This ties into the 'more and better' mentality that seems so toxic for mental health.

## The internet typhoon

The addictive nature of the internet makes it is so easy to scroll through Instagram, click on a link or two and end up deeply embedded into the internet world with no visible escape route. It is so easy to lose hours, swept away with more and more links, ending up nowhere near where you started, nor where you would have planned to be. Similarly, with gaming, it is always just one more level.

And at the end of the scrolling or gaming, what do you find? Is it nice? Is it kind? Is it enjoyable? Does it support your values? Does it enhance your life?

Or is it superficial? Cruel? Does it reflect an extreme position or culture? Does it take you further from the person you want to be? Is it full of rubbish, leaving you feeling slightly grubby?

The young people I see are often worried about safety and their future. They are often concerned about e-numbers and colours in food, or care that the food they eat is organic, sustainable, ethical. They neither smoke nor drink as much as previous generations. They care what they put in their body. And yet not a single young person has ever come to me concerned about what they are putting in their mind. The content, the amount, the pace of the stuff they are exposing themselves to. A lot of the stuff on the internet is rubbish – unproven, mean, superficial. It could be analogous to a diet entirely made up of junk food.

## Values and The Happiness Trap

In the chapter about friendship, I introduced the work of Russ Harris, author of *The Happiness Trap*, on values (see page 76). Values are the antithesis to the outcome model of living your life: they are about how you want to live your life and not about what you want to achieve. They are about the quality of the journey not the destination. I enclose Russ Harris's list below and I would like you to go through and follow the instructions to pick which ones are very, quite or less important to you.

This is how Harris introduces the concept and meaning of values in his book:

'Values are your heart's deepest desires for how you want to behave as a human being. Values are not about what you want to get or achieve; they are about how you want to behave or act on an ongoing basis; how you want to treat yourself, others, the world around you.

'There are literally hundreds of different values, but below you'll find a list of the most common ones. Probably, not all of them will be relevant to you. Keep in mind there are no such things as "right values" or "wrong values". It's a bit like our taste in pizzas. If you prefer ham and pineapple but I prefer salami and olives, that doesn't mean that my taste in pizzas is *right* and yours is *wrong*. It just means we have different tastes. And similarly, we may have different values. So pick a domain of life that you want to improve, and read through the list below and write a letter next to each value: V = Very important, Q = Quite important, and N = Not so important – *for the specific domain of life you have picked to work on.*

1. Acceptance: to be open to and accepting of myself, others, life etc

2. Adventure: to be adventurous; to actively seek, create, or explore novel or stimulating experiences

3. Assertiveness: to respectfully stand up for my rights and request what I want

4. Authenticity: to be authentic, genuine, real; to be true to myself

5. Beauty: to appreciate, create, nurture or cultivate beauty in myself, others, the environment etc

6. Caring: to be caring towards myself, others, the environment etc

7. Challenge: to keep challenging myself to grow, learn, improve

8. Compassion: to act with kindness towards those who are suffering

9. Connection: to engage fully in whatever I am doing, and be fully present with others

10. Contribution: to contribute, help, assist, or make a positive difference to myself or others

11. Conformity: to be respectful and obedient of rules and obligations

12. Cooperation: to be cooperative and collaborative with others

13. Courage: to be courageous or brave; to persist in the face of fear, threat, or difficulty

14. Creativity: to be creative or innovative

15. Curiosity: to be curious, open-minded and interested; to explore and discover

16. Encouragement: to encourage and reward behaviour that I value in myself or others

17. Equality: to treat others as equal to myself, and vice-versa

18. Excitement: to seek, create and engage in activities that are exciting, stimulating or thrilling

19. Fairness: to be fair to myself or others

20. Fitness: to maintain or improve my fitness; to look after my physical and mental health and wellbeing

21. Flexibility: to adjust and adapt readily to changing circumstances

22. Freedom: to live freely; to choose how I live and behave, or help others do likewise

23. Friendliness: to be friendly, companionable, or agreeable towards others

24. Forgiveness: to be forgiving towards myself or others

25. Fun: to be fun-loving; to seek, create, and engage in fun-filled activities

26. Generosity: to be generous, sharing and giving, to myself or others

27. Gratitude: to be grateful for and appreciative of the positive aspects of myself, others and life

28. Honesty: to be honest, truthful, and sincere with myself and others

29. Humour: to see and appreciate the humorous side of life

30. Humility: to be humble or modest; to let my achievements speak for themselves

31. Industry: to be industrious, hard-working, dedicated

32. Independence: to be self-supportive, and choose my own way of doing things

33. Intimacy: to open up, reveal, and share myself – emotionally or physically – in my close personal relationships

34. Justice: to uphold justice and fairness

35. Kindness: to be kind, compassionate, considerate, nurturing or caring towards myself or others

36. Love: to act lovingly or affectionately towards myself or others

37. Mindfulness: to be conscious of, open to, and curious about my here-and-now experience

38. Order: to be orderly and organized

39. Open-mindedness: to think things through, see things from other's points of view, and weigh evidence fairly.

40. Patience: to wait calmly for what I want

41. Persistence: to continue resolutely, despite problems or difficulties.

42. Pleasure: to create and give pleasure to myself or others

43. Power: to strongly influence or wield authority over others, e.g. taking charge, leading, organizing

44. Reciprocity: to build relationships in which there is a fair balance of giving and taking

45. Respect: to be respectful towards myself or others; to be polite, considerate and show positive regard

46. Responsibility: to be responsible and accountable for my actions

47. Romance: to be romantic; to display and express love or strong affection

48. Safety: to secure, protect, or ensure safety of myself or others

49. Self-awareness: to be aware of my own thoughts, feelings and actions

50. Self-care: to look after my health and wellbeing, and get my needs met

51. Self-development: to keep growing, advancing or improving in knowledge, skills, character, or life experience.

52. Self-control: to act in accordance with my own ideals

53. Sensuality: to create, explore and enjoy experiences that stimulate the five senses

54. Sexuality: to explore or express my sexuality

55. Spirituality: to connect with things bigger than myself

56. Skilfulness: to continually practice and improve my skills, and apply myself fully when using them

57. Supportiveness: to be supportive, helpful, encouraging, and available to myself or others

58. Trust: to be trustworthy; to be loyal, faithful, sincere, and reliable

59. Insert your own unlisted value here:

60. Insert your own unlisted value here:

'Once you've marked each value as V, Q, N (very, quite, or not so important), go through all the Vs, and select out the top three that are most important to you *in this domain of life, at this point in time.* The next step is to start looking at ways to live these values, in this area of life; things you can say and do, guided by these values.'

*(Copyright Russ Harris, 2021* www.actmindfully.com.au. *Reprinted with permission)*

## Deciding and keeping to your values

When I use this list with patients, some, at first, believe they should make all the values very important to them. They are falling for the myth of perfection again. This list shouldn't be used as another stick to beat yourself with. It is impossible to subscribe to all these values as they are often incompatible. For example, it's difficult to hold the value of 'order' and also the value of 'flexibility'; similarly, the values of 'fun' and 'humour' may find it difficult to co-exist with those of 'respect' or 'responsibility', as humour is often on the edge of what is respectful. I also think it's a list designed for adults and the responsibility/respect axis is over-represented, and there should be more of the spontaneity/excitement stuff. But look through and identify five or six that really resonate with you. Which ones really sum you up? Or do you want to sum you up in the future?

While my point here is about whether the internet enhances your values or not, I also want to put in a note of caution about adopting too many responsibility/control/respect/order/industry-type values from this list. A lot of my patients seem to overvalue these at the expense of friendliness/fun/humour/spontaneity and then wonder why they are unhappy or anxious!

Once you have identified which values are most important to you, I want you to ask yourself how often the stuff you do on your phone or screen takes you towards your values and how often it takes you away? I hope the answer is that generally it enhances your values, that it makes you a better friend, or funnier. But if it does take you away from your values, how long does it take you away for? While it is very important that you have relaxing down-time, and the screen can be fab for that, the typhoon nature of it means that once it whips you in, it is difficult to stop.

You can start by thinking, 'Who wrote that song I've got stuck in my head?' You search on Spotify but then sign up to follow your friend's new playlist. Google throws forward that that singer has just been caught punching a photographer and has split up with his girlfriend . . . 40 minutes later, you realise you have been swept away. Or you start with a YouTube TED talk about global warming and, as one video morphs into the next, you find yourself on an endless loop of make-up tutorials and cat videos. You start gaming, thinking that you'll just chill out for half an hour before you do your homework and get hooked on just getting to the next level. It's never a good time to stop. Until your mum makes you stop for dinner or you realise you are about to pee your pants.

*In Maria's therapy, half the battle was in her identifying the processes going on. We thought about what her values were and she realised that it was OK that she and her parents had different values. She valued affection and connection, and she thought her parents valued conformity and order more highly. However, she also realised that her parents were unlikely to change and so she might need to 'make her own family' with her friends. But we also worked on her being able to set some boundaries in friendship and on the unrealistic standards she set herself, such as, 'I should be there for my friends all the time.' She set some screen times on her phone so it didn't ring and ping at night, and so she wasn't tempted to game and scroll. She committed to only using audio books or real books at night. Her friends accepted that was the way she was and they laughed at her fondly for liking her early nights, but in no way did it impact on the intensity of their relationships.*

So, not only does the internet have no natural start and finish, it has no boundaries and structure, no rules or instructions. A world with few restrictions or laws can be exciting but it can also be toxic, especially when it hooks you in and goes on forever.

Indeed, the vast, lawless internet often appeals not to your values but to the very opposite, your weaknesses. It tempts you into being nosey, competitive, comparative, jealous, envious, lazy and avaricious. Afterwards, you can be left with a 'screen hangover' – you feel slightly grubby about the stuff you looked at, which you probably know wasn't great, and resentful of the time you wasted. You may feel anxious about what you should have been doing instead. You may have rowed with your family about it and defended your position, probably while knowing you were wrong and being annoyed at yourself. Yet the algorithms embedded in your device will then continue to tempt you with similar stuff next time you go online.

This endless, addictive, online vortex drags you in, keeps you in and gives you an occasional 'hit' of pleasure, but it also sometimes takes you to a different world where some strange things go on. All this time online leaves less time for activities less easy to access or immediately pleasurable but which are, in the medium or long term, good for your mental health (as outlined in the emotions chapter). That includes spending time with your family, shared activities, being outside, physical exercise and, most importantly, sleep. None of those might seem as instantly appealing as flopping in an armchair and scrolling for half an hour but they are – in that most dreaded of phrases – oh, no! They are GOOD FOR YOU (sorry).

## Comparison and perfectionism

Screens and phones can be completely wonderful tools for breaking down barriers and loneliness. They can allow pro-social, marginal interest groups of people to meet each other. They can allow distant family and friends to share joy, jokes and be in an almost constant conversation. They can enhance a sense of belonging, which is so important to good mental health. Whatever your special interest, favourite band or particular style, you can find your tribe out there.

But the other side of that coin is that there are masses of people to compare yourself to. Comparison is, to some degree, completely normal for adolescence: you look to your peer group and your wider social context to help with your thinking about yourself and separating from your parents. It is also an issue that has always troubled some young women but, this seems to have been intensified and increased by the internet.

*Fatima was always immaculately presented: neat hajib, perfect clothes, carefully made up. She hadn't been born in the UK and had*

*had to move here after experiencing trauma in her country of origin. She had supportive parents, her family was well settled and she was doing well in her studies. She had a boyfriend who, for religious and cultural reasons, she didn't meet in private but they attended sixth-form college together and talked on the phone. Despite her modest dress and strong values, she was almost addictively drawn to looking at Instagram lifestyle models in bikinis showcasing vacuous lives, focused on 'healthy' food, fashion and fitness. She scrutinised photos of herself, comparing herself to both influencers and her friends. She obsessed about unflattering photos of herself or photos in which the angle or perspective allowed her to think she looked bigger than other people. She would say, 'Look, they are thinner than me,' when they were further away or if they were angled so they were standing slightly sideways and she was standing square on to the camera.*

When you compare yourself to others, you are likely to compare your own insides with other people's outsides. Inside of you, you are acutely aware of your own imperfections, the times when you have been mean, screwed up and made mistakes. In adolescence, there is a greater chance of making mistakes because you have not quite figured out your own values, plus you have high hormone levels and a high capacity for risk taking.[18] Then you look at your friends and peers and it's easy to think they are better than you. What you see is their best and bravest faces. You don't see their worst points, their insecurities, their imperfections and their mistakes, because, generally, you don't look for them and because they (like you) hide these from the world. You wear your 'positive and kind' glasses to look at

---

18 Part of the fun of adolescence. Enjoy. The times you have now will keep you in stories until you are old.

them. You will therefore be comparing your worst self to others' best selves and if you do that, you will likely find yourself lacking. Thus, it has always been, but the internet has amplified this process.

I often explain this to my patients by analogy to icebergs: only 10 per cent of an iceberg is seen and 90 per cent is hidden below. We tend to show the best things about ourselves to the world and hide the more shameful stuff under the waterline – although we have a lot of lovely stuff hidden too. What other people show you and what you look for in others is often the tip of the iceberg. Think about it: when you go to see your friends, you look for the bits you like; you don't scrutinise them for flaws. You don't examine their thighs, close up, naked, for example, to check out their cellulite; you don't know what name they called their mother that morning and, if you do, you justify it in the *Love-Island*-girl-chat ('You are right. She deserved it. She was being a bitch.'). In teenage life, you are often comparing the

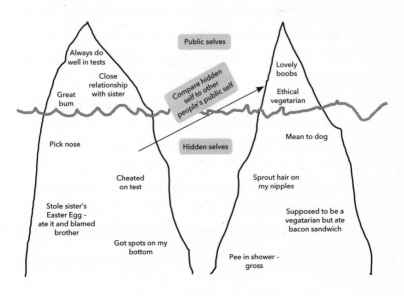

worst of your hidden 90 per cent to the best of other people's 10 per cent public display. This is a recipe for triggering sadness and/or worry.

The explosion of images and of curated narratives of life on social media over the last 20 years has intensified this process. The ability to take, upload and edit photos instantly and the Instagram-mindset of flaunting success has made the perfection shown in public more visible, more frequent and, indeed, simply more perfect. And other people's perfect lives seem more magnetic when you are feeling down, leading you to a greater sense of comparative insecurity, which can lead to thoughts of 'everyone's better than me'. While young people used to find themselves lacking compared to the girl they sat next to in class, now you can compare yourself to the whole world via a screen, 24/7. The internet provides an infinite comparison mirror: it is a petri dish in which to grow comparison anxiety.

The internet fuels those absolute standards that you are put under (and you put each other and yourselves under). It fuels the belief that you *must* have this to be happy or you *have to* watch that to belong; it drives the thought that *everyone* is doing something and you are not; it feeds that endless list of expectations on you that you need to ... you should ... you ought to ...

And it does so in such an insidious, infinite and visual way.

- Insidious, because you enjoy using it and don't notice the pressure that it puts you under.

- Infinite, because there is always another standard, another expectation to judge yourself on.

- And gosh, yes, visual: the endless images of perfection that surround you now. The painstakingly prepared images that have become people's lives to create, curate and feed back to you as achievable.

*Fatima thought she wasn't pretty, clever, likeable. She looked at all her friends' posts and thought they were gorgeous, trendier, funnier and more popular than her. She struggled to post on her Instagram at all, often agonising over which picture to put up and sometimes taking them down soon after. She never believed the comments her friends put on her posts and would dismiss them by saying, 'Well, they have to say that, don't they?' She knew in her rational mind that she and her friends would sometimes hang out taking photos, setting up exactly the right shot: the right angle, lighting, facial expression, make-up, hair and clothes. Yet in evaluating herself, she only used her emotional mind, comparing her non-made-up, non-staged self in baggy clothes to other people's perfect poses without bearing in mind the editing at all. It was like she put on negative, unkind glasses to judge herself and judged her friends with warmth and affection.*

It is very tempting to use the internet to constantly seek out people who you deem to be 'better' versions of whatever criteria you choose to judge yourself on in that moment. And if you don't find what you're looking for, you can just shift the criteria. If you are physically fit, you can compare yourself to the academic girls. If you get top marks you can beat yourself up for not being invited to the party. If you're mentally ill, you can find people who appear more unwell than you, so you don't even feel like a 'good enough' mentally ill patient.

When everyone and everything becomes comparative, it drives feelings that you are not good enough. Dominique Thompson, a former GP in a British university health centre, reflected on the approximately 78,000 consultations she had with students over her career in her 2021 TED talk. She talks about how, over the years, her patients reported increased levels of pressure, comparison and competition. They were arriving in the first term of the first year of university, worried about what class of degree they'd get. Joining societies became an opportunity to further their careers rather than to pursue leisure. Her mentally ill young patients were so driven that nothing was fun: photos posted became a 'likes' contest; making a cake was imbued with *Bake Off* standards. Dr Thompson argued that this sort of competition[19] drives perfectionism.

The online world has ratcheted up what it means to be perfect. Perfectionism is the seeking of perfection, a goal you can never achieve, because as we know 'being perfect' is a myth. There is no agreed, universal standard for being human, it is an Emperor's New Clothes illusion; an illusion that society seems to collude in. Meanwhile, most perfectionists think they are awful and rubbish but the seeking of being better, of being more, is ruining their lives. It is toxic for mental health.

*It was understandable that Fatima didn't believe she was good enough as she had been hurt in the past. She kept herself inscrutable behind a mask of internet-perfection and an immaculate*

---

19 Here I am referring to the global, all-encompassing competition we see young people feel on 'life' or 'being the best person' (if there were any agreement what that was). That if they don't win, they are a loser. Not the short-term, relatively low stakes competition of sport or games.

*appearance. However, she could see in time that the constant comparison got in the way of her connecting to people. She needed to accept who she was so she could relate to her friends without comparing herself to them.*

*We looked at Fatima's values, which included being a strong independent woman, doing well in her studies, being able to provide for herself and being part of her family. She introduced a women's self-defence course into her routine. We thought about whether the hours she spent scrolling appearance-driven content on the internet took her towards or away from her values. It also seemed to be implicated in warped ideas about what her body should look like and what she should eat, which took her away from eating with her family and meant she was frequently hungry and found it hard to complete her studies. She deleted the influencers one by one and started to 'like' other content, which was more in line with her values but still fun. For example, she loved animals and children. She wanted to be a teacher and she got an after-school job babysitting in her neighbourhood.*

## Loneliness and vulnerability

As well as the effects of perfectionism, I think this constant comparison, this striving for likes and streaks and watching of others and being watched by them, can have an insidious impact on your ability to actually connect to other people. Some young people, in their desperate attempts to be their best version of themselves, alienate those around them. In their preoccupation to be clever, pretty, thin, ethical, nice or even the most mentally ill, they missed actually finding a shared mental space with people. They forgot empathy as they were too busy trying to be liked or the best or perfect. They never got to know the hidden part of anyone else's iceberg.

The key to this shared mental space is vulnerability; female friendships are often based on vulnerability. But vulnerability is tricky. I meet a lot of young people who have no confidence and constantly self-deprecate. They manage other people's expectations by saying things like, 'I did terribly in that test', 'You are so much prettier and thinner than me'. A certain game goes on around exams: some young people say, 'I have hardly done any work, I don't know anything, I am going to fail' and then go on to get straight As. Others will say, 'I've worked eight hours today, I'm fully up to date on my revision plan, which I started three months ago.' Both make everyone around them feel awful. I know mostly this is done with no ill intent; the motives behind it are generally to eye up how much work other people are doing because they are feeling anxious themselves. But the net effect is to psyche each other out as effectively as two heavyweight boxers, eye-to-eye at the world championship weigh in. This is a pseudo-vulnerability.

True vulnerability is about giving up seeing yourself as a product, as the sum of your accomplishments. Think about it: generally you don't pick your friends for what they achieve, you like them for who they are and how they make you feel when you are with them. If you consistently strive to be the best, it can actually make other people uncomfortable. Striving for more, for better, while deprecating your efforts elicits a comparison reaction in others. True vulnerability involves letting go of your attempts at improvement and perfection and allowing people to see you for who you are. It means letting people connect with your 'true' self: your interests, your humour, your wobbly bits, your mental blocks, your moods, your weaknesses. True vulnerability is about making a mistake and *forgiving yourself* so you can be there for someone else. Of really and truly screwing something up, and being honest in that, and dusting yourself down to start again. It's being accepting of your faults but not defined by them. Ultimately, vulnerability allows connection and comparing inhibits it.

So, I find myself wondering whether the internet inhibits that vulnerable connection and instead contributes to loneliness.

I sometimes tell my patients a story about a friend I didn't make, Hannah. We had both moved into the same street and were at the same stage of our lives. We were introduced by a mutual friend. So far so good, right? Every time I ran into her she looked perfectly made up and dressed nicely; even though we lived on the same street, I never bumped into her running to the corner shop in a tracksuit, dirty hair pulled back into a ponytail (she frequently spotted me like that!). When I asked her how things were, they were always fabulous. She'd never had a row with her partner; she was never fed up with anything; work was always great.

Then, one year, she went away for a week to a little British seaside town. It was one of those weeks when the weather was crazy and that particular seaside town was pictured in my newspaper with the coast being battered. And I thought, 'Oh poor Hannah, stuck in some holiday cottage with the whole family driving each other mad.' When I next bumped into her I said, 'OMG, I was thinking of you last week, the weather was crazy, poor you, did you all drive each other mad?' and she said, 'No, we had a great time, the weather was fine, so relaxing, we all loved it,' and I thought, 'I can never be friends with you.'

I can never be friends with someone who can't be real. Who can't let me in behind the show; who is always trying to be perfect; who won't share their vulnerability with me.

## It's not enough; I've had enough; I'm not enough

I am often reminded of this quote as I listen to my patients. It seems so many young women feel that what they have achieved (with school tests or their friends or their appearance) is not enough. It doesn't meet some exacting standard created by their families, their schools, the internet, society and then, most worryingly, internalised by themselves.

Constantly striving for the perfect outcome is a lonely place to be. The internet is at its best when it is used to connect you to other people and not when it's used to compare and contrast with others. The screen has contributed towards the seemingly innocuous phrase 'just do your best', which has become laden with endless standards of best. My advice? Be yourself. Being your true self involves being vulnerable. It means facing the anxiety that you can't control everything. It involves taking what is important to you, your values, and knowing that some people won't like you. They will have different values, different interests, a different way of being. And do you know what? That is OK. It is hard to accept but infinitely better for your mental health than this striving for perfection.

On that assembly line of your childhood, collecting achievements and qualifications, you have grown up in a context that encourages you to view yourself in the third person, as a product, meeting (or failing to meet) a checklist of standards. Internet-based comparison, I fear, makes this a whole lot worse. Social media particularly encourages you to post content and open yourself to external judgements – 'likes' and the like. It puts you in the producer position – the producer but also the product. Being an influencer is literally selling yourself as the product but that mindset is endemic in the social media phenomena.

Adults, I find, are keen to blame social media for the ills of your generation and responsible for all the mental ill health. I don't see it like that. But I do see social media as part of the assembly line: a perfect storm of factors, in conjunction with the outcome-based education system, the corresponding parenting zeitgeist and a fever-pitch of consumerism pushing 'more and better'. Together, that has whipped young women up to believe that they are not good enough. They have internalised that *they* are not (clever/ kind/pretty) enough. And ultimately, and very sadly, they often feel they've had enough of trying, so self-harm or not eating, or even killing themselves, seems to be the answer.

## Screen freedom or screen slave?

There are so many pleasures and perils of the internet and I have really only touched on a few. Over the last few years, the young people I have known have been lured in by internet fraud, become addicted to internet porn, have used it to access drugs and been arrested with those drugs. They have tortured themselves with perfect pictures of other people's appearance or with food that they are not allowed to eat. They have had unsolicited pictures of self-harm sent to them; they have discovered suicide notes. They have sought out the most toxic, damaged people to hang out with. They have had their friends lie to them to the extent of making up a whole new friend, who doesn't actually exist.

It can be crazy down that yellow brick road. Weird stuff happens.

But, of course, wonderful things happen as well: you learn stuff; you connect to people; you have fun; you develop interests; you entertain yourself. It's clever, creative and stimulating. You just need to check in with yourself about whether you are in control of your screen or whether it in control of you. It's all about you keeping some balance when the internet is trying very hard to lure you into addiction. A theme throughout this book is balance, and balance is really tough: it's trying to not topple over when different forces are pulling at you. And the internet is a tough, strong, ubiquitous force; it's there all the time. It never sleeps.

So, similar to how you wouldn't eat a diet of only pizza and chocolate, but pizza is great at least once a week and chocolate is essential every day (IMHO), you want to find the right balance with being on your screen. One that also gives you the chance to spend some time with your family (annoying as they are), speak to people face-to-face, move your body, be outside, be with pets, read from a page and live in a world that's 3D rather than 2D.

And while it's fine to have the pleasure of Minecraft or TikTok, you also want to seek out stuff that's congruent with your values and not against them. Hardest of all, I think, is that you need to learn to notice the point when you are on your screen and it tips from constructive to destructive. Where online stops being enjoyable and fun, and starts to be mindless, obsessive or unpleasant. Experience says that just at that point, the addiction will kick in and it will be hardest to stop.

We are all figuring this stuff out. Civilised societies need structure and boundaries but these haven't been established on the internet yet. I would wager it is going to be far more regulated in another generation. That probably means that you need to make some rules for yourself. Don't rely on your willpower to control yourself on the internet, as the internet is as addictive as crack cocaine for young people – an analogy, not scientific fact – and your willpower is unlikely to be strong enough to resist. I can't tell you what your rules should be as only you know what your particular problem is with your screens. Are you missing sleep because of it? Are you over-stimulated? Are you constantly comparing yourself to others? Are you missing out on real life? I don't know but I do know that rules, structure and boundaries work better than willpower and good intentions when we are changing any behaviour. Some young people (or their parents) keep their phone somewhere else overnight or have set monitoring apps or time blocks. Others make rules for themselves, such as they put the phone away before homework or go Instagram-free for a month a year.

The internet and screens are not going anywhere and you have to learn to master them to serve your best purposes and values, and not be a slave to their tyranny. I've seen young people come back from Oz and release themselves from the hold it had on them. Resisting the urge to be online 24/7 for their friends, allowing their brains to rest from the stimulation and freeing themselves of constant comparison. It's hard but if it's impacting on your mental wellbeing, you may need to give it a go.

# CHAPTER 9

# ATTRACTION, RELATIONSHIPS, SEX AND LOVE

'Love is a temporary madness'

**LOUIS DE BERNIÈRES, *CAPTAIN CORELLI'S MANDOLIN***

'One day, someday, my prince will come, so the fairy tale said;
Thirty years later it's still in my head
That if I screw a frog, I'll wake in a 4-poster bed'

**TIM MINCHIN, 'ONE DAY', FROM *GROUNDHOG DAY: THE MUSICAL***

As with the internet, the changes in romance and relationships have been seismic for your generation. You have more knowledge, more choices and more freedom than the generations before you, and that is great. But with choice comes complexity. And with complexity comes psychological angst.

Yet you continue to be sold a dream of happy-ever-after, romantic love. This story is ubiquitous through history and across continents: boy meets girl; conflict and uncertainty between them creates a will-they-won't-they dilemma, ending with boy declaring love to girl; girl gratefully accepts his love and the two walk off into the sunset together, hand in hand. Books, songs, films and plays all perpetuate this heteronormative and privileged narrative of fidelity and commitment. I think that this story plays on the overwhelming feelings of love and lust you experience as a young person to keep you tied into a gendered stereotype, a dynamic linked to power and inequality.

So, we are now at a time where you get to break out of that narrative. Up until relatively recently, the majority of womankind throughout history had only two socially approved choices: marriage or the life of a spinster. Girls didn't ask themselves if they were gay or straight (or neither); they didn't get to try out lots of partners; they didn't have many opportunities to earn their own living or make their own choices. Now, in your sexual and romantic life, you have many different ways to express yourself and choices to make. Oh, how wonderful! What choice, what freedom . . . and yet, how complicated.

*Bo came to see me during her first year at university. She was feeling off, jangly, anxious every day. She wasn't sure why. Prior to that, she had been uber confident. In her sixth form, she had been right at the centre of a large social group that spanned several schools, and so to feel so out of it was a shock for her. She described how she had gone through puberty early and was sexual from an earlier age than many of her peers. She was also completely comfortable with her fluid sexuality: she got with boys and girls at parties and in clubs all the time. Her parents were liberal and cool; they liked her social life and weren't beyond joining her friends for a joint at the kitchen table; they let her bring lovers home. There were no boundaries between their life and her life. She was super close to them.*

## LGBTQ+

A word about sexual diversity. It is perhaps surprising that so many of these narratives about love and sex are stuck in such a narrow rut when there has been a huge change in most young people's attitudes in relation to sexual identity. In the Western world, young people have more freedom to express their sexuality than at any point in history. For many of the young people I see now (in my liberal corner of north London) their sexuality (i.e., the sex of the people they are attracted to) is accepted in their friendships, their families, their schools and their communities. I see many girls who are attracted to girls and boys, and it is fabulous to see the freedom and liberation so many have, and the lack of inhibition and guilt. So it should be. However, this is not the whole story: there are still hetero-normative assumptions and homophobic prejudices endemic in society, and you may feel reluctant to own your own sexuality, or share it with others. As a cis-gendered female therapist I can only try to understand the impact on the mental health and wellbeing of these factors on the young people I work with.

I see the same freedom for many young people about being non-binary or gender-fluid, with a choice of pronouns. I know many of my generation struggle with this, but I see it as part of each generation pushing at a boundary which allows for progress to be made in a civilised society. I see adolescence as a time of forming your identity and if this is a positive expression of that which gives you a sense of belonging or connection, that's a great thing. That doesn't mean I always remember to use someone's correct pronouns – this is new to older generations – we are learning.

Sexuality (who you are attracted to) and gender identity (how you identify) are separate issues to gender dysphoria (a feeling of discomfort in the gender you were assigned at birth). In the multiple edits that a book has gone through to be published, this section has been rewritten time and time again. I rather get the feeling people don't want me to say anything about it. And maybe I shouldn't.

But I am going to venture in. Why? Because I keep imagining you – perhaps thirteen, fourteen, fifteen – scared and confused with this possibly terrifying, definitely overwhelming, feeling that you are being identified as the wrong gender by everyone around you. What should you do? Who can you tell? Maybe you've found this book helpful so far and then to find there is nothing on this particular worry that you have got, well, then I'd feel that I was letting you down. It sounds terrifying – like being in a deep dark forest, completely lost, lonely and no idea which way to go.

So, I feel that I need to come in to this forest with you, and be with you, because we don't know which way you need to go. What did other people do when they were lost here before? Well, for some people their way out of the forest was that their gender dysphoria was set at birth, like their sexuality or their race, and that they needed to transition to a different gender to find their way out. They are likely have spent a lot of time finding that path, and experienced lots of abuse and prejudice on the way. They may (or not) have wished they had been supported to transition earlier.

But the thing is there are infinite ways out of the forest and others will have found a different way out, that in the formal psycho-medical language of professionals, sounds like they had body dysmorphia or ASD or transitioned socially but not physically. They may have transitioned but that did not take them out to where they wanted to be, and actually were forced back in the forest, to transition back. That doesn't sound a brilliant way out tbh.

So I guess if I were sitting in that forest with you, I wouldn't know which way was the right way *for you* to go, specifically *for you*, and you alone. What I'd want to do is sit with you whilst you were sad and lonely, until you didn't feel so sad and alone anymore. And then what I'd want to do is be very curious about which way was the right way to go *for you*. I'd be a bit sceptical if anyone came along sure that they had the right way for you very quickly. And I guess what I'd want to say is "it's not nice here, but let's try and bear it whilst we figure it out. Let's not rush, but even if we don't rush, we might go down some wrong paths, have some horrible experiences, but I will be by your side, until we find a place that is completely right for you."

I wish everyone who is experiencing gender dysphoria that support. I wish you the opportunity to explore it from all different angles, without judgement nor sanction, and find people who are both neutral and supportive of you finding *your* right way. Your experience of this won't be exactly the same as anyone else's and you will have to find your own path. Sadly, there are no simple, nor quick, answers. All through this book, I've railed against simple answers. Education is about more than grades; food about more than its nutritional content; feelings more than happy and sad. Our sexuality is complicated stuff and simple answers may be appealing when you are in distress but are likely to be 'an easy way out' rather than 'the answer'.

If you are struggling with family or community judgements of your sexuality or your gender, please do seek help. Freedom to express your sexuality is the law in this country and you should be supported if you let your school, sexual health clinic or GP know. There are resources in the 'Want to know more?' section.

In this chapter, I have tried to be inclusive of everyone's sexuality, of everyone's gender expression. Any failures to do so, I deeply apologise for.


## Love and the wise mind

Being attracted to someone and falling in love are the biggest threat to your wise mind. Why? Because they are wonderful, exciting, exhilarating, powerful emotions that place you so firmly into your emotional mind it is easy to forget a rational mind exists. Being in love *is* a temporary madness: research shows that when people fall in love their mind is dominated by their loved one in the same way that a mental illness will dominate your mind.

That's why there are all those books and plays and songs about love and lust. They are amazing, potentially overwhelming and life-changing emotions, for everyone.

And, of course, that is exactly why you do need to listen to both your emotional and your rational mind now more than ever. I hope you have flexed your wise-mind muscle before you get to feeling sexually attracted to someone because if anything is going to give your wise mind a challenge, it is this.

*Bo had thought she was going to be fine leaving home to go to university as she had always been pretty independent. And the first few months had been fine. She made a lot of friends really quickly and continued to have a number of casual romantic relationships through meeting people in clubs and on Tinder. However, one of these people had become quite a good friend as well as a lover and one night someone had described Bo as their girlfriend. Bo had immediately (vehemently?) said she wasn't and that it was just casual, but they were there and Bo had seen their face fall. She had felt really uncomfortable with this and unsettled. She had really strong emotions for them but now wanted to avoid them, which was difficult as they had overlapping groups of friends and similar interests. They continued to hook up occasionally when drunk.*

## Why are you attracted to someone?

Adolescence is all about change. You have been a child, going to school, living with your family, and it's probably been all a bit the same. Then your body starts developing, school gets harder and leaving home is on the horizon. As we have seen, all this change makes you unsure of yourself at times and you will make mistakes.

You may switch friendship groups or get stuck in a friendship group you don't really like, or chase a friendship group you are not really sure like you. Separation and individuation inevitably mean that there are more disagreements with your parents. It is normal to have doubts and be unsure of yourself at times.

And along comes someone who says they like you. They laugh at your jokes, they hold your gaze a moment too long, they tell you that you are pretty. Remember the iceberg from the last chapter? While your mind may repeatedly go to the bits of yourself you don't like, the parts buried beneath the surface, this person focuses on the tip of your iceberg. Being with someone who is sexually attracted to you is like looking in a mirror and having the tip of the iceberg – your best bits – reflected back to you.

Many young people fear no one will ever like them like this. So familiar are they with their faults, the underneath part of their iceberg, that they fear they are unlovable. I hope that is not you. I hope you don't fear that you are so deeply flawed or unattractive that you will never find anyone who is attracted to you. Because you are not. I can almost hear you saying, 'Yes, I am,' but you are not. Let's challenge that negative automatic thought: do you really think, of everyone in the world, you are so uniquely hideously special that you are incapable of being loved? Is there a type of egocentricity in thinking that you are the worst? But also, doesn't it show a lack of faith in humankind to believe that there isn't someone out there who is capable of loving your quirks and (as you see them) faults?

Everyone else has faults too. Everyone else makes mistakes. When you meet someone, you see the top of their iceberg: their projected image. Underneath the surface, they will have insecurities and things they don't like about themselves. Weird feet. That they pick their nose. They like BTS. They might be worried their penis is too small or that it won't work right. In fact, most other people are grateful to be liked. Most other teenagers are quite grateful to have someone flirting with them or kissing them. If they are nice, they will tolerate your foibles.

That 'I'm uniquely horrible and no one will like me' thinking is also dangerous because it means that you may feel too grateful to reject the first person who comes along and shows you some attention, even if they don't suit you or they are awful or they have bad intentions. You may be so caught up in them liking you that you don't stop to think about whether or not you truly like them.

Because when you meet someone who pays you compliments or gives you positive attention, it can feel wonderful. Especially when you are feeling insecure; then it can be almost addictive. However, there are so many reasons for potential partners to say lovely things to you: it might be because they are falling in love with you but it also might be because they are a manipulative slime-ball trying to have sex with you regardless of what you want.

Of course, the most likely reasons are somewhere between these extremes. They think they like you but they might, *at any time*, decide they don't. Romantic relationships come with a lifetime receipt: they can change their mind at any time. **And so can you**. Are you familiar with the get-out-of-jail-free card in Monopoly? Well, in attraction, love, sex and relationships, you and they have an unequivocal, lifetime, get-out-of-this-free card that can be played at any time. You can play it without warning, without explanation, without consultation, in every sexual and romantic encounter you have and however it feels for the other person. This is another key message of the book.

## Attraction and attachment

When you start to like someone in a romantic or sexual way, it evokes your attachment blueprint: the shadows of your previous relationships with your parents, family and friends. This is sometimes referred to as your love-map. We have come full circle: like the attachment we discussed in the first chapter, romantic or sexual relationships are an intricate dance of backwards and forwards give and take, them responding to your cues and you to theirs. In sex and love, you will be held, metaphorically and physically, in someone else's arms and reciprocity is required for the dance to work.

As you start to 'dance' with someone, you have to show yourself and that is a risk because you are making yourself vulnerable. Your vulnerabilities will be linked back to your attachment blueprint, to those early relationships, as well as being embedded in the values and expectations of your community, religion and society. But it's not as simple as X sort of attachment leads to Y sort of relationship; it's about how your particular personality experienced those early relationships in that particular context.

*In therapy, we thought about why Bo was so uncomfortable with the closeness. We linked it back to her close but boundary-less relationship with her parents. She didn't associate closeness with friends and lovers but with her parents. We established that she had a love-map where initially when she met new people she came across as friendly and open, used to sharing stuff with others. But when people then opened up emotionally to her, she pulled away: the intimacy was too much. Although she loved her parents to bits, she did sometimes feel intruded upon by them and that stopped her wanting to commit in relationships. Bo realised that in her parents and her being so close hadn't allowed room for her to individuate and find her own way in life: she hadn't quite figured out who she was.*

Take, for example, overparenting. We saw in Chapter 2 how some parents hover over you, watching your every move, creating a very intense relationship. Even with siblings in the same family, there will be different responses to this, which is prompted by your own innate personality. Some of you may have enjoyed that type of parenting and that might mean you seek out intensity in romantic relationships and rush in too quickly or come on too strongly. Or, alternatively, you may have hated it and found it suffocating. Then you may be repelled by any closeness in romantic relationships: it might make you feel trapped, to be answerable to someone.

The opposite sort of attachment history can lead to similar patterns, too. Those of you who have parents low on warmth or involvement may struggle to show warmth or commitment in romance. You may fear intimacy. You are not used to the feeling of being too close to someone and you might find it hard to trust them. Or you may have a well of loneliness, which may lead to you overinvesting in someone and that may be off-putting or even overwhelming to the other person.

What is your own love-map as you start to flirt with romance? What are you attracted to and what might your pitfalls be?

*Bo's natural inclination with her friend-with-benefits was to pull away when things got too close or intimate. And yet, she also desperately wanted to hang out with them and missed them when she wasn't with them. Bo had to acknowledge she had strong feelings for them and she and her friend did start a relationship. She allowed herself to be vulnerable, to really share and to be open with them. And when they split up she felt broken-hearted and joked with me that it was my fault. But really, we both thought it was progress. Progress both in transferring her need for closeness from her parents to her peers and progress because it is only through being vulnerable that we truly connect.*

## Attractiveness and power

As we saw in the friendship chapter, in secondary school as romantic relationships start, being popular can start to be linked to being pretty or attractive. If your peer group sees you as 'good-looking', that can give you power in all your relationships. That is a bit of a warning sign as it can make you think of your appearance as the most important thing about you, which it isn't. When you are feeling awkward and self-conscious, someone else (or lots of people) finding you attractive can define your social status or the social hierarchy of your peer group. It can make you popular and when you are popular it's harder to remember to be kind.

Or the opposite can happen. Many women struggle to let go of the judgement of their teenage self or their teenage peers long after it is relevant or useful and allow that perception to cloud their judgement of themselves for years to come.

Another key message of this book: despite a media largely dominated by similar images, there is not one type of attractiveness. Beauty really is in the eye of the beholder. While that might not feel true when you are in your early teenage years, it is certainly true as you get older. In younger years, when teenagers are judging themselves and others as attractive or not, they will often just follow the crowd or the zeitgeist of the time. That can mean a heteronormative, conventional standard of attractiveness is adopted. If your particular looks do not or did not meet the tastes of your group at that time, don't worry – and certainly don't hold on to that as a definition of your attractiveness going forward. Please, please don't hold what some 13-year-old boy thought of your looks as your defining judgement. Thirteen-year-old boys are awash with hormones and have no idea what they think or feel about what or who they are attracted to. They just want to fit in like everyone else at that age and will tend towards the conventional judgements.

## The thrill of the chase

When you are attracted to someone it can be an overwhelming feeling: there is the thrill of the chase; your reflected positive image; the romance; the status it might give you in your peer group; the curiosity to figure that person out. There are lots and lots of things that are great about *the process* of attraction. Please don't confuse *the process* of attraction being great with *the person* you are attracted to being great: they may be or they may not be. You may have to kiss a lot of frogs. Don't confuse the thrill of the chase with the value of the catch. And even if they are a prince, they may be entirely wrong *for you*.

And you might be entirely wrong for them too, without that meaning that you are unattractive or awful, or that you'll always be alone. Finding out whether or not you are right for each other is what a relationship is for.

*Chloe was struggling with her mental health during sixth form: she often felt sad and anxious. She had been raised by her grandparents, and only occasionally saw her mum who had troubles of her own and she didn't know her dad at all. Her grandparents were fab, very warm and loving to her and each other, and had been very involved in her activities, schoolwork and friendships. But in her teenage years, she hadn't felt close to them, they were just kind of out of touch and she couldn't talk to them. They were pretty strict too, they didn't want her to go 'off the rails like your mum', and so she was the only one in her group who had to be home early and hadn't been allowed on a post-GCSE group trip away, where friendships seemed to have been sealed. Her friends' parents were more laid-back. Now, she wasn't confident in her friendship group; it was a bit on and off. She wasn't confident in her looks, either. Chloe had got with a few boys but not in a serious way. Then she started seeing one boy who was right at the heart of the friendship group. He seemed really into her. Their relationship became quickly intense. He had a difficult home life and he talked to her about his family and emotional life, and she cared about him. When they were alone together she got the closeness that she had always craved. He was very loving to her in public too, always draping his arm over her or holding her hand. For a while, she felt great. She felt as though she had arrived socially.*

The trouble is that all the heady feelings of fancying someone combine with all those messages from books, TV shows and songs about a one true love, and can lead you to think your relationship is more than it is. It can make you believe that you are in love with them. You can end up projecting attributes and characteristics onto them that they don't have. You so want 'love like in the movies' that you don't see that 'he's just not that into you' and make excuses for your love interest.

The 'hurdles to be overcome' narrative of all the books and movies is particularly insidious in this situation: when they don't call, when you argue, when they are jealous, possessive or even aggressive, this fits into the narrative of great love overcoming obstacles to finally be together. Or . . . they could just be a prick.[20] So steeped are we in a cliched story of romance that you can continue to fool yourself that they like you when the signs are all there that either (a) they are not that into you or (b) they are a prick. Hurdles to romance intensify a feeling of sexual attraction or love because they allow the fantasy to exist; you project your love-map, your needs for love, onto that person, without using your rational mind at all (let alone your wise mind). You ignore their faults and the glaring inconsistencies in your compatibility.

Which brings us to the on/off boyfriend – you remember the on/off friend? The on/off boyfriend is an even more toxic version of that dynamic. If you were burnt by an on/off friend at school (and who wasn't?) the on/off boyfriend is additionally addictive, as our psyche has an annoying habit of repeating patterns that are unresolved. It is more addictive as it has the added complication of hormonal attraction plus the drama of that 'hurdles to be overcome' narrative we are told everywhere. The on/off boyfriend will play on that. It's a three-act play: the first act is of intense passion; the second act a period of anger, jealousy and coldness (allegedly triggered by your behaviour and faults); the third act is reconciliation, with the tears and the apologies, the flowers and the declarations that you are the only person he loves and trusts, the only one who understands him. It's as if you have a role as the heroine in this story and that makes you feel special and important – the often-told story of the love of a good woman healing a man who has suffered so.

This is all nonsense: the on/off boyfriend is a coercively controlling husband-in-waiting and that is now illegal.

---

20  Girls can be pricks too. And many of my gay and bisexual clients seem to meet them.

*It wasn't all perfect between Chloe and her boyfriend. Sometimes he picked fights with her out of nowhere about her phoning or not phoning, or not answering her phone when she was studying or having dinner with her grandparents. She was also not meant to have her phone in her room at night but he didn't like that as he liked to talk to her late at night. She liked it too, she felt close to him then, but even when she bent the rules and stayed up late chatting to him, he still sometimes picked fights when she had to go. Then it was counter-productive because if he got cross she couldn't sleep anyway, worrying. Sexually, he pushed her into stuff she wasn't 100 per cent confident with: he had sort of guided her head down to give him a blow job. She worried about this – it seemed wrong. He complimented her a lot and told her she was beautiful but he also gave her the kind of compliments that were a bit back-handed: 'I love your big bum' for example, or, 'Wow, that's a low-cut top'. He never quite said, 'Are you wearing that?' but she felt he thought it.*

Warning signs for the on/off boyfriend: he has few friends; no one understands him (except for you); he's never felt like this before; it's your fault that he's angry. Run, girl, run. This is about valuing yourself. Do not be scared of being alone: it is only by being alone that you will be able to find someone genuine to love.

Now, of course, the on/off boyfriend might be exciting and exciting might be what you want when life is quite dull. Being with your family, school uniform and homework: all that can be quite boring. Some girls, maybe you, like a drama and a romantic entanglement is certainly a good way to liven up life. It can be passionate and fun as long as their unkindness to you when they are in the 'off' part of the cycle doesn't mirror your own self-doubt and become a truth: don't internalise their off version of you. And of course don't confuse it with love. Love is something different.

## Playing hard to get?

Over 20 years ago, there were a couple of books published, one called *The Rules* and one called *Why Men Love Bitches*, which both advised women to play hard to get if they want to 'snare' a man. Both books have a central premise that men are, at heart, hunters, who are attracted by the chase and want to set the pace. Therefore, if she wants to 'get a man', a woman must pretend that she is not interested in him or artificially put hurdles in the way to increase the chance a man will be interested.

#whymenlovebitches has recently become a popular hashtag on TikTok. And that narrative continues to dominate dating now.

I hate this narrative.

I hate that it continues to tie men and women into gender stereotypes of the man as the strong, silent provider who needs to be won by a clever, cunning woman who competes against the rest of their gender. In being a 'bitch', a woman is using the hurdles-to-overcome narrative to intensify the romance, and the man, not really knowing her, projects his fantasy woman onto her.

But, and it's a big but, just because I hate the narrative, that doesn't mean that I don't recognise that there is some truth in it. Girls and women generally tend to be more emotionally literate than boys and men, as talking about your feelings is a key part of girls' chat from an early age. Sold the romantic dream of love-in-the-movies, girls can get more intense, more quickly. Girls often look for the same reciprocity in boys, wanting them to be in touch all the time, to share thoughts and feelings.

*One weekend when Chloe was studying for a big test, she wouldn't go to a party with him. He was really mad at her and ended up getting with another girl. Everyone saw so he couldn't hide it. He was so, so sorry, and cried and said he loved her. She felt heartbroken and desperately wanted to stay with him, but also felt humiliated and that made her end it. However, she missed him dreadfully and hoped that they would reconcile. She thought he would chase her. Within two weeks, he was with someone else in the group. Every time she went out she had to see them together: him with his arm draped over the new girl, whispering in her ear, them giggling together. It was excruciatingly painful to see. She felt humiliated but also missed him like crazy.*

So when you are really enjoying fancying someone and them flirting with you, you can keep wanting that little hit of anticipation and pleasure that comes from a message sent or received. This can result in you sending too many, giving them constant attention. For many people – and again I think this has a gender component and is truer of boys – this is overwhelming as they are still figuring out what they are feeling. It can be off-putting and can cause them to withdraw.

Why off-putting? Let's turn it around a moment to think about why this might be. Have you ever met someone totally in their emotional mind? Someone in their emotional mind does not respond to you, they respond to their own emotional mind. You go to them with your problems and they make it about them. It's all about their feelings; they are a bit out of touch with reality and that feels a bit jarring when you are on the receiving end. That's how the object of your affection might be feeling.

However, I don't think you should hold back because you want to trap them into liking you. You should hold back because you need to use your rational mind as well as your emotional mind. The sensations of lust, flirting and sex are so strong, and so entwined with each other. For women, for pretty much the whole history of time, the context of these feelings has always assumed to be triggered only by love: the romantic narrative. This creates the perfect conditions for your thinking to become fused to your emotions – for you explaining your feelings with the 'true love' narrative rather than recognising that it is lust or excitement or on/off addiction. That leaves you vulnerable to being completely stuck in your emotional mind and makes it more likely that your rational mind or wise mind will not show up to the party.

And that is a problem, why? It is a problem in two ways. It is only by being in your rational mind that, over time, you can see someone's character and decide whether you can trust that their intentions are good and that they are going to be kind to you. By good intentions, I don't mean that he wants to marry you. We are not in *Pride and Prejudice*. I just mean that he is not a prick. That he's not going to tell all his mates he banged you, or cheat on you with your best friend. You need to use your rational mind to separate the thrill of the chase from the value of the catch.

And, secondly, you need your rational mind to see that, even if they are good and kind, they just might not be that into you. They might tick all your boxes and you only tick some of theirs. Inevitably, love, sex and relationships involve the coming together of two emotional minds, theirs and yours, and only when there is a connection between them can the love, sex or relationship progress. But, as we've seen, when your emotional mind is firing on all cylinders it can be very hard to accurately tune into theirs.

You should use your wise mind because a relationship is about two people and if the person you're into is not responding regularly to you, you need to respect that and respond to it rationally, not with all your unspent passion. Rationally, that's not part of a hurdles-to-overcome narrative; it's a sign that he is not that into you. And indeed, this is what the ghastly #whymenlovebitches hashtag is picking up on: some women's tendency to be too much in their emotional mind early on, which can be off-putting early in a relationship and do more harm than good.

We're back to our two icebergs again, but instead of hiding the stuff under your waterline, your feelings about this other person are clearly on display. In fact, you dump them on the other person and they go, 'Whoa, hold on a minute; too much too soon.'

And now, a quick word about your girl-tribe. Your friendship group may struggle to tell you the truth when the subject of your attraction is not that into you. Why won't they tell you? Firstly, because they care about you and they don't want to hurt your feelings, but secondly, because they are steeped in the same romantic fantasies as you and while you are recounting the trials and tribulations of what his text (or absence of text) means, they are living vicariously through you. As I discussed in the emotions chapter, a show like *Love Island* brilliantly illustrates this – the women gathering around one poor love-struck girl to convince her that her partner really, really likes her, they can tell, she's got to have faith. The camera then cuts to Casa Amor where the man in question is clearly going after another girl. Learn from this: cultivate some friends who will cut the BS and tell you the truth, rather than letting you live in your happily-ever-after fantasy emotional mind. Sometimes a frog is just a frog. And sometimes he is a prince – but he's not your prince, he's someone else's prince.

A sexual relationship between two or more people in a

friendship group can cause complexity, whether it is boys or girls. However, girls often have very close-knit groups of other girls, so when girls in the same friendship group start crushing on each other or dating, this can cause tension. Your girl group of friends are often your substitute family and the people who have your back. Misread cues or hurt feelings when girls are attracted to each other within the group can undermine the strength of the group as a whole. For example, it's completely normal for girls to lie on each other's beds, to change in front of each other, to hug, to say 'love you' and it can be hard to differentiate between this in friendship and a sexual advance. The only way out of this is communication. Being honest and open is the only way to avoid confusion and feelings getting hurt.

## Love and self-respect: congrats, hun

As we are on *Love Island*, I name this section in honour at the great dignity of one of the contestants Shaughna Phillips, who after a week of pining for an absent boyfriend had to face him dumping her for a new girl. She bravely looked straight at him, cool as a cucumber and yet broken-hearted, and uttered the immortal words: 'Congrats, hun.'

In anything and everything you do, it is great to win but statistically you are unlikely to always win. You are going to have plenty of opportunity at coming second, third, fourth *ad infinitum*. And that is OK. All great success stories have their fallow periods or backsteps along the way and the same is true in love and sex. These inevitably involve the excruciating torture of loving someone who doesn't feel the same and it often involves being dumped.

*Over the weeks watching her ex-boyfriend with the new girl, Chloe could see that his behaviour was borderline controlling. She began to understand that his possessiveness was not because she was the love of his life but because he liked to show off. She recognised in herself that it wasn't him she loved, she could see now he had not been the best person for her. But she had loved being loved, and she was perhaps particularly vulnerable to this having missed out being raised by her own parents. But she was no fool: she had seen her grandparents' love for each other and knew what a real relationship was. She had loved being at the centre of the group, not him. She felt angry at him, and herself for falling for it.*

*And now it felt excruciating to her. She had the choice to stay at home, bored and resentful with her grandparents, or head out with the group and hold her head up high and pretend it didn't hurt. She couldn't wait for school to end and to escape to the next part of her life.*

In your school and work career, backsteps will be failing tests, not getting the grades you want or the job you want, or making a big mistake when you do. There should also be periods of being on your own. While for some, single life feels like a glorious period of freedom, for others, once you get used to being in a couple, single life can feel quite hard to go back to: you have become accustomed to having your self-esteem boosted by someone else finding you attractive and it's difficult to get by on your own resources. There is a huge temptation to go straight back to another person or a relationship. This is usually a mistake. This isn't about loving yourself but it is about valuing yourself and re-connecting to yourself. I am sorry that this sounds like new-age psychological-bullshit, but it is true.

In relationships, you compromise and it is inevitable in that process that you lose something of yourself. Something about the way you think, what you feel, what you like, who you like, what you want in life, how you spend your time. Of course, you may gain things from a relationship too, like new interests or new friends, and keep these long after the relationship has ended. The period on your own helps you recalibrate all that back together again for the next phase. To know who you are is so, so important in a relationship at any age but particularly as a teenager with the swaying hormones dragging you elsewhere. I don't believe that you have to love yourself for someone else to love you. But I do believe that you have to value yourself to find a relationship based on respect and equality, otherwise you risk giving too much or not enough.

In the series *Modern Family*, Gloria has a secret stash of money in case she ever needs to run away from her marriage: 'my disappear bag'. But the challenge is for you to hold an emotional disappear bag: you need to be robust enough to be out of a relationship and the only way to do that is to have times when you are on your own. Have some dignity in defeat, walk away and lick your wounds. Re-evaluate before you get out there again. And if you do this broken-hearted with your head held high, congrats, hun.

## Nurturing your sexuality

Since the swinging sixties, girls' sexuality has been increasingly accepted outside of the story of love 'n' marriage and celebrated in its diversity, including LGBTQ+. Women are beginning to challenge the stereotyped narratives of romantic, heterosexual marriage being the only way, although it is still pervasive in society.

But, despite this progress, I still hear a whole heap of sad stories in my therapy room. Stories of degradation, humiliation, violence, force. Since the #metoo and #everyonesinvited campaigns, I feel we are only beginning to understand what impact the catcalling, up-skirting, slut-shaming, harassing, sexual pestering, insulting and assaulting has had on girls and women, and how, previously, we all just accepted this as the norm. Since these campaigns started, I have explored with lots of girls how this sort of casual misogyny has triggered, contributed to or perpetuated their mental health difficulties. When comments about their body have been made; when their intimate photos have been shared; where they have bruises on their body after what was meant to be consensual sex; when their drinks have been drugged and they've been raped. I fear I didn't ask about this enough in the past.

Is this linked to the availability of porn and the extremity of that porn? We have gone from a situation a couple of generations ago where young people were taught about sex in biology lessons without any reference to relationships or feelings and had a narrow window of sexual exploration, which was linked strongly to marriage and heterosexuality. This was hardly ideal. But now, many young people, especially boys, are viewing hardcore porn before they get an opportunity to experiment with actual relationships. That gives them a warped view of sex. Particularly, it creates a distorted perception of women's bodies and a twisted understanding of issues of consent and violence. It's like growing up having only had a choice of food from a cake shop: lots of what is there is quite nice but it's bad for you if that's all you eat. I have seen young men for therapy who have found themselves addicted to porn and appalled by the way it makes them look at women – though, of course, men who seek therapy are the least of the problem because they are showing a self-awareness and a wish for things to be different.

Where is the middle ground in this? If sex education wasn't going to come from a biology lesson or hardcore pornography, what would I want you to know about sex? I think it is this:

- Everyone's sexuality kicks in at a different age and you should feel comfortable about what is right for you. You are not weird or immature if that is different from your peers. You shouldn't feel pressure or be embarrassed. It's a bit like any developmental stage – for example, when you learnt to walk and talk. It makes no difference to you now whether you walked or talked at ten months or two years old; you got there in the end. Some of you will be cool with one-night stands; others will want to save yourselves for 'the one'. Both are fine and normal and just who you are.

- Sexuality is about how you feel inside – who you are attracted to, how that makes you feel, what you enjoy. Don't confuse your sexuality with whether other people think you are sexy, which is often about how you look. That is being sexualised – it's someone else's judgement put on you.

- Your sexuality is all about what you want and feel, so don't confuse that with pleasing someone else. Remember, sex and love are an intricate dance, in which you respond to their movements and notice what they want, but not at the expense of your sexuality – your feelings about what you want to do. Too much, too often and for too long, women have subjugated their sexuality for men's sexualisation of them, to make a man happy and so as not be criticised for leading them on or being frigid. That is a trap, which you can't win it, as double standards are applied to women: sluts if they do and frigid if they don't. The only way out of this trap is to hold on to what you want and feel sexually and keep your wise mind close at hand. That will help you bow to no one's judgement but your own. You do not have to accept sexual slurs, name-calling or slut shaming. Ignore it or call it out. And, of course, don't inflict it on the sisterhood.

- Watching other people have sex in porn or mainstream media seems to contribute to you taking a third-person stance to yourself during sex: that is, judging yourself as sexy against these images, rather than being in touch with your own sexuality – your own feelings and desire. Instead, sex becomes something of a performance act, rather than a shared activity. Porn particularly seems to take some of the fun of exploration away and give you extreme, misogynistic views about what is sexy. Avoid watching it if you can before you are regularly sexually active, so you can discover what you like in reality without having pre-conceived ideas in your head, as once it is in your head, it is hard to get it out. A bit like the scary film you always remember when you are on a dark street or alone in your home.

- In a sexual or romantic relationship, your partner should not make you feel weird or ashamed because of the way your body is and if they do, that is their problem and not yours. Just for the avoidance of doubt: women's bodies are meant to have hair on them and come in all shapes and sizes. You should not be body-shamed in any sexual encounter, you should be respected and made to feel beautiful for the honour of sharing your sexuality with them. And most people do.

- Sex is meant to be fun for everyone involved. It's meant to be nice for you as well as them. Psychologist Lisa Damour talks in her podcast of imagining a Venn diagram of what you want to do and what they want to do, and the overlapping bit is what you *can* do. This isn't just about consent – because consent is too low a bar. Their or your hesitation and doubt should be felt in the intricate sex dance and responded too accordingly: they need to be as sensitive to your hesitation as they are your cues to move forwards, as you should be to theirs. This is about active participation and not just either of you dragging the other round our metaphorical dance floor.

• If you do choose to enter a physical relationship with someone, remember you have your get-out-of-this-free card to use at any time: you have an unequivocal right to say no to anything and everything for ever, and you can use this card as much as you like. You are allowed to say no to kissing, touching, penetration, giving or receiving anything at any point during flirtation, romance, sex, relationships and marriage without feeling guilty. It is perfectly OK to change your mind about something, as sometimes you might find something sexy in fantasy but not in reality. If you've previously messaged about doing something sexually and then find that when you are, you don't like it, you don't have to follow through. You don't 'owe' them it. You do not have to protect anyone's ego from rejection if you don't want to kiss them or them to touch you. If they are nice and just not for you, tell them with kindness and respect their vulnerability. But being coerced into something that doesn't turn you on is a big warning sign that this person is a bad egg. A 'popular' coercion seems to be boys guiding girls' heads down to give a blow job: if you don't feel that is what you fancy doing, don't do it. If they are trying to force you, you have the right to call it out, or scream it out, or report them to the police.

- Sex can be incredibly intimate: it's a risk. It's a risk because you make yourself physically and emotionally vulnerable, which is why your rational mind needs to have shown up to the party.

- Why physically vulnerable? Because most rapes and sexual assaults are not carried out by strangers walking down the street at night. Most rapes and sexual assaults happen with a boy that you know and probably like. Maybe you've fantasised about him kissing you for a long time, maybe you've flirted with him regularly, maybe you willingly go to a bedroom or behind the bush at the park with him, maybe you know his sister and parents. You may have liked it when he first kissed you, felt excited when he touched you intimately, but then he pushes your head down on to his dick and holds it there and you feel like you're gagging. Or he pushes his fingers or willy into you and you don't want him to, or it's with force, or into your bum and not your vagina. You, arguably, take a physical risk every time you are alone with a boy when you don't know if they are trustworthy. Often rape happens with girls saying no and boys not listening. But it can also be rape when a boy doesn't respond to your cues, your hesitation, and pushes through your boundaries. Sometimes after sex, girls aren't clear themselves about where they stopped consenting, but they know they did. And again, my language is gendered but rape and sexual assault happen in gay relationships too.

- Why emotionally vulnerable? Because you may fall in love with him and he may fall in love with you, or he may be using you to get a blow job or sex and boast to all his friends about it and immediately dump you.

- Generally, young people take more risks than older people but you will all have a different relationship with risk. You need to know yourself if you are a sentimental type who is likely to fall for someone in the intense experience which sex is. In the short term, do you trust this person in this encounter? To stop when you say stop? do you trust them not to force you? In the longer term, do you trust this person to treat you with respect once the lust has gone?

- If anyone hurts you in a sexual relationship, that is wrong, unless you have explicitly asked them to. They shouldn't assume your consent – that should be pre-discussed. When the fun stops, stop. I believe in your utter right to say no and be respected.

- It should not be on you to protect yourself; it should be on the other person to respect your 'no'. Unfortunately, Sarah Everard's rape and murder has reminded us this is still not our reality. Use your emotional mind to tune into your intuition about a situation and your rational mind to know that your 'no' might not be respected. Make wise decisions to protect yourself on this basis. I hope that in your generation this will change.

- Sending or just taking naked pictures can make you as psychologically vulnerable as walking down a dark street. Your emotional mind might want to. It might feel sexy; you might want to make someone happy and show them you trust them. But once someone else has a naked photo of you, you lose control over it. Nearly all romantic relationships end, sometimes in bitterness and recrimination, and will you want them to have it then? Do you trust that they won't ever share it? Or worse, use against you?

• Sex and alcohol/drugs: it is rape if you are too drunk/ drugged to consent. For many reasons, it's rarely a good idea to be that drunk/drugged but that doesn't make it your fault if something happens. Watch out for 'roofing' (slipping the sedative Rohypnol into a drink) – it's ubiquitous.

The hashtag #everyoneinvited has been incredibly powerful for the girls and women I've seen in helping them understand their past experiences and the impact of those on their current lives. They could finally name that the sexual slurs, body shaming, spiked drinks, forced physical contact was wrong and not their fault. They could begin to unpick how it had led them to withdraw into themselves, feel uncomfortable in their bodies, avoid standing up and speaking out and accept less-than-good relationships because they had been conditioned by this to believe that was all they deserved. It seems obvious now but it was a bit of a revelation to me at the time how much a toxic, misogynistic, highly sexualised culture had contributed towards their anxiety, depression, eating disorders and other mental health difficulties. I feel proud of your generation that you have started to call this out more often than my generation. It's only in this way that attitudes will change. Sadly we are not there yet.

## Final thoughts on love

Ultimately, kissing, making out, having sex, being in a relationship and being in love should involve you and that person being mutually kind to each other. Both of you should be putting something good in the space between you. They should be your friend who you fancy and they should have your back and generally think you are great. Of course, there will be things you don't like about them (and them, you) and there are bound to be some hurdles, but mostly it should be a relaxed pleasure. Don't sell yourself short, chasing for someone's love or tiptoeing around someone who isn't very nice. You can't define your self-worth through whether someone wants you or not. If you are unlucky and don't find that, it doesn't make you one iota less special. Get on with being your best self. Hug your girl-tribe close. You don't need to wait to be with someone before you start to live your life. Live it today.

# LAST WORDS

*'Here's to the fools that dream;*
*foolish as they may seem.*
*Here's to the hearts that ache;*
*here's to the mess they make.'*

**FROM 'THE AUDITION', *LA LA LAND***

So, what have we learnt? What do I want you to remember so you maximise your chances for mental wellness?

I want you to remember that you get to be your own person: you don't have to live according to what your friends, family or lovers think. Don't try to do your best but instead be your truest self. Who you are inside matters more than what you look like or how good your outcomes are. You are not a product to be moulded into other people's standards. Know your own values and, within reason, try to live according to them. Know that it's impossible to hold all the values, because being perfect is a dangerous myth: it's a myth that, if you subscribe to it, will, in all likelihood, harm your mental health.

I want you to understand the importance of vulnerability,

empathy and connection, and that comparison, competition and perfection are their enemies. Connection is made by the way you feel when you are with people and not by being the best person. Find people who make you feel good and gently drop the ones who don't. Don't confuse lust or excitement with love.

Don't forget the boring stuff: eat enough, sleep enough, move your body. Avoid extremes – nearly always mental health is about balance and the middle road is the one with the best chance.

Your feelings are like the waves in the sea: they will go up and down. Like the waves, they need to be respected and you mustn't let them drown you. Don't be too wedded to your emotional mind; let your rational mind in. Make wise choices using both. Being vulnerable doesn't mean being a victim. Wise choices are sometimes letting go and walking away and giving up.

Being scared or frightened is sometimes necessary and being sad inevitable if you want to live and love. Sometimes you will have times when you are alone and a bit lonely, and while it's OK to be a little scared of that, hold your values tight, keep offering empathy, vulnerability and connection and you will be alright.

Good luck to you, my young friend, be brave.

# ACKNOWLEDGEMENTS

I would have never written this book without my colleague and friend Cynthia Rousso, who made me believe in myself as a psychologist and that I had something interesting to say. She also has read countless drafts of nearly everything I have written and passes the Love-Island test of giving me honest (sometimes ruthlessly honest) feedback about my work and my life. You are a kidney-friend.

Thanks must go to my mum and dad too who taught me a lot about attachment before I knew the word attachment and then let go of me, and took up tap dancing. Legends.

I want to thank all my domestic substitutes over the years but particularly Jackie and Miley, for looking after my home and my kids while I worked and wrote. Shout out to Mihaela and Cheyenne too for the same reason.

Thank you to my young guinea pigs who read earlier drafts: Freya; Lily; Catherine; Emma, Joe and Ella. Your feedback was utterly amazing – each time you were spot on. I think I used every one of your comments to make an edit. Thank you to Dr Vic Chapman for her comments and support after reading an earlier draft.

Thank you, Victoria Hobbs, for taking a risk and taking me on amongst all your other high-profile and high-powered authors, and to both the Jessicas, Raynor and Lee, for your support and diligence. To the team at Bonnier: Margaret Stead, for her belief; Susannah Otter, for her enthusiasm; Justine Taylor, for her sensitive, diligent editing and Sophie Nevrkla, for her youth view. Thanks to Nikki, Eleanor and Frankie on the marketing and PR side, and Beth, who I have never met but apparently came up with the book's title. Liz Marvin, you are a bit of a genius copyeditor: so glad to have your help.

# WANT TO KNOW MORE?

Psychologists pride ourselves on being scientists and when I was writing a book for you, I wanted it to be based on scientific research as well as my experience over 25 years. I didn't want to patronise you but instead treat you as active agents in your own mental health. But also I wanted to make it readable. I hope I got the balance right.

But for some of you, there may not be enough material or science on any of these topics. You might want to know more because you are interested or because you are struggling in this area and want a bit of extra help. Or you might be an A level, degree or doctoral psychology student writing an essay or paper. You might want a broad but scientific overview to the area in question, or you might want to know which specific references back up my points. So, in this section, I'm trying to offer a variety of different levels of resources that might be of interest to you, starting with the lighter reads and going on to the more academic texts, and then the references for any research I quote.

One other thing to note: sometimes when I returned to the research or theoretical literature to reference the content, I found my memory of it had changed or, to put it more positively, my views on it had changed over the 25 years that I have been practising psychology. Thus, I sometimes give a reference for the purpose of you understanding the roots of my ideas rather than this content being a direct quote or representation of the work. I've tried to make it clear when this is the case. Similarly, sometimes there is so much research in an area it is hard to pick just one article.

Links to webpages are given in good faith but I cannot guarantee that they will always work.

# ENDNOTES

## INTRODUCTION

**p. 4 Self-harm among girls of 16–24 years old has shot up from around 6 per cent in 2000 to around 20 per cent**

McManus, S. et al (2019), 'Prevalence of Non-suicide Self Harm and Service Contact in England 2000–14. Repeated Cross-Sectional Surveys of the General Population', *The Lancet*

**p. 6 One of my favourite psychology articles ever is called 'On Knowing What You Don't Know'**

Puckering, C. (1996) On Knowing What You Don't Know. Clinical Child Psychology and Psychiatry, 1(1), 157-160.

## CHAPTER 1: ATTACHMENT AND BELONGING

**p. 10 A baby gosling will look for a moving stimulus . . .**

See work by Korad Lorenz, e.g. www.youtube.com/watch?v=2UIU9XH-mUI or www.youtube.com/watch?v=JGyfcBfSj4M

**p. 10 A baby monkey separated from its mother will cling to a cloth mother-substitute**

See work by Harry Harlow e.g. https://www.youtube.com/watch?v=znBa3lap5jQ .

**p. 10 Young children separated from their parents while in hospital or orphanages and not given adequate connection ...**

See work by Rene Spitz, e.g. www.youtube.com/watch?v=iW3UHcYfCPI

**p. 10 Footage of Romanian orphanages from 1989 ...**

See www.youtube.com/watch?v=JGyfcBfSj4M

**p. 13 'A psychoanalyst called Donald Winnicott...'**

Feel free to read Winnicott in the original but I like this book about him: Phillips, A. *Winnicott*, Penguin, 2007

**p. 14 Still-face experiment**

I would like you all, general interest readers or psychologists, to watch the still-face experiment video: it tells you so much about human psychology. You can find it at: www.youtube.com/watch?v=apzXGEbZht0

**p. 14 Attachment theory**

The British Psychological Briefing Paper on attachment (exact reference below) has is a very good psychological summary of attachment theory, and its cheap! If you want the info for free, see: positivepsychology.com/attachment-theory/.

**p. 23 ... being hit has very serious consequences for that child's sense of being loved and cared for and of knowing how to relate to people in the future**

Cecil, C.A. et al (2017), 'Disentangling the mental health impact of childhood abuse and neglect'

**p. 28 'We [parents] need to give them [adolescents] space and hold them tight all at the same time'**

Hohnen, B., Gilmore, J. and Murphy, T., *The Incredible Teenage Brain*, Jessica Kingsley Publishers, London, 2019

## CHAPTER 2: YOUR FAMILY.

For more information about the psychology of the family and parenting I think Nancy Darling's work is a brilliant place to start. Her research work is amazing and she kindly disseminates it widely through her blogging: www.psychologytoday.com/gb/contributors/nancy-darling-phd

### p. 34 Families are complex systems . . .

These ideas stem from a branch of therapy called 'family therapy' or more accurately now 'family and systemic psychotherapy'. This book is old but probably the seminal text in the area: Burnham, J. *Family Therapy* , Routledge, 1986

### p. 40 being dragged round to various different specialists

I am not doubting the validity of diagnoses like sensory-processing difficulties nor dyscalculia, nor the distress that is caused by them. However, in a sub-population they are over-diagnosed, and extra time is over-represented amongst the wealthy who pay for private reports. See: www.bbc.co.uk/news/education-38923034

### p. 43 Discipline, boundaries and rules

For a good overview, see: Smetana, J.G. (2017), 'Current research on parenting styles, dimensions and beliefs, *Current Opinion in Psychology*, 15: 19–25.

### p. 49 Legitimacy to parent

See Nancy Darling: www.psychologytoday.com/us/blog/thinking-about-kids/201001/the-language-parenting-legitimacy-parental-authority

### p. 52 95 per cent of adolescents lie to their parents...

Again, see Dr Nancy Darling's work, e.g. www.psychologytoday.com/gb/blog/thinking-about-kids/201703/why-do-teens-lie-part-1

### p. 59 It's an ego boost that comes from denial (that you make the same mistake) and comparison (I'm better than them)

Kristin Neff's work on self-compassion is a good place to understand why the self-esteem boosts we get from compassion are not a great thing. The 'Hidden Brain' podcast is a good introduction to her work: hiddenbrain.org/podcast/being-kind-to-yourself/or her self-compassion workbook: Neff, K and Garner, C., *The Mindful Self Compassion Workbook*, Guildford Press, 2018

## CHAPTER 3: FRIENDS.

For general reading on friendship, I would recommend Lisa Damour's book *Untangled* (Atlantic Books, 2016), which is very, very good on teenage friendship. Although it's written to parents, you will probably find that it explains your friendships to you well. Similarly, *Queen Bees and Wannabees* by Salind Wiseman (Hachette, 2002; 2009). This is apparently the book that the film *Mean Girls* was based on.

### p. 75 . . . in the secondary school years, that there is a confusion between 'being liked' and 'being popular'

Parkhurst, J.T. and Hopmeyer, A. (1998), 'Sociometric Popularity and Peer-perceived Popularity: Two Distinct Dimensions of Peer Status', *The Journal of Early Adolescence*, 18 (2), 125–144

### p. 75 Russ Harris . . . lists around 60 possible values

Adapted from Harris, R., *The Confidence Gap: From Fear to Freedom*, Penguin Australia, 2013. Russ Harris lives his own values by freely handing out useful worksheets on the website. russharris@actmindfully.com.au

### p. 77 Fitting in – finding your tribe

I'm not sure who first cornered the market in girls' friendships as a tribe, but I got the idea from Damour, L., *Untangled*

### p. 81 Social awkwardness

Holly Smale has spoken about her experience of being a socially awkward spectrum girl, and (although I haven't read them) her 'Geek Girl' books are about this experience. More academically, see: Kim, C., *Nerdy, Shy and Socially Inappropriate*, Jessica Kingsley Publishers, 2014. This is a good first person account.

### p. 82 . . . it is helpful to use a simple brain model of three layers

This model of the brain is called the triune brain. It was proposed by Paul McLean in the 1960s. It is not a literal description of the brain but a model to help us understand different functions.

### p. 83 Social anxiety

This section is based on David Clark and Adrian Wells' 'A Cognitive Model of Social Phobia' (1995), which is published in a very expensive book and so the original is probably for the psychology students amongst you with access to a library (*Social Phobia: Diagnosis, Assessment and Treatment*; Guildford Press, 1996). For those of you who want to understand yourself, Psychology Tools www. psychologytools.com/resource/social-anxiety-formulation/ has a good summary.

## CHAPTER 4. EMOTIONS, THOUGHTS AND FEELINGS

Daniel Goleman's seminal book *Emotional Intelligence* (1995) is very readable as a psychology student or generally if you want to know more; the exact reference is below. There's an updated twenty-fifth anniversary edition out too. I also think Matthew Walker's book about sleep is excellent. For help with your mental health advice and support see www.themix.org.uk and www.verywellmind.com. Also check out Brene Brown's work on feelings, especially empathy www.youtube. com/watch?v=1Evwgu369Jw, and vulnerability – www.ted.com/talks/brene_ brown_the_power_of_vulnerability continue to blow me away.

### p. 94 In psychology, there is a concept of 'high expressed emotion'

This is a well-established psychological construct with easy googleability. This meta-analysis is often quoted as the seminal article. Butzlaff, R.L., Hooley, J.M. (June 1998), 'Expressed emotion and psychiatric relapse: a meta-analysis', *Arch. Gen. Psychiatry*. **55** (6): 547–52.

### p. 95 . . . there are debates among psychologists about what constitutes basic, universal emotions

Ortony, A. (1990), 'What's Basic About Basic Emotions?' *Psychological Review* 97(3), 315–331

### p. 95 . . . more recent research on facial expressions is more suggestive of four: anger, happiness, sadness and fear

Jack, R.E. et al, 'Dynamic Facial Expressions of Emotion Transmit an Evolving Hierarchy of Signals Over, *Current Biology* 24, 187–192

### p. 99 Your emotional mind and your rational mind

Based on the work of Marsha Linehan. See www.youtube.com/watch?v=X_ BmPxd0Eiw

**p. 104 At any point in time, you can be in one of four places in relation to your own feelings and those of others**

Goleman, D., *Emotional Intelligence: Why it Can Matter More than IQ,* Bloomsbury, 1996

**p. 109 self-harm in the Western world . . . has gone from being incredibly rare to something used by approximately 20–30 per cent of young women in the UK and America**

McManus, S. et al. (2019), 'Prevalence on non-suicidal self-harm and service contact in England, 2000–2014', *Lancet*, 6 *and* Lim, K-S. et al. (2019), 'Global Lifetime and 12-month prevalence of suicidal behaviour, deliberate self-harm and non-suicidal self-injury in children and adolescents between 1989 and 2018: A meta-analysis', *Int. J. Environ Res Public Health,* 16(22), 458

**p. 114 research shows only 23 per cent of you like school PE**

Women in Sport and Sport England, 'Puberty and Sport: An Invisible Stage. The impact on girls' engagement in physical activity', August 2018

**p. 116 the most important thing a school can do is to find a physical activity that a young person loves that will sustain them for the rest of their life**

Porter, T. 'The key to good mental health? Physical Activity', *Times Educational Supplement,* 6 June 2019

**p. 116 a massive study of over a million Americans found a surprise result that being active was the most powerful factor correlated with good mental health**

Chekroud, S.R. et al. (2018), 'Association between physical exercise and mental health in 1.2 million individuals in the USA between 2011 and 2015: a cross-sectional study', *The Lancet,* August 2018

**p. 119 There are whole books devoted to why sleep is important**

Walker, M., *Why We Sleep*, Penguin, 2018

**p. 130 There is also evidence that writing down things you are grateful for every day – sometimes called gratitude journaling – improves mood**

See The Greater Good Science Centre for lots of gratitude research, e.g. ggsc. berkeley.edu/images/uploads/GGSC-JTF_White_Paper-Gratitude-FINAL.pdf

**p. 130 be kind to yourself . . . self-compassion**

See Kristin Neff's work on self-compassion, referenced in the notes to chapter two, above

## CHAPTER 5: ANXIETY AND WORRY

For a general introduction, see Jud Brewer's work. Ted talk: www.youtube.com/ watch?v=-moW9jvvMr4&t=564s or podcast: podcasts.apple.com/gb/podcast/ whats-essential-hosted-by-greg-mckeown/id1513285647?i=1000514396071 . He has a habit mapper for anxiety here: drjud.com/mapmyhabit/

**p. 135 Because survey after survey indicate that anxiety is currently rife**

See www.ons.gov.uk/peoplepopulationandcommunity/wellbeing/bulletins/ youngpeopleswellbeingintheuk/2020

**p. 135 It seems like the stuff you worry about is similar to previous generations**

Relatively similar but not exactly the same, according to www.childrenssociety. org.uk/good-childhood. There are increases in young people's worries in two areas: education and appearance which is why the next two chapters are on education and weight and shape

**p. 136 we didn't focus so much on the physiology bit, by which I mean what happens in your body, but this is really important in understanding anxiety**

There's a pretty good summary of the stress response here: www.health.harvard. edu/staying-healthy/understanding-the-stress-response

**p. 149 Physiological management of anxiety**

I see lots of young people who have given up on mindfulness and relaxation as they were taught it in their classroom with 29 other pupils by someone who wasn't an expert. That seems a perfect formula for finding it unhelpful. Lots of other kids messing around, fidgeting. You worrying about whether they are judging you or laughing at you or what the cool kids are doing in relation to it. Now, you may like relaxation/mindfulness or you may not but you can't judge it from that experience. That is like being taken to a film made by your teacher and deciding you don't like movies. If you are anxious, I thoroughly recommend that you try a lot of different resources before you decide it's not for you. www.freemindfulness. org/download has lots of free different types of mindful and relaxation exercises.

See also: donothing.uk. The apps Calm and Headspace are both excellent and have a couple of free exercises but for most content you need to pay.

### p. 157 Absolutes: shoulds, oughts and musts

From the work of Albert Ellis. E.g. iveronicawalsh.files.wordpress.com/2012/06/cbtafg_mustshouldought.pdf

### p. 157 first identified by psychologists almost 100 years ago

See William James. I love this anti-perfection podcast: www.cbc.ca/radio/ideas/should-we-aim-for-mediocrity-1.5493778 . As well as the William James stuff, there is so much other interesting stuff– I listen to it over and over and get new stuff every time. Winnicott is in there with his concept of a good enough parent and this is expanded to the concept of having good enough life.

### p. 159 Other types of Negative Automatic Thoughts

Based on the work of Aaron Beck. There are lots of free resources through Beck Institute. E.g. beckinstitute.org/resources-for-professionals/patient-pamphlets/. This is a good list of NAT: www.cci.health.wa.gov.au/~/media/CCI/Mental-Health-Professionals/Anxiety/Anxiety---Information-Sheets/Anxiety-Information-Sheet---04--Unhelpful-Thinking-Styles.pdf

### p. 160 The Ah Ha test: Accurate and Helpful

I didn't make this up, someone else did. I thought I had an article on it filed in my 'favourite articles' file, but when I went to search for the reference, I couldn't find it. The article would be about 20+ years old I reckon, so thank you to that nameless psychologist who I borrowed this concept from.

### p. 165 In the 1980s, a book was published called *Feel the Fear and Do It Anyway*

Jeffries, S., *Fear the Fear and Do It Anyway* (25th anniversary edition), Vermillion, 2012. This is a lovely little summary: www.youtube.com/watch?v=o8uIq0c7TNE

## CHAPTER 6: EDUCATION AND QUALIFICATIONS

### p. 178 kids who are happy generally and like their school at 11 get better results

www.natcen.ac.uk/media/1813898/Final_AW_6635_AYPH_6PP_NatCen_SinglePages.pdf

**p. 180 An idea which I, and lots of people who know much more about education than me, believe is fundamentally wrong**

I personally feel everyone in the world should watch the wonderful Ken Robinson TED talk deconstructing all the nonsense about education www.ted.com/talks/ sir_ken_robinson_do_schools_kill_creativity. It is funny, engaging, clever and thought provoking. He was a professor of education so he should know what he is talking about.

**p. 181 teenagers are often not so pro-social when coping with being disenfranchised from school . . . use drugs, alcohol or cigarettes to numb the pain, or to crime and gangs to get status**

Bonell, C. Et al (2019), 'Role theory of school and adolescent health', *The Lancet*. Published online 11 July 2019

**p. 183 school is often the area where young people rate themselves as most unhappy**

The Children's Society, 'The Good Childhood Report', 2018

**p. 183 Test anxiety is much higher among girls than boys**

Howard, E. (2020), 'A review of the literature concerning anxiety for educational assessment', Ofqual.

**p. 192 If finances are really important to you, academic jobs *on average* have better salaries but there are lots that don't**

I really hate telling you this, but being male, on average, gets you a better graduate salary. Graduate Labour Market Statistics (2018), UK Government www.gov.uk/ government/statistics/graduate-labour-market-statistics-2018. This is probably in part due to more males studying Economics and Management and STEM and not taking maternity leave, and more women studying humanities and nursing. Or, to put it another way, the subjects women are more interested in, either genetically or due to societal pressures, are less well paid.

**p. 196 The Teaching Excellence Framework**

www.officeforstudents.org.uk/advice-and-guidance/teaching/about-the-tef/. For a review of Russell Group universities not getting gold standard TEF see here: www.theguardian.com/education/2017/jun/22/many-top-uk-universities-miss-out-on-top-award-in-controversial-new-test

**p. 199 Study smart not long**

For psychology students looking for a summary of the psychology of teaching and learning, 'Mr' Craig Barton has kindly done all the work for us in *How I Wish I'd taught Maths*, John Catt Educational Ltd, 2018. The memory model I propose here isn't 'right' or 'perfect' but is more or less useful. It's influenced by the memory work of Alan Baddeley and Robert and Elizabeth Bjork and they summarise it beautifully for free here: bjorklab.psych.ucla.edu/research/

**p. 200 Procrastination**

If you are a procrastinator watch this by Tim Urban:_www.ted.com/talks/tim_urban_inside_the_mind_of_a_master_procrastinator?language=en

(The perfectionists among you should look at the links in chapter eight)

**p. 200 the pareto principle . . . states that 20 per cent of your efforts account for 80 cent of your marks**

science.ubc.ca/students/blog/how-to-increase-your-productivity-by-doing-less

## CHAPTER 7: FOOD, EATING, WEIGHT AND SHAPE

IMHO the very best two books on these topics are Laura Thomas's *Just Eat It* and Rick Kausman's *If Not Dieting then What?* I would also rate Bob Schwartz's *Diets Don't Work* and I recommend Roy F. Baumeister and John Tierney's brilliant book *'Willpower: Why Self-Control is the Secret to Success* to all psychology students particularly but it is a *New York Times* bestseller and very readable for anyone . It is not about food, eating, weight and shape per se, but there is one chapter on this topic. If you are a psychology student looking for a good overview of the theory and research in this area, *The Psychology of Eating: From Healthy to Disordered Behavior* by Jane Ogden is very thorough. I would also direct you to the work of Polivy and Herman, and Marika Tiggemann._ www.flinders.edu.au/people/marika.tiggemann. And there is Renee Engeln's work, which you can access through_bodyandmedia.com/home.html_for an overview of the area._

**p. 211 Analysis of social media content suggests it is dominated by a mix of appearance-driven content**

Hu, Y. et al., 'What We Instagram', Proceedings of the Eighth International AAAI Conference on Weblogs and Social Media

**p. 217 There is evidence that even when you don't consciously see the thin bodies . . . they will still increase your body dissatisfaction.**

Chatard, A. (2017), 'The woman who wasn't there', *Journal of Experimental Social Psychology*, 73, 1–13

**p. 217 there is some evidence that if images are labelled as altered it makes them *more* likely rather than *less* likely to increase your body dissatisfaction**

Engeln, R., *Beauty Sick*. Harper, 2017

**p. 220 the mental image you have of yourself is unlikely to be how other people see you**

Garner, D.M., Garfinkel, P.E. and Bonato, D.P. (1987), 'Body image measurement in Eating Disorders', *Adv. Psychosom Med.*, vol 17, 119–133.

**p. 221 What we 'see' is not 'true': it is a 2D representation of a 3D reality based on the brain's previous experience and assumptions it makes**

Take a look at this incredible demonstration of selective attention: www.youtube.com/watch?v=MFBrCM_WYXw. Or there's a good selection of visual illusions here: illusionoftheyear.com proving that visual perception is a top down processing influenced by stored knowledge as well as actual visual input

**p. 221 'For that our brain would need to be bigger than a building'**

Susana Martinez-Conde quoted from www.bbc.com/future/bespoke/story/20150130-how-your-eyes-trick-your-mind/index.htm. For a selection of her research and popular science writing on the tricks of perception see: smc.neuralcorrelate.com

**p. 223 what size is your body in the mirror?**

See Bertamini, M. (2010), 'Mirrors and the Mind', *The Psychologist*, 23, (2) thepsychologist.bps.org.uk/volume-23/edition-2/mirrors-and-mind for an easy explanation or www.bertamini.org/lab/Publications/BertaminiParks2005.pdf. For some mind-bending demonstrations of the impact of a 3D object being seen in 2D see www.isc.meiji.ac.jp/~kokichis/3Dillusionworld/3Dillusionworlde.html

**p. 226 the media presents women with 'a constant barrage of idealized images of extremely thin women . . . that are nearly impossible for most women to achieve'**

Tiggemann, M. and Pickering, (1996), 'Role of Television in Adolescent Women's Body Dissatisfaction and Drive for Thinness', *International Journal of Eating Disorders*, Vol. 20, No. 2, 199-203 (1996)

**p. 226 'Try everything once except folk dancing and incest'**

Attributed to Sir Thomas Beecham. Assuming you are going to avoid incest, BTW, there are probably about half a dozen other things I would add to the list, but two makes for a niftier quote. What Beecham had against folk dancing I'll never know.

**p. 227 research shows that dieting is predictive of both eating disorders and obesity**

Lowe, M.R. et al (2013), 'Dieting and restrained eating as prospective predictors as weight gain', *Frontiers in Psychology*; Patton, G.C. et al (1999), 'Onset of adolescent eating disorders: population based cohort study over 3 years', *BMJ*, 318(7186),765–768.

**p. 229 80 per cent or more of diets fail to result in significant weight loss over two years**

Mann et al (2007), 'Medicare's search for effective obesity treatments: diets are not the answer', *Am Psychol.*, Apr;62(3):220–33; *Le Journal de Femmes Sante*'s review of the Dukan diet, reviewed here in English: www.nhs.uk/news/food-and-diet/dukan-diet-tops-list-of-worst-celeb-diets/. Or see this good summary of the impact of low carb diets:_www.independent.co.uk/news/people/profiles/pierre-dukan-yes-slimmer-teenagers-do-deserve-better-exam-grades-8229932.html

**p. 230 whatever random diet you go on . . . while you might lose a bit of weight, the core brain will fight back**

As I write this in 2020, the only diet where their initial research shows some health benefits for older, obese people is intermittent fasting. These have not been demonstrated on a younger population whose health and metabolic needs are very different. Older people need significantly fewer calories than you as your body is growing, strengthening and renewing.

# ENDNOTES

**p. 230 In some legendary experiments in the 1950s, Ancel Keys studied the effect of starvation**

Keys, A., Brozek, J., Henschel, A., Mickelsen, O. & Taylor, H. L., *The Biology of Human Starvation, Vols. I–II*, University of Minnesota Press, Minneapolis, 1950

**p. 233 Dieting fails because of a combination of these physiological, psychological and societal factors**

Polivy, J. and Herman, C.P. (2020), 'Overeating in Restrained and Unrestrained Eaters', *Front. Nutr.* 7:30.

**p. 237 Baumeister and Tierney . . . call dieting 'the nutritional catch-22'**

Baumeister, R.F. and Tierney, J., *Willpower*, Penguin, 2011

**p. 241 The core brain responds as though it is in another famine and therefore it must make the body more efficient**

Brownell, K. et al (1986), 'The effects of repeated cycles of weight loss and regain in rats', *Physiology and Behavior*, 38, 459-464; Schwartz, B. *Diets don't work*, Breakthru Publishing, 1996; Hill, A. J. (2004), 'Does dieting make you fat?' *British Journal of Nutrition*, 92(1), S15–S18.

**p. 241 Ancel Key's experiments also show us the after-effects of dieting**

Ekbert, E.D. et al (1987), 'A 57-year follow-up investigation and review of the Minnesota study on human starvation and its relevance to eating disorders', *Archives of Psychology*, 2(3).

**p. 244 The internet has allowed movements such as health at every size and body positivity to flourish**

Penney, T.L. and Kirk, S.F.L. (2015), 'The Health at Every Size Paradigm and Obesity. Missing Empirical Evidence May Help Push the Reframing Obesity Debate Forward', *Am J Public Health*, 105(5). This website has multiple links to research, blogs, podcasts, etc.: haescommunity.com. For body positivity, have a look at www.verywellmind.com/body-positive-influencers-4165953 for a whole heap of body positive influencers – I love #jiggleforjoy @kate_speer; powertoprevail. co/about-me/ and www.healthyisthenewskinny.com but feel free to choose your own inspiration. Sonia Renee Taylor rocks Body Positivity as radical self-love: www.sonyareneetaylor.com.

**p. 246 [intuitive eating has] already been done brilliantly for a female teenage/ young adult audience**

Thomas, L, *Just Eat It*; Kausman, R., *If Not Dieting, Then What?*

## CHAPTER 8: SCREENS AND THE INTERNET

'In this chapter, I argue for the negative impacts of perfectionism on friendship but perfectionism impacts negatively on nearly every part of life. Two videos that can help you understand this are Dominique Thompson's TED talk www. tedxbath.co.uk/2018/videos and Brene Brown's masterclass on the importance of letting go of control and perfection and embracing vulnerability, which I've already recommended in the chapter four, but it's so good I am recommending it twice: www.ted.com/talks/brene_brown_the_power_of_vulnerability.

The research section on screens and the internet is smaller than some of the others in this book and I think that is because the definitive research isn't in yet. It's all too new and it has been changing all the time so difficult to subject to research conditions. My thoughts come more from clinical observation than research. There have been a couple of different debates between 'mainly researchers' on one side and 'mainly clinicians' on the other about how harmful it is or isn't. The researchers often say there is no evidence to say it is harmful, whereas the clinicians basically say that's not what we are seeing. For example, see Palmer, S. et al (2016), 'Letter to Guardian, 25 December' on one side, and Etchells, P. et al (2017) reply 7 January. Or Bell, V. Bishop, D.V. and Przybylski, A. (2015), 'The debate about digital technology and young people', *BMJ*, 351, on one side and Greenfield, S. (2015), 'The Impact of Screen Technology', *BMJ*, 351. I must note that sometimes clinicians do notice things before researchers confirm it, e.g. the negative effects of smoking back in the 1940s.

**p. 253 digital natives**

The term 'digital native' is generally attributed to Marc Prensky in 2001. I became familiar with it through Greenfield, S., *Mind Change: How Twenty-first Century Technology is leaving its mark on the brain*, Random House, 2014.

**p. 254 there are lots of great things about the digital revolution**

If you want 'evidence' of the benefits of technology on young people, see: www. oii.ox.ac.uk/people/andrew-przybylski/?research – though I must say that I am a bit sceptical of about this research because it seems to focus more on the positives than any negatives. By the law of averages, I would have thought there were some negatives.

**p. 263 statistics show that, on average, there is a bit of a gender split on what young people use their screens for**

Ofcom, 2020, 'Children and parents. Media use and attitude report' 2019

## CHAPTER 9: ATTRACTION, RELATIONSHIPS, SEX AND LOVE

For a general introduction, I would recommend the 'Ask Lisa' podcast on consent, number 38: podcasts.apple.com/us/podcast/38-how-do-i-teach-my-kids-about-consent/id1525689066?i=1000520002212. I would also recommend Peggy Orenstein's book *Girls and Sex: Navigating the Complicated New Landscape*, Harper, 2016. This book made me think a lot about female masturbation. I realised I'd never write a chapter to boys about sex without mentioning masturbation and that made me reflect on just how taboo masturbation is for girls and women still, as I rarely talk or hear about it in therapy. There are so few topics that don't get touched on in therapy and maybe that's 'my bad' as you lot say, for not bringing it up. However, having said that, I haven't talked to girls in therapy about it, and given Peggy Orenstein has talked to lots of girls about it, I'll leave it to her. Her TED talk is a good introduction: www.ted.com/talks/peggy_orenstein_what_young_women_believe_about_their_own_sexual_pleasure?language=en. Those looking for a bit more information or for proper psychological research can look to Deborah Tolman's extensive research, and this podcast is a good start: sexologypodcast.com/2017/07/24/female-sexual-desire-with-dr-deborah-tolman/. Her activism gender work is at www.sparkmovement.org. and her research work for a general audience at www.sexgenlab.org.

**p. 290 LGBTQ+**

I have tried to write about what I know and whilst I regularly see LGBTQ+ patients in my clinic and at times discuss their sexuality and gender, their struggles with their sexuality or gender have rarely been the main reason for them being there. Also in relation to trans issues, my clinics are very near the only Gender Identity Service in the country, where those people struggling with these issues would be more likely to be seen. I read a lot about this area even in writing this small section but if you are struggling with these issues I would first direct you to everydayfeminism.

com/2016/08/transgender-101/ (and generally to everydayfeminism.com) and www.sexgenlab.org and also amysmartgirls.com. These are the websites I found that seemed to be having the most nuanced, inclusive stories, research and debates about issues of gender and sexuality. Stonewall - https://www.stonewall.org.uk/young-stonewall - offer support to LGBTQ+young people and have some great YouTube videos about conversion therapy etc.

https://mermaidsuk.org.uk/ and https://genderedintelligence.co.uk

are both charities for transgender and gender diverse young people.

### p. 304 Playing hard to get?

I don't think these books are 'good' but I do think they are important as a document of some of the dynamics that go on in male–female relationships. Only read them if you carefully put on your critical feminist glasses first: Fein, E. and Schneider, S. *The Rules*, Warner Books, 1995; Argov, S. *Why Men Love Bitches*, Adams Media, 2009

### p. 317 Sending or just taking naked pictures can make you . . . psychologically vulnerable

Plus, in the UK, it is illegal to do this under 18 and your school has the legal right to search your phone if they reasonable grounds to assume you have. It is a law that is enacted though young people seem unaware of it. childlawadvice.org.uk/information-pages/sexting/

# PERMISSIONS